UNTOUCHABLE

UNTOUCHABLE
Dalits in Modern India

edited by
S. M. Michael

LYNNE
RIENNER
PUBLISHERS

BOULDER
LONDON

Published in the United States of America in 1999 by
Lynne Rienner Publishers, Inc.
1800 30th Street, Boulder, Colorado 80301

and in the United Kingdom by
Lynne Rienner Publishers, Inc.
3 Henrietta Street, Covent Garden, London WC2E 8LU

© 1999 by Sage Publications India Pvt. Ltd.
English-language world rights excepting South Asia
reserved by Lynne Rienner Publishers, Inc.

Library of Congress Cataloging-in-Publication Data
Untouchable: dalits in modern India /   edited by S. M. Michael.
    p. cm.
    Includes bibliographical references and index.
    ISBN 1-55587-697-8 (hc : alk. paper)
    1. Untouchables—India—Political activity. 2. India—Politics
and government—20th century. I. Michael, S. M. II. Title: Dalits
in modern India.
DS422.C3U54   1999
305.5'68—dc21   99-11837
                                                                                       CIP

British Cataloguing in Publication Data
A Cataloguing in Publication record for this book
is available from the British Library.

Printed and bound in the United States of America

The paper used in this publication meets the requirements
of the American National Standard for Permanence of
Paper for Printed Library Materials Z39.48-1984.

5 4 3 2 1

To
Dr. Stephen Fuchs

Contents

List of Tables ix
Acknowledgments xi

    Introduction
    S. M. Michael 1

1 Who Is a Dalit?
    John C. B. Webster 11

Part 1 Dalit Visions

2 Dalit Visions of a Just Society
    S. M. Michael 25

3 Phule's Critique of Brahmin Power
    Mahesh Gavaskar 43

4 Ambedkar, Buddhism, and the Concept of Religion
    Timothy Fitzgerald 57

Part 2 Positioning Dalits

5 Representing Hinduism
    S. Selvam 75

6 Misrepresenting the Dalit Movement
    Gopal Guru 93

| 7 | Becoming Hindu: *Adivasis* in South Gujarat
Arjun Patel | 103 |

Part 3 Dalits and Development

8	State, Market, and the Dalits *B. L. Mungekar*	131
9	Dalits and Economic Policy: The Contributions of B. R. Ambedkar *Gail Omvedt*	145
10	Dalits and Rural Development *S. P. Punalekar*	155

The Contributors	173
Index	175
About the Book	183

Tables

8.1 Socioeconomic Profile of Scheduled Castes   134

8.2 Percentage of Scheduled Castes in the Central Government, PSUs, and Nationalized Banks, 1 January 1987   136

8.3 Percentage of Scheduled Castes in Employment in Forty-one Educational Institutions, 1987   137

8.4 Employment Scenario at a Glance, 1992–1997   140

8.5 Welfare Expenditure as Percentage of Total Public Expenditure in Selected OECD Countries, 1977   141

8.6 Expenditure by Center, States, and Union Territories on Social Services as Percentage of GDP, 1985–1986 to 1996–1997   142

Acknowledgments

Stephen Fuchs, the founder of the Institute of Indian Culture, a research center in anthropology and sociology in the megacity of Mumbai, has been a source of inspiration to a large number of scholars who have undertaken research on the marginalized people of India. After a long period of committed scholarly work, spanning more than sixty years in India, he has gone back, reluctantly, to Vienna for medical care and rest. This volume is dedicated to him in appreciation of his enormous contribution to Indian anthropology and sociology.

This book is a product of teamwork. First of all, I express my profound sense of gratitude to J. V. Ferreira for his valuable suggestions throughout the book. I am indebted to Teresa Menezes for typing the manuscript. I am also grateful to Elizabeth Reuben, Kaj Tougaard, and Mark R. Hooper for their editorial assistance.

Last, but not least, I express my sincere thanks to the contributors to this volume.

S. M. Michael

Introduction

S. M. Michael

Sociology grows and changes continually in response to new phenomena within world societies, to discoveries and insights within the discipline itself, and to the mandate for ever-increasing relevance that comes from the very people whom sociologists study. Today, prominent aspects of world economic, political, and social relations revolve around issues of inequality based on class, caste, race, and gender. In the context of India, anthropological and sociological attention to the study of the Untouchables, now known as Dalits, represents a major trend in Indian sociology.

Throughout history, sociocultural and political situations have been changed by the power of certain ideals and visions. Such a tremendous change is in progress in traditional India, and the old values related to caste relationships are under great strain. One of the profound changes in contemporary Indian society has been the Dalit transformation of our times. As will be shown in brief in this introduction, and more fully in this volume, the Dalit vision of Indian society is different from that of the upper castes. It is appropriate, therefore, to explore the social, economic, and cultural content of this transformation and to focus, as well, on its relevance for the nation and its future implications. This book studies the aspirations and struggles of the marginalized masses for a new society based on the values of equality, social justice, and human dignity.

It might be suggested that we should dispense with visions entirely and deal only with reality. But that may in fact be the most utopian vision of all, for reality is far too complex to be comprehended by any single mind. Visions are like maps that guide us through a tangle of bewildering complexities, and like maps, visions have to leave out many concrete features in order to enable us to focus on a few key paths to our goals (see Sowell, 1987: 13–17). As the term is used here, a "vision" is not a dream, a hope, a prophecy, or a moral imperative, though any of these things may ultimately derive from some particular vision.

The aspirations of contemporary Dalits are completely different from those of Dalits in traditional India. This change is due to the difference in vision of Untouchables of the past and of today. Visions set the agenda for both thought and action; philosophical, political, or social theories are built on them. Believers in one vision will view themselves in a very different moral role from the followers of another. The ramifications of such conflicting visions extend to economic, judicial, military, philosophical, and political spheres. This is made clear in the case of Untouchables in the history of India.

Untouchables by Various Names

To be an Untouchable in the Indian caste system is to be very low in and partially excluded from an elaborately hierarchical social order. Untouchables are persons of a discrete set of low castes, excluded on account of their extreme collective impurity from particular relations with higher beings, both human and divine. They make up about 16 percent of the Indian population and number about 138 million. They have been called by various names, such as "Untouchables," "Harijans" (a glorified term coined by Narasimha Mehta and adopted and popularized by Mahatma Gandhi), "Exterior Castes" (used by J. H. Hutton), "Depressed Classes" (used by British officials), "Outcastes," and "Pariahs" (undoubtedly derived from the Tamil word *para* or *parai,* the drum [see Deliege, 1997]). In more ancient times, the terms "Mlechha," "Chandala" (used by Manu), "Panchama" (the fifth class), "Avarna" (i.e., outside the four *varnas*), "Nishada," "Paulkasa," "Antyaja," and "Atishudra" were used.

The term "Scheduled Castes" appeared for the first time in April 1935, when the British government issued the Government of India (Scheduled Caste) Order specifying certain castes, races, and tribes as Scheduled Castes. Prior to that, these population groups were generally known as Depressed Classes. The term "Dalit," first used in journalistic writings as far back as 1931 to connote the Untouchables, did not gain currency until the early 1970s, with the Dalit Panther Movement in Maharashtra. As it is now used, it implies a condition of being underprivileged and deprived of basic rights and refers to people who are suppressed on account of their status at birth.

The Origins of Caste and Untouchability

The origins of caste and of untouchability lie deep in India's ancient past, and the evidence of these origins provided by the archaeological and literary sources now available is, at best, circumstantial. Consequently, scholars have been forced to engage in considerable speculation in their efforts to reconstruct the past history of untouchability. What we now have are not hard and clear facts but a variety of competing theories, all of which have proved difficult to substantiate in a convincing manner.

The dominant view traces the origins of caste and untouchability to the Aryans and to their ways of relating to the peoples of India with whom they came into contact. The Aryans, a set of related and highly self-conscious tribes sharing a common language and religion, began their invasions of India from the northwest around 1500 B.C. For centuries they remained in seemingly constant conflict with the indigenous peoples, whom they looked down upon as culturally inferior and shunned as ritually unclean. Once conquered by superior military technology, some of these peoples withdrew into regions as yet unoccupied by the Aryans, whereas others were incorporated as separate and inferior castes within Aryan-dominated society. In post-Rigvedic literature, there are more frequent references to primitive forest-dwellers who were kept on the fringes of Aryan society in the conquered regions. Among these were the Chandalas.

Although the Chandalas were severely stigmatized in the later Vedic age, it was only in the period between 600 B.C. and A.D. 200 that untouchability appeared as such (Webster, 1994: 2). In the *Dharmasutras* and in Kautilya's *Arthasastra* the Chandalas are treated as Untouchable, and the "mixed-caste theory" of the origins of untouchability is enunciated. However, it is in the *Manusmriti* that this theory, as well as the *varna* theory and the classification of castes in a hierarchy based on occupation and degree of pollution, receives its classic statement.

According to Manu, the ancient Indian lawgiver, untouchability is the punishment for miscegenation between a member of a high caste and that of a low caste or an outcaste. The children of such an unequal pair become Untouchables, and the greater the social gap between the two parents, the lower the status of their children. The consequences are also more severe if the mother is of the superior caste. Thus the offspring of a Brahmin father and a Shudra mother is called Nishada; the child becomes a fisherman. The offspring of a Shudra father and a Brahmin mother is called Chandala; he is the most degraded of all mortals. To Manu, a degraded occupation is not the cause of untouchability; rather, untouchability condemns a person to a low and impure occupation. In later times, racial mixture was added as a factor of impurity. In the period after Manu, increasing numbers of the members of the lower castes belonged to different races and cultures. The practice of untouchability was intensified and applied to more groups in the years following A.D. 200, and Chandala become a label not simply for a tribe but for all whom the Aryans considered to be at the very bottom of society.

What has been described thus far relates to northern India. The literature from southern India suggests that the people whom the Aryans conquered were Dravidians, who subsequently moved south, subjugating the indigenous people. It was only later, when Aryan influences spread to the south, that the *varna* system and untouchability came into being there.

J. H. Hutton, eminent anthropologist and author of one of the best books on caste, *Caste in India* (1963), locates the origins of caste in the taboos and divisions of labor in the pre-Aryan tribes of India as well as in their efforts at self-preservation in the face of invasion. In his opinion, untouchability is the consequence of ritual impurity. He says: "The origin of the position of the exterior castes is partly racial, partly religious, and partly a matter of social custom. There can be little doubt but the idea of untouchability originates in taboo" (Hutton, 1963: 207). Von Fuerer-Haimendorf, another eminent anthropologist, believes that untouchability is an urban development and is the result of an unclean and ritually impure occupation (see the foreword in Fuchs, 1950). Once untouchability had developed in urban or semiurban settlements, its gradual spread to the villages was inevitable.

B. R. Ambedkar's thesis on the origin of untouchability, as expounded in his book *The Untouchables* (1948), is an altogether novel one. The distinction between the Hindus and the Untouchables in its original form, before the advent of untouchability, was the distinction between "tribesmen" and "broken men" from alien tribes. It is the broken men who subsequently came to be treated as Untouchable. There are two roots from which untouchability has sprung: (1) contempt and hatred for the broken men, as for Buddhism by the Brahmins, and (2) continuation of beef eating by the broken men after it had been given up by the others. Ambedkar tries to explain what he means by "broken men." He proposes an ingenious hypothesis: When primitive society began to settle down and to cultivate, certain tribes remained nomadic and warlike. They began to attack the settled tribes because the latter were wealthier. In addition, they had grain, which the nomads wanted but did not possess. The settled men needed defenders because they had lost their warlike spirit. They employed broken men—defeated nomads and stray individuals who needed protection and shelter. These became mercenaries of the settlers but were not allowed to stay within the settlement. They were kept at a distance because they belonged to a different tribe and were treated with disrespect. Ambedkar provides supporting evidence for such a process from Ireland and Wales. The difference was that in those countries the outsiders were absorbed into the settled community after nine generations, but this did not happen in India.

At first sight this theory may seem rather farfetched. However, agreeing with the views of Ambedkar, Stephen Fuchs says:

It is a well-known fact that the nomadic animal breeders of Inner Asia, for example, enjoyed nothing more than raiding and fighting. When a tribe was defeated and routed, the survivors often used to be sold into slavery by their conquerors. Those who managed to escape had to seek the protection of another tribe. Being powerless they had often to content themselves with menial jobs, tending horses and cattle, making and repairing saddles and other leather-work, such as tongs and bridles, making and cleaning weapons, etc. As these animal-breeding nomads generally despised menial and manual work, this contempt was also extended to those who had to perform it. (Fuchs, 1981: 13)

There was a deep social cleavage between the masters and their servants. Ambedkar believes that the root cause of untouchability therefore lies in a pronounced cultural or racial difference coupled with a close economic dependence of the inferior society on the superior one.

Fuchs proposes a new theory regarding the origin of untouchability (1981: 15ff.). According to him the previously proposed theories, as well as various others presented by a number of Indologists, seem to suffer from one great defect: they do not penetrate deeply enough into the past of the dominant Indian peoples. They restrict themselves unduly to happenings in India. It is true that the caste system and untouchability developed after the arrival of the Aryans and, most probably, of the Dravidians in India; that the caste system, as it has grown in India, is unique and not found elsewhere in the world; and that nowhere in the world are Untouchables found in such vast numbers—138 million! Yet, the roots must be sought in an age when both population groups lived on the steppes of Inner Asia. Here the animal-breeding societies developed a pronounced hierarchical structure. These animal breeders gave up cultivation completely and regarded manual work of any kind as unworthy of a shepherd and a warrior. They also developed a social structure of their own: an extended joint family system with a patriarch at its head in whom all power was vested.

According to Fuchs, there is sufficient evidence to prove that the Aryans as well as the Dravidians on their arrival in India still belonged to such an animal-breeding culture. They must have brought along their aversion to manual work and to foreign people. The Aryans, on their slow advance through northern India, and the Dravidians, wandering down along the west coast into southern India, encountered on their way a multitude of earlier settlers who either submitted passively to their conquest or were defeated in fierce battles. As conquerors they managed to impose many of their cultural values and prejudices on the subject peoples of India. Adding to their inherited attitude toward manual work and racial purity a new dimension, namely that of ritual purity, they gradually developed the unique Hindu caste system that is intimately connected ideologically with the concept of untouchability.

None of these explanations for the origin of untouchability are conclusively proven facts. As so often happens with human institutions, no single cause can explain untouchability. It is deeply rooted in Indian history, in the agrarian social order that dominated the Indian economy until the advent of the British and that remains today India's largest economic sector. Though the relation of India's rural Untouchables to this social order has shifted in subtle ways in the past two centuries, there remain pervasive continuities, especially of meaning and of cultural construction, with this deeply rooted past.

From Untouchability to the Dalit Movement

"Dalit," which means ground down, downtrodden, or oppressed, as shown earlier, is now being used by the low castes in a spirit of pride and militancy. The name "Dalit" is not merely a rejection of the very idea of pollution or impurity or untouchability; it reveals a sense of a unified class or a movement toward equality. It speaks of a new stage in the movement of India's Untouchables, which is now a century old. Dalit self-assertion manifests itself today in a debate on several contrapositions: Mohandas Gandhi versus Ambedkar, Harijan versus Dalit, *varna* versus *jati*, *Manuwad* versus casteless society.

In view of the social location of the Dalits, it should occasion no surprise that they were the last community in colonial India to be influenced by those liberal notions that reached out to the country as a part of the cultural hegemony of the West. Perhaps the first modern Dalit voice was that of Jotirao Phule, a powerful advocate of social and gender equality based in Maharashtra. Another Dalit deeply influenced by liberal values was the Ezhava leader of Kerala, Narayan Guru, who attacked the institution of caste in a regional society where the Adi Shankara had argued, long centuries ago, of the essential oneness of things in his metaphysical formulation of *advaita* (nondualism) as the true basis of reality. There was a fair sprinkling of Dalit leaders elsewhere holding out identical messages. Their principal argument was loud and clear. Humankind was made up of a vast community of individuals, all of whom, in principle, were entitled to the same social status and economic and cultural dignity.

Though the Dalit voice expressed itself eloquently from the outset, it was left to B. R. Ambedkar, a second-generation Dalit leader, to articulate the abject condition of his community in the idiom of modern politics. Ambedkar also spelled out why Hindu discourse offered no route to liberation for the oppressed classes located within the Hindu social matrix. The Dalit communities, Ambedkar argued, were not the stratified constituents of an associational social order. Instead, they constituted the nethermost stratum of an organically integrated social body held together by the worldview of Brahminical Hinduism. The only way to liberation for the Dalits, therefore, was to opt out of the Hindu fold.

In the course of empowering his Dalit caste fellows, Ambedkar was drawn into an epic conflict with Gandhi, on the critical question of the Dalit location within the Hindu social order. Ambedkar felt that once India got freedom, his people, the Untouchables, would once again be subjected to the hegemony of caste-Hindus and be forced to scavenge and sweep for them. To safeguard their interests, he proposed that there should be a number of special seats in parliament for the depressed classes, which would be filled through elections from special constituencies. While drafting a new Constitution for India in the 1930s, the British extended to the Dalit communities the privilege of voting as a separate electoral constituency. Gandhi opposed this constitutional provision with all the strength at his command, since he believed a separate Harijan electorate would damage Hindu society beyond repair. Instead, he offered the Dalits reserved seats in the central and provincial legislature(s) on a scale more generous than promised by the British. The so-called Pune pact of 1932 was a triumph for the Mahatma because it ensured the social cohesion of Hindu society.

According to Gandhi, "the most effective, quickest and the most unobtrusive way to destroy caste is for reformers to begin the practice with themselves.... The reform will not come by reviling the orthodox. The so-called higher classes will have to descend from their pedestal before they can make an impression upon the so-called lower classes." Ambedkar, however, believed that India required a cultural revolution to destroy the caste system and his call to his followers was "educate, organize, and agitate." Thus, Ambedkar's project rested on questioning the traditional social order in order to build a just and egalitarian society, whereas Gandhi's interest was to preserve the traditional social equilibrium. In addition to providing leadership, Ambedkar engendered among the Depressed Classes the vital element of self-respect, without which the Untouchables' movement could not have arisen. Under his leadership, they realized that it was possible for them to organize, resist, and challenge injustice.

Ambedkar's followers formed the Republican Party of India immediately after his death, mainly for representing the interests of the Scheduled Castes and other weaker sections. But the leadership crisis in the Republican Party and growing attacks on the Dalits have made Dalit youths reject their leadership and adopt more militant methods. These Dalits, especially the educated Dalits in Maharashtra, have come forward and taken up the task of bringing all the Scheduled Castes onto one platform and mobilizing them in the struggle for their rights and justice. The caste stigma, which remained even after its legal abolition, was deeply painful to these sensitive youths. They firmly believe in what Frantz Fanon says: "Hunger with dignity was preferable to bread eaten in slavery" (Fanon, 1965: 143). They are struggling at various levels in villages, cities, educational institutions, and working organizations by means of a number of political and social organizations: Dalit Panther, Dalit Liberation Army, Youth Republican, Dalit Sangharsha Samiti, and so on. These organizations, dominated mostly by youth wings of the Dalit force, work as pressure groups for educating and mobilizing the Dalits and demonstrating in order to get their problems resolved. Dalit consciousness is also expressed in events like the formation of Bhim Sena, Dalit Sena, and the Dalit Sahitya Movement and the emergence of Dalit Reng-bhoomi (Dalit theater), the All India Backward SC, ST, OBC, and Minority Communities Employees Federation, Bahujan Samaj Party, and Bharatiya Republican Party.

With the growth of democratic institutions and the "politics of numbers," the Dalits began to assume some importance in national politics in independent India. The leaders among the Untouchables, in order to take due advantage of the situation and bring about their liberation, started to mobilize forces in their favor. Today the Dalit voters have successfully undercut the dominance of the upper caste and intermediate castes and have thrown up a new leadership reflecting a social resurgence from below that provides, contemporaneously, an altogether novel complexion to democratic functioning. This novel politics, which is Ambedkarite in inspiration, rests on a grand strategy that seeks to turn the Indian world upside down and shape an order of things wherein the hitherto deprived shall not only inherit the earth, literally and metaphorically, but also shape the principles of governance for the entire polity. In its strategic design, therefore, the Dalit upsurge of our times is a development of the highest significance.

* * *

The collection of chapters in this book represents the major concerns of the Dalits already described. It is divided into four parts. The preliminary chapters, including this introduction, deal with the origin and development of untouchability in Indian civilization. John C. B. Webster's chapter follows, dealing broadly with the genesis of the term "Dalit." After a historical search on the problem of who is a Dalit, he concludes that caste alone, not class or religion, has determined who is a Dalit.

Part 1 is concerned with the difference between the Dalit vision of Indian society and the upper-caste Hindu vision. The chapter by S. M. Michael outlines the main ideas developed by eminent social philosophers like Jotirao Phule, E. V. Ramaswamy Periyar, and Babasaheb Ambedkar, whose influence is very strong in the Dalit movement today. Mahesh Gavaskar then studies the contributions of Jotirao Phule, who laid the foundation for the contemporary Dalit movement and who is also known as the father of the Indian social revolution (see Keer, 1964). The next chapter, by Timothy Fitzgerald, further develops the social implications of the ideas of Ambedkar on Indian society.

Part 2 considers the methodological and procedural aspects of being Dalit in Indian society. S. Selvam critiques traditional Indian sociology, which looks at Indian society mainly from a Sanskritic perspective. In the course of this critique, he also makes an attempt to propose a method for the study of the complex nature of Hinduism and Indian society. He is of the opinion that Brahminical ideology swayed the lower castes in a relatively peaceful and subtle manner so that subordination in the Brahminical ideological domain was accepted. He proposes that in order to unravel the ways in which first the Dalits and now the tribals have been incorporated into the Brahminical social organization, studies should be undertaken at the micro, regional, and macro levels. Next, Gopal Guru takes up the question of the Dalit movement in mainstream sociology. According to him the ideological position of scholars will shape their approach to a Dalit sociology. If some scholars believe that the Dalit movement is limited to achieving partial changes in the existing social order, then their view of Dalit sociology will be different from that of those scholars who believe in the total transformation of Indian society. In the next chapter, Arjun Patel studies the Hinduization of *adivasis* in southern Gujarat, and shows how the tribals are brought into a Sanskritic way of life at the expense of the tribal culture.

Part 3 concentrates on the economic condition of the Dalits. At present there is a lot of discussion on the impact of the New Economic Policy on the Dalits; accordingly, this is the concern of the chapter by B. L. Mungekar. Gail Omvedt next discusses the Dalits and economic policy, taking inspiration from the contributions of Ambedkar. Keeping to the same themes, S. P. Punalekar considers the problem of empowerment of the Dalits on the basis of his rural studies in Maharashtra and Gujarat.

References

Ambedkar, B. R. 1948. *The Untouchables*. Bangalore: Dalit Sahitya Akademy.
Deliege, Robert. 1992. "Replication and Consensus: Untouchability, Caste and Ideology in India," *Man* (n.s.) 27: 155–173.
———. 1997. *The World of the "Untouchables": Paraiyars of Tamil Nadu*. Delhi: Oxford University Press.
Fanon, Frantz. 1965. *Wretched of the Earth*. UK: Macgibbon and Kee, Penguin Books.
Fuchs, Stephen. 1950. *The Children of Hari: A Study of the Nimar Balahis in the Central Provinces of India*. Vienna: Verlag Herold.
———. 1981. *At the Bottom of Indian Society: The Harijan and Other Law Castes*. Delhi: Munshiram Manoharlal.
Fuerer-Haimendorf, Von. 1950. "Foreword," in Stephen Fuchs, *The Children of*

Hari: A Study of the Nimar Balahis in the Central Provinces of India. Vienna: Verlag Herold.
Hutton, J. H. 1963. *Caste in India*. Oxford: Oxford University Press.
Keer, Dhananjay. 1964. *Mahatma Jotirao Phooley: Father of the Indian Social Revolution*. Bombay: Popular Prakashan.
Sowell, Thomas. 1987. *A Conflict of Visions: Ideological Origins of Political Struggles*. New York: Quill William Morrow.
Webster, John C. B. 1994. *The Dalit Christians: A History*. Delhi: ISPCK.

1

Who Is a Dalit?

John C. B. Webster

Dalit (oppressed or broken) is not a new word. Apparently it was used in the 1930s as a Hindi and Marathi translation of "Depressed Classes," the term the British used for what are now called the "Scheduled Castes."[1] In 1930 there was a Depressed Classes newspaper published in Pune called *Dalit Bandu* (Friend of Dalits) (Pradhan, 1986: 125). The word was also used by B. R. Ambedkar in his Marathi speeches. In *The Untouchables*, published in 1948, Ambedkar chose the term "broken men," an English translation of "Dalit," to refer to the original ancestors of the Untouchables. The Dalit Panthers revived the term and in their 1973 manifesto expanded its referents to include the Scheduled Tribes, "neo-Buddhists, the working people, the landless and poor peasants, women, and all those who are being exploited politically, economically and in the name of religion" (Omvedt, 1995: 72). There has thus been a narrow definition, based on the criterion of caste alone, and a broader one to encompass all those considered to be either similarly placed or natural allies. Since the early 1970s, the word has come into increasingly wider usage in the press and in common parlance where it is normally used in the original, narrower, caste-based sense.

Scholars also have written about Dalits in different ways. Two views predominate. Those using a class analysis of Indian society subsume Dalits within such class or occupational categories as peasants, agricultural labor, factory workers, students, and the like. This can be seen in most Marxist historical writings, the subaltern studies volumes, and, to a lesser degree, in the Dalit Panther manifesto. To those using a communal analysis of caste, Dalits are the people within Hindu society who belong to those castes that Hindu religion considers to be polluting by virtue of hereditary occupation. The histories of the Dalit movement by J. R. Kamble (1979), S. K. Gupta (1985), Atul Chandra Pradhan (1986), and Trilok Nath (1987) are based on this premise. Both views require critical reexamination.

Class Analysis

The analytical frameworks within which the Census of India set its descriptions and enumerations of the Dalits provide a useful starting point for such a reexamination. On the one hand, the census takers sought to depict Indian social reality as they found it; on the other, what they depicted was not always accurate, and such was its power that the census could play an important role in shaping that reality. Dalits were listed in the chapters of the census devoted to castes and tribes. The 1881 Census simply described and enumerated castes in the various provinces and states. *Varna* categories were often used to group them, and so the Dalit *jatis* generally appeared at or near the end of the lists. The 1891 Census, however, adopted a standard classification of castes according to the occupation assigned to each by tradition. Dalit castes were thus included within such occupational categories as field laborers, leather workers, scavengers, watchmen, and village menials. The 1901 Census classified Hindu castes in order of social precedence "as recognized by native public opinion" (Pradhan, 1986: 197). The 1911 Census provided a separate enumeration of those castes and tribes that either did not conform to or were excluded from certain aspects of what was considered to be generic Hindu religion.[2] Ten criteria were used to determine whether a caste or tribe was, to quote Ambedkar, "one hundred percent Hindu" or not (Ambedkar, 1969: 92). The five that applied to Dalits pertained to the denial both of various services by Brahmina priests and access to the interior of temples, and to causing pollution by proximity or contact, as well as to the Dalit practice of eating beef and not reverencing the cow (Pradhan, 1986: 197).

However, under special instructions from the Government of India, which wanted more information about them, an entire appendix of thirty pages in the 1931 Census was devoted to what J. H. Hutton, the census commissioner, chose to call the "exterior castes." Hutton's instructions to the various superintendents of census operations advised them to develop their own criteria in determining which castes should or should not be included, since such criteria might vary throughout India. Nevertheless, he did point out subsequently that the defining characteristic of the exterior castes was that contact with them requires purification on the part of high-caste Hindus: "It is not intended that the term should have any reference to occupation as such but to those castes which by reason of their traditional position in Hindu society are denied access to temples, for instance, or have to use separate wells or are not allowed to sit inside a school house but have to remain outside or which suffer similar social disabilities" (Hutton, 1933: 417).

Later in his report, Hutton did ponder two criteria that would indicate that pollution and hence interaction with high-caste Hindus might be a consequence of a caste's socioeconomic position (ignorance, illiteracy, poverty) or occupation, both of which are changeable, rather than of its traditional position in Hindu society, which was not, but he did not consider those criteria to be functionally operative (Hutton, 1933: 472–473). In the end, he stayed with an inherited pollution inherent in one's caste, which seriously affects interaction with those belonging to other castes, as the distinguishing characteristic that made these castes exterior. He placed their disabilities into three categories:

> Firstly, that under which they are barred from public utilities, such as, the use of roads and tanks, and secondly, their religious disabilities which debar them from the use of temples, burning grounds, *mats* and some other institutions. In addition to the above, but arising out of the second of these, there are the disabilities involved in relation with private individuals, such as the services of barbers and the admission to tea-shops, hotels or theatres owned by private individuals. (Hutton, 1933: 482)

This analysis was largely supported by contemporary witnesses. On the one hand, Ambedkar had testified to the Simon Commission in 1928 that the Bombay labor unions wished to preserve caste distinctions, whereas at a Bihar Depressed Classes Conference in 1937, Jagjivan Ram said that members of the Kisan Sabhas were exploiters of the Dalits (Webster, 1994: 127). From their Dalit perspective, caste was much more powerful than class. On the other hand, not only Mohandas Gandhi's antiuntouchability and Harijan uplift campaigns, which sought to remove the stigma of inherited pollution and change patterns of social interaction, but also the opposition that his campaigns aroused bore eloquent testimony to Hutton's understanding of what set Dalits apart from other Indians of the same social class.

A number of recent sociological studies indicate that, despite all the changes that have occurred in the past sixty years, the idea of their inherent pollution continues to be what sets Dalits apart. The assumption underlying the Government of India's constitutionally mandated compensatory discrimination policy has been that if Dalits can raise their class status through the educational, employment, and political opportunities opened up to them, then their caste status, defined in terms of interaction with people belonging to other castes, will also be raised. This assumption has, however, proven to be only partially true. Even the integration of the middle-class Dalits into wider middle-class society was only partial and incomplete at best, more obvious in public than in private settings.[3]

Class analysis thus not only fails to take account of the basic contradiction and oppression that Dalits face but also hides these by using categories that divert attention away from them. It is therefore no accident that historians using class analysis have largely ignored the Dalits, whereas those who have written histories of the Dalits do not make class analysis the basic framework of their histories.[4]

Communal Analysis

The census also provides a useful entry point into the communal analysis of caste in Indian society. As noted earlier, the census saw caste as a religiously sanctioned Hindu pattern of social organization. The Muslim pattern was seen as primarily tribal, at least at its upper levels. At the same time, census reports often provided statistics on the religious affiliations of members of various castes, thus opening up the possibility that caste might not be a strictly Hindu phenomenon. When the 1911 Census had to determine which Hindu castes and tribes had to be enumerated separately for reasons of nonconformity or exclusion, religious criteria were used.

The 1931 Census treated the exterior castes as Hindu castes occupying a "degraded position in the Hindu social scheme" (Hutton, 1933: 473). They were Hindus because "they worship the same deities and, though refused entry to the temples, boxes are placed outside, at the limits to which they can approach, to receive their offerings" (Hutton, 1933: 484). Thus Hutton's entire appendix is devoted first to those disabilities that high-caste Hindus impose upon their co-religionists that define the latter as exterior castes and then to naming the castes so defined. It is significant that "it was decided that Muslims and Christians should be excluded from the term 'depressed class.'" The reason for the decision may have been practical, but the decision had a very definite ideological dimension.[5] It was in keeping with that kind of thinking that the British government used when introducing separate electorates for Muslims in the 1909 Constitution, extending them to Sikhs in the Punjab and Indian Christians in the Madras presidency in the 1919 Constitution, and continuing them in the 1935 Constitution. The fundamental divisions within Indian society are religious; each religious community constitutes a watertight compartment; each has its own distinct social patterns, religious beliefs, and political interests that require that each community be represented by co-religionists of its own choosing. Thus, despite evidence to the contrary (Hutton, 1933), the stigma of untouchability and its accompanying disabilities were seen as affecting relationships only among Hindus. The Order in Council specifying the Scheduled Castes referred to in the 1935 Constitution turned this communal view of caste into law by specifically stating that "no Indian Christian shall be deemed to be a member of any Scheduled Caste."[6] Gandhi was also wedded to this communal view of caste; not only his fast in response to the Communal Award but also his scrupulousness in having the Harijan

Sevak Sangh confine its uplift activities to Hindu Harijans was based on this premise. Ambedkar, however, came to the opposite conclusion; although agreeing that Hindu religion was clearly a, if not *the,* major source of Dalit oppression, he did not consider the Dalits themselves to be Hindus.

The same communal view of caste that initially defined the Scheduled Castes in 1936 was stated even more strongly in the President's Constitutional (Scheduled Castes) Order No. 19 of 1950, which designated these castes to be considered Scheduled Castes in the constitution of independent India. It stated that "no person who professes a religion different from the Hindu religion shall be deemed to be a member of a Scheduled Caste." This was amended in 1956 to include the Sikhs and in 1990 to include the Buddhists. Moreover, in 1985, this religious criterion for determining caste membership was upheld by the Supreme Court, which argued that caste was a peculiarly Hindu phenomenon. When one moves out of the Hindu community into the Christian community, then one must show equal disabilities and backwardness *within* the Christian community in order to be considered a member of the Scheduled Castes according to the constitution.[7] The assumption here is that Indian society is divided into totally separate compartments according to religious community, that an Indian lives *exclusively* within one community or another and is affected *only* by that community's norms.

Historians as well as social scientists have also based their work on this set of assumptions by consciously or unconsciously applying a religious in addition to a caste criterion to determine whether or not a person is a Dalit. This is understandable. The colonial government, through the provision of separate electorates as well as in its census procedures and categories, had shaped the history about which historians now write in those terms, and the government of independent India, while dropping communal electorates, continues to use the old categories in areas of "social policy." In their histories of the pre-independence Dalit movement, Kamble, Gupta, Pradhan, and Trilok Nath treated those Dalits who converted to other religions as no longer Dalits and therefore no longer part of the history of the Dalit movement, whereas Mark Juergensmeyer (1982) included Christian Dalits in his history of the movement against untouchability in the Punjab.[8] Most sociologists and political scientists in studying Dalits since independence confine their samples to "Hindu"[9] and, where relevant, Buddhist Dalits. Suma Chitnis, however, included Christians and Sikhs as well in her national survey on the grounds both that conversion had not changed their situation and that several state governments had recognized this (Chitnis, 1981: 20–22).

Research on the history of the Dalit Christians indicates that this "communal" framework of analysis does not do justice to the complexity of either Dalit social reality or the modern Dalit movement. In fact, it breaks down at three crucial points. The first is in its assumption that the social consequences of conversion to Christianity were the same for Dalits as for members of the higher castes. In fact, they were quite different. Back in the last quarter of the nineteenth century and the first quarter of this century when most of the Dalit mass conversions occurred, high-caste people were completely cut off from family and *jati* upon conversion to Christianity. For them, the Supreme Court's assumption proved to be substantially correct; they moved out of their *jati* community into the Christian community and were to be governed only by the latter's norms.[10] However, this did not happen to Dalit converts. They were not outcaste but almost always continued to live with their caste fellows on the periphery of the village or, in the south, in the *cheri* outside the village. They also continued to marry within their own *jatis,* preferably with co-religionists. Moreover, their place in the village economy and social system was not altered by conversion. This is not to suggest that conversion produced no strains in self-understanding and social relationships or no alterations in the lifestyles and attitudes of the converts. It is to say that these strains and alterations occurred without totally changing their social identity and relationships within the village. These could change only if the converts left the village, which the vast majority of them could not and did not do.[11]

A second point where the communal framework of analysis breaks down is in its assumptions about Dalit Christian political activity during the 1920s and 1930s. In 1919, Christians in the Madras presidency, where the vast majority of Dalit Christians lived, were granted separate electorates. Dalit Christians there were placed in the Christian rather than in the general constituency. (Elsewhere in India, all Christians were part of the general constituency until 1935.) There is not much evidence of Dalit Christian political activism during this period; Ambedkar was right about that (Ambedkar, 1989: 472). However, what evidence there is indicates that they were more active as Dalits on Dalit issues than as Christians on general Christian issues. They had no voice in the All-India Conference of Indian Christians or other Christian political organizations, and these bodies were as guilty of patronizing neglect as were the Congress, other non-Dalit political parties, and the government. Where Dalit Christians were politically active was in Dalit caste associations[12] and in protesting against caste discrimination within the churches.[13] In fact, in 1929, a deputation of Dalit Christians gave evidence before the Simon Commission in Madras, arguing that they should be put in the general constituency, where they expected fairer treatment than they had received in the Christian constituency (Indian Statutory Commission Oral Evidence, 1929: 14–20). It would seem, therefore, that the modern Dalit movement was not just a movement within the Hindu community alone, but, like the nationalist movement, it included people on all sides of the neat communal boundaries that the British had built up.

Finally, the communal framework of analysis breaks down because it accepts as exclusively valid the "sacral view" of caste according to which castes are treated as "components in an overarching sacral order of Hindu society" and does not include the more secular associational and organic views of caste, which can be equally oppressive to Dalits (Ambedkar, 1946; Joshi, 1982).[14] Here too, research on caste in the Christian community and churches since independence, although of uneven quality, is nonetheless instructive. Caste exists in and affects the Christian community today, even though caste and castes are rarely part of the "Christian sacral order." Moreover, caste does not function within the Christian community in the same ways throughout India. Three variables account for virtually all the differences: location (rural versus urban), region (north versus south), and denomination (Protestant, Roman Catholic, or Syrian Orthodox).

Denomination is a significant variable because historically these different branches of the Christian church have viewed caste differently. The Protestants have been the most consistent in attacking it as part of the Hindu sacral order and in trying to establish among Christians a community without caste. The Roman Catholics adopted an organic view of caste, treating it as simply the Indian system of social stratification, and until recently have chosen to work within its constraints. The same can also be said of the Syrian Orthodox churches, which have tended to function as one caste among many in Kerala society rather than as a multicaste community (Koshi, 1968). Region is an important variable because the patterns of conversion have not been the same in the north as in the south. Whereas in the north a small number of converts from miscellaneous castes as well as from Islam combined with large numbers of converts from only one Dalit caste (e.g., the Chuhras in the Punjab and the Bhangis in Uttar Pradesh) to form the Christian community (Webster, 1976: 46–53, 227–234), in the south large numbers of several castes of differing status converted to form the Christian community.[15] Thus it has been possible in the south, as it has not been in the north, for two, three, or four castes to carry on within the churches the same competition for status and precedence as their Hindu caste fellows were carrying on in other arenas. Location is also a variable because it is generally recognized that caste sanctions are more strictly enforced in rural than in urban settings. Given these variables, one would expect to find caste weakest in urban Protestant congregations in the north and strongest in rural Roman Catholic or Syrian congregations in the south. One simply cannot generalize for India as a whole.

Given these variations, it is possible to make a few additional generalizations about caste in the Christian community and its impact upon

Christian Dalits. First of all, the Christian population, like the Indian population as a whole, is predominantly rural.[16] In the overwhelming majority of villages where Dalit Christians live, the dominant castes are Hindu, and so social identity and social relationships are determined by Hindu rather than by Christian norms and values. There the sacral view of caste still generally prevails; Christian Dalits are simply categorized with other Dalits and treated accordingly. Second, within the urban Christian community, caste seems to have been replaced by class in the north (Alter and Singh, 1961: 87–115), whereas the associational view of caste prevails in the south. There, caste often provides the social networks necessary for getting jobs or winning elections to positions of leadership within the churches. Because Dalit caste networks are less effective than those of the higher castes, Dalits often lose out in the competition. Third, those studies of southern Indian villages where both the dominant castes and the Dalits are Christians not only indicate that the distinctions of status and precedence on the basis of caste exist but also suggest that considerations of purity and pollution still affect relations between Christians of differing castes (Koilparampil, 1982: 154–168; Japhet, 1987: 59–87; Fuller, 1976: 63–65; Mosse, 1986: 264–280), even though, as C. D. F. Mosse has pointed out, both Hindus and Christians alike recognize that Christian deities are less concerned about purity and pollution than are Hindu deities (Mosse, 1986: 276). Thus, in Christian rituals Dalits play subordinate roles.

In the face of this body of evidence, it is difficult to retain a basically communal view of caste when Dalits did not automatically cease to be Dalits upon conversion to Christianity, and the vast majority of them remain victims of the very disabilities that Hutton listed back in 1931. Instead, the evidence points to the conclusion that, at least for Dalits, the stigma of untouchability and its accompanying disabilities based on caste are an Indian, rather than exclusively Hindu, phenomenon. A communal view of caste imposes a framework for studying the history of the modern Dalit movement that seriously distorts the empirical realities of the Dalit situation and Dalit movement. A more inclusive framework is thus required.

Conclusion

A historian, when using concepts and labels, is under obligation to be as faithful to the complexities of past empirical reality as possible. Concepts and labels carried over from the colonial past, even when enshrined in law, cannot be utilized without testing their ideological biases, particularly with regard to what they leave out. The same would be true of those brought to study the past from present-day political struggles and controversies. This critical examination of alternate referents for the label "Dalit" indicates that the original definition of who is a Dalit is empirically the soundest one for the historian to work with. Caste alone has determined who is a Dalit, not class or religion. Social stigma and a variety of disabilities were based on caste; these were and, to a significant degree, still are the defining characteristics of a Dalit, even if a Dalit moves up in social class or changes religion.

Notes

This chapter is a revision of a paper first presented at the Indian Institute of Advanced Study, Shimla, in October 1995. The author wishes to express his thanks to the director, Professor Mrinal Miri, and fellows of the institute for their comments and suggestions.

1. See Gail Omvedt (1995: 77). The 1931 Census made reference to the possibility that in the Punjab members of the "exterior castes" would list themselves in the Census returns as Dalits (J. H. Hutton, 1933: 488).

2. The use of "Hinduism" in modern times has come in for serious review. For two examples, see Romila Thapar (1985: 14–22) and Robert Eric Frykenberg (1989).

3. For a summary of some of these findings of Nandu Ram and other studies, see Nandu Ram (1988) and John C. B. Webster (1994: 153–154).

4. Gail Omvedt's critique in the first chapter of her *Dalits and the Democratic Revolution: Dr. Ambedkar and the Dalit Movement in Colonial India* (1994) is relevant at this point.

5. See the comments from the Madras report referred to in Hutton (1933: 499).

6. Cited in Pradhan (1986: 339). The same also applied to Buddhists in Bengal.

7. The 1985 judgment is published in full in Jose Kananaikil (1986: 43–50). The anomaly of including Sikh Dalits among the Scheduled Castes was first accepted on the basis that these "were originally Scheduled Caste Hindus who had recently been converted to the Sikh faith and 'had the same disabilities as the Hindu Scheduled Castes'" (Kananaikil, 1986: 48). This was taken as proven in the case of the Sikh Dalits but not of Christian Dalits.

8. Mark Juergensmeyer (1982). See also Joseph Mathew's treatment of the Pulayas in *Ideology, Protest and Social Mobility: Case Study of Mahars and Pulayas* (1986).

9. "Hindu" is often used as a residual category for those Dalits who are neither Muslims, Buddhists, Christians, nor Sikhs.

10. The only exceptions to this were those high-caste people who converted to Christianity in large groups rather than as individuals or nuclear families. They tended to carry their old norms over into the Christian community.

11. Discussion of the issues presented in this paragraph may be found in John C. B. Webster (1994: 63–70; 1976: 65–72), James P. Alter and Herbert Jai Singh (1961: 24–36), Duncan B. Forrester (1979: 69–96), Dick Kooiman (n.d.: 168–196), and G. A. Oddie (1975: 61–79; 1969: 259–291).

12. This was particularly true of the Pulayas in Travancore. See J. W. Gladstone (1984: 343) and *Census of India 1931* (1933: 439).

13. Evidence for this is given in John C. B. Webster (1994: 88–89, 105–106, 115–116).

14. This typology, which also includes the sectarian view of caste, is that of Marc Galanter (1968: 300–301).

15. In Kerala there were the Syrian Christians (who either migrated to India or converted to Christianity well before the sixteenth century and were about equal to the Nairs in status), the Izhavas, and the Pulayas; in Tamil Nadu there were the Vellalas, the Nadars, and the Adi Dravidas; in Andhra Pradesh there were the Kammas, Reddys, Malas, and Madigas.

16. In the 1971 Census, 74.8 percent of the Christians were rural, as compared with 80 percent for the population as a whole. In the 1981 Census these figures were 70.8 and 76.3 percent respectively; in 1991 they were 68.7 and 74.3 percent. Thus Christians, while slightly more urban than the population as a whole, remain predominantly rural.

References

Alter, James P., and Herbert Jai Singh. 1961. *The Church in Delhi.* Lucknow: National Christian Council of India.
Ambedkar, B. R. 1946. *What Congress and Gandhi Have Done to the Untouchables* (2nd edition). Bombay: Thacker.
——. 1969. *The Untouchables* (2nd edition). Balrampur: Jelavan Mahavir.
——. 1989. "The Condition of the Convert," in Vasant Moon (compiler), *Dr. Babasaheb Ambedkar: Writings and Speeches.* Bombay: Education Department, Government of Maharashtra.
Caplan, Lionel. 1987. *Class and Culture in Urban India: Fundamentalism in a Christian Community.* Oxford: Oxford University Press.
Census of India 1931. 1933. *Volume xxviii, Travancore Part I: Report.* Delhi: Manager of Publications, Government Press, p. 439.
Chitnis, Suma. 1981. *A Long Way to Go: Report on a Survey of Scheduled Caste High School and College Students in Fifteen States of India.* New Delhi: Allied Publishers.
Forrester, Duncan B. 1979. *Caste and Christianity.* London: Curzon Press.
Frykenberg, Robert Eric. 1989. "The Emergence of Modern 'Hinduism' as a Concept and as an Institution: A Reappraisal with Special Reference to South India," in Gunther, D. Sontheimer, and Hermann Kulke (eds.), *Hinduism Reconsidered.* Delhi: Manohar.
Fuller, C. J. 1976. "Kerala Christians and the Caste System," *Man* 11: 63–65.
Galanter, Marc. 1968. "Changing Legal Conceptions of Caste," in Milton Singer and Bernard S. (eds.), *Structure and Change in Indian Society.* Chicago: Aldine Publishing Co.
Gladstone, J. W. 1984. *Protestant Christianity and People's Movements in Kerala 1850–1936.* Trivandrum: Seminary Publications.
Gupta, S. K. 1985. *The Scheduled Castes in Modern Indian Politics: Their Emergence as a Political Power.* Delhi: Munshiram Manoharlal.
Hutton, J. H. 1933. *Census of India, 1931: Vol. I—India: Part I—Report.* Delhi: Manager of Publications, Government Press.
Indian Statutory Commission Oral Evidence. 1929. Fourteenth Meeting, Madras. 1 March.
Japhet, S. 1987. "Christian Dalits: A Sociological Study, on the Problem of Gaining a New Identity," *Religion and Society* 34, September: 59–87.

Joshi, Barbara R. 1982. *Democracy in Search of Equality: Untouchable Politics and Indian Social Change*. Delhi: Hindustan Publishing Corp.
Juergensmeyer, Mark. 1982. *Religion as Social Vision: The Movement Against Untouchability in 20th-Century Punjab*. Berkeley: University of California Press.
Kamble, J. R. 1979. *Rise and Awakening of Depressed Classes in India*. New Delhi: National Publishing House.
Kananaikil, Jose. 1986. *Scheduled Castes in Search of Justice. Part II: The Verdict of the Supreme Court*. New Delhi: Indian Social Institute.
Koilparampil, George. 1982. *Caste in the Catholic Community in Kerala*. Kochin: CISR.
Kooiman, Dick. n.d. *Conversion and Social Equality in India*. Columbia: South Asian Publications.
Koshi, Ninan. 1968. *Caste in Kerala Churches*. Bangalore: CISRS.
Mathew, Joseph. 1986. *Ideology, Protest and Social Mobility: Case Study of Mahars and Pulayas*. New Delhi: Inter-India Publications.
Mosse, C. D. F. 1986. "Caste, Christianity and Hinduism: A Study of Social Organisation and Religion in Rural Ramnad." Unpublished diss., University of Oxford.
Nath, Trilok. 1987. *Politics of the Depressed Classes*. Delhi: Deputy Publications.
Oddie, G. A. 1969. "Protestant Missions, Caste and Social Change in India," *Indian Economic and Social History Review* 6, September: 259–291.
―――. 1975. "Christian Conversions in the Telugu Country 1860–1900: A Case Study of One Protestant Indian Movement in the Godavery-Krishna Delta," *Indian Economic and Social History Review* 12, January–March: 61–69.
Omvedt, Gail. 1994. *Dalits and the Democratic Revolution: Dr. Ambedkar and the Dalit Movement in Colonial India*. New Delhi: Sage Publications.
―――. 1995. *Dalit Visions: The Anti-Caste Movement and the Construction of an Indian Identity*. New Delhi: Orient Longman.
Pradhan, Atul Chandra. 1986. *The Emergence of the Depressed Classes*. Bhubaneshwar: Bookland International.
Ram, Nandu. 1988. *The Mobile Scheduled Castes: Rise of a New Middle Class*. Delhi: Hindustan Publishing Corporation.
Thapar, Romila. 1985. "Syndicated Moksha," *Seminar* 313, September: 14–22.
Webster, John C. B. 1976. *The Christian Community and Change in Nineteenth Century North India*. New Delhi: Macmillan.
―――. 1994. *The Dalit Christians: A History* (2nd edition). Delhi: ISPCK.

Part 1

DALIT VISIONS

2

Dalit Visions of a Just Society

S. M. Michael

The Dalits are socially weak, economically needy, and politically powerless, despite protective policies followed by the government under provisions of the constitution that guarantee them educational concessions and scholarships, employment, political reservations, and socioeconomic welfare benefits. The word "Dalit" particularly emphasizes the dehumanizing caste oppression that makes them outcastes and Untouchables (a degradation not shared by the tribals, or *shoshits*) within the context of the Hindu caste system with its religio-social organizing principle of "purity and pollution" (see Zelliot, 1992; Prabhakar, 1990: 24–25; Massey, 1990: 40–41; Irudayaraj, 1990).

The ideology of the Dalits for a just society has mainly been developed by eminent personalities like Mahatma Jotirao Phule (1826–1890), E. V. Ramaswamy Periyar (1879–1973), and Babasaheb Ambedkar (1891–1956), with many others throughout India: Narayan Guru in Kerala, Achhutanand in Uttar Pradesh, and Mangoo Ram in Punjab (see Omvedt, 1995). They attacked the system of exploitation at all levels—cultural, economic, and political. They developed their vision of Indian society as an alternative to the upper-caste understanding of India. Hence it is important to pay some attention to the historical context in which the Dalit ideology developed.

Two Visions of Indian Nationhood

During its almost 5,000 years of history, the vast Indian subcontinent has nourished the growth of a great civilization, characterized by the diversity of many cultural and racial groups, castes, religions, and languages and vitalized through cross-cultural contacts. In the early stages, unity was achieved by recognizing this plurality and the autonomy of various groups. According to Rajni Kothari, "in the absence of centralised political authority it was the Indian civilizational enterprise which over the centuries achieved a remarkable degree of cohesion and held together different subsystems in a continental-size society' (Kothari, 1988: 2223). Thus, the unifying force of Indian civilization was the acceptance of multiculturality and linguistic diversity rather than political ideology.

The modern nationalism that emerged in Western Europe in the second half of the eighteenth century quickly spread throughout the world in the nineteenth. In India, it can be traced to the political and administrative unification, which was later followed by economic unification. The first expression of national consciousness in India was in the form of social and religious reform movements. The important question then was, what was the cultural foundation of Indian society and how was it to be reconstructed as a modern nation on par with other modern nation-states? Two strands of thought emerged: one led to an attempt at reconstructing Indian society on the basis of Western ideas originating in the "Ages" of Reason, the Enlightenment, and Liberalism; and the other wanted the reconstruction to take place on the foundation of ancient, upper-caste, Brahminic Hindu traditions.

Indian Nation Built on a Rational Approach to Culture

The Enlightenment philosophy of the West began to have its impact on the newly Western-educated Indian during the colonial period. It gave rise to the "Indian renaissance." The spirit of English education was liberal, rational, and utilitarian, a spirit that challenged the very presuppositions on which the orthodox Hindu systems of conduct were based. With ruthless self-criticism, reformers sought to lay the ground for a total social transformation, to weld science and rationality to Indian culture, to re-create India.

The beginning of this social revolt can be easily identified with the thought of Rammohun Roy (1772–1833). Roy vividly described the degraded state of society and acknowledged without embarrassment the virtues of Western learning, liberal thought, legal and social institutions, and social ethic (see Damle and Aikara, 1982: 77). With a view to cleansing Hindu culture and society of its weaknesses and incongruities, he founded the Brahmo Samaj. The purpose of the Brahmo Samaj was to restructure Hindu culture in terms of modernity. His revolt against contemporary Hindu society and his appeal to Indians to purify their religion and reconstitute their social institutions echoed throughout the century after his death.

Indian Nation Built on Aryan Vedic Culture

Whereas Rammohun Roy envisioned an Indian society ultimately renovated by centuries of exposure to Western science and Christian morality,

Dayananda Saraswati (1824–1883) urged a regeneration of Hindus through adherence to a purified "Vedic-faith." The Arya Samaj was founded by Dayananda Saraswati in 1875. Its aim was to bring about social and religious reform through a renewal of early Hindu doctrines, and its favorite dictum ran thus: "Back to the Vedas and Aryavarta for the Aryans" (William Roy Smith, 1938: 57). It is in this context of the upper-caste Hindus' identifying the "nation" and the "national culture" as basically Hindu, as deriving from Vedic times, and as fundamentally a creation of the Aryan people that we should view the alternative vision provided by Jotirao Phule, who was born in a Shudra caste.

The Vision of Jotirao Phule for a Just Society

Jotirao Phule was the first Indian to proclaim in modern India the dawn of a new age for the common man, the downtrodden, the underdog, and Indian women. It was his aim to reconstruct the social order on the basis of social equality, justice, and reason. As we have just seen, the "Aryan theory of race" constituted the most influential common discourse for discussing caste and society in Phule's time. European Orientalists like William Jones, Charles Wilkins, James Prinsep, and others (see Marshall, 1970: 1–44) conveniently used it to assert an ethnic kinship between Europeans and the ancient Vedic peoples (see O'Hanlon, 1985: 57–59). The constant interest of European scholars like H. H. Wilson, C. Lassen, H. T. Colebrooke, Monier Williams, Max Mueller, and others (see Kejariwal, 1988) in ancient Aryan society and their appreciation and praise of this society provided an important moral boost to high-caste Indians. Thus, Indian civilization was seen as primarily derived from Aryan civilization, and the caste system was lauded as a means by which people of diverse racial and cultural backgrounds were brought together and subjected to the civilizing influence of the Aryans (Omvedt, 1976: 103).

At one level, Phule simply reversed this notion, arguing that the low castes, whom he sometimes called "Shudras and Ati-Shudras" and who were simply listed as "Kunbis, Malis, Dhangars . . . Bhils, Kolis, Mahars and Mangs," were the original inhabitants of the country, enslaved and exploited by conquering Aryans, who had formulated a caste-based Hinduism as a means of deceiving the teeming masses and legitimizing their own power. It was the confirmed and sincere view of Jotirao that the ancient history of India was nothing but the struggle between Brahmins and non-Brahmins (Keer, 1964: 120). Hence, Phule consciously sought to bring together the major peasant castes (besides the Kunbis, or cultivators, the Malis or "garden" cultivators, and Dhangars, or shepherds) along with the large Untouchable castes of Mahars and Mangs in a common "front" against Brahmin domination (see O'Hanlon, 1985: 131). Phule's attack on

Brahminism was uncompromising. He realized that the seeds of the Brahmins' power, supremacy, and privileges lay in their scriptures and *Puranas,* and these works and the caste system were created to exploit the lower classes (see O'Hanlon, 1985: 122–132). Phule also reinterpreted sacred religious literature, for example, by reading the nine avatars of Vishnu as stages of the Aryan conquest and using King Bali as a counter-symbol to the elite's use of Ram, Ganapati, or Kali (see O'Hanlon, 1985: 137; Keer, 1964: 90–125). Thus, he attacked the Brahminical scriptures and *Puranas,* revolted against priestcraft and the caste system, and set in motion a social movement for the liberation of the Shudras, Ati-Shudras (Untouchables), and women.

Phule realized that the strongest hold of religious tradition on the people derived from the extensive integration of Hindu religious literature into the popular culture and oral traditions. Phule's answer to this was to provide alternative accounts of the texts, myths, and stories most common in popular Hinduism. He linked these with important symbols and structures from contemporary Maharashtrian society in order to convey the real community of culture and interest that united all lower castes against their historical and cultural adversaries: the Brahmins.

To fulfill his life's ambition to establish a casteless society, Phule founded the Satya Shodhak Samaj (truth-seeking society) on 24 September 1873. The Samaj set up the first school for girls and Untouchables. Phule also organized marriages without Brahmin priests, widow remarriages, and so on. According to Phule, the performance of any religious ceremony by a Brahmin priest for a member of another caste expresses in a concrete form the relations of purity between them that make up the basis for Hindu religious hierarchy. It is the Brahmin priest alone who, in his ritual purity, has the power to mediate between the human world and that of the high gods, and so it is he who controls the entry of divine power into the world (see Babb, 1975: 31–67). For this reason, Phule felt that the employment of Brahmin priests negated the very principle upon which he hoped a community of the lower castes would be based. The Satya Shodhak Samaj actively encouraged marriages without Brahmin priests. Thus, it assumed a vital role as the ideological conscience for all those who identified themselves with the lower castes, whether they belonged to the Samaj or to one of the numerous other groups working for lower-caste uplift.

A fundamental difference between the "historical" religions—Christianity and Islam—and Hinduism consists in their attitudes toward history. Whereas the latter conceives of human history as the eternal recurrence of illusion, the historical religion works out its destiny within those very processes, organized around the church, the visible body of the faithful, the book, and the incarnated savior. All human history takes its meaning from the struggle (Weber, 1958: 167). As we have seen, one of Phule's main concerns was to locate the struggle of the lower castes within history, to transform myth into history and establish a diachronic relation between present and past oppression. King Bali had stood as the symbol and mainstay of the pre-Aryan realm. Here, it is possible to see how Phule's perception of human history strengthened his scheme more generally. On the mass level, history became purposive (see O'Hanlon, 1985: 203–205).

Thus, the nineteenth century saw the beginning of a violent and controversial movement of protest among western India's low and Untouchable castes, aimed at the effects of their lowly position within the Hindu caste hierarchy (see O'Hanlon, 1985).

Cultural Controversies in the National Congress

A second stage in the modern development of Indian nationalism emerged in 1885 with the foundation of the Indian National Congress by an Englishman, Allan Octavian Hume. The congress tried to define a new India in terms of ideas borrowed from European political experience and Western social ethics (see Donald Eugene Smith, 1963: 880). All the same, by the end of the nineteenth century, there was a mighty struggle for the control of the congress. The two factions, namely the moderates and the extremists, held radically different views about the proper ends and means of the nationalist movement. Whereas the moderates in the congress, such as Dadabhai Naoraji, Madhava Govinda Ranade, and Gopal Krishna Gokhale, stood up for reforms in Hindu culture, extremists like B. G. Tilak glorified Hindu culture and opposed any kind of reform. The moderates, or liberals, envisioned a modernization of India through the adoption of the Western parameters of justice, order, rationality, and the secular state, Tilak, however, glorified the deeds of the Vedic civilization (Parvate, 1959: 463). Tilak's overall consideration was the promotion of solidarity and unity among the Hindus, and hence he emphasized the superiority of their religion, encouraged revivalism, politicized the Ganapati festival, and converted Shivaji into a cult figure, thus serving both religious and political objectives (Michael, 1986: 91–116). The style of the revivalists like Tilak was aggressive and tended to reflect a Kshatriya (warrior) worldview.

When Mohandas Gandhi publicly emerged on the Indian political scene after World War I as the Mahatma, he received widespread revivalist support. Indeed, many believed him to be one of them. Although Gandhi had much in common with the revivalists, many came to oppose him as they gradually became better acquainted with his ideas. Gandhi declared that his Hinduism included all that he knew to be best in Islam, Christianity, Buddhism, and Zoroastrianism. Gandhi strove unceasingly for Hindu-Muslim unity, convinced that ultimately both religions were true and valid (see Gandhi, 1949). His deepest conviction was that God, truth, and *ahimsa* (nonviolence) were all one and the same. *Satyagraha* (truth-force, nonviolent resistance) was thus based on Gandhi's personal religious faith and outlook.

The revivalists were disturbed by Gandhi's ascetic non-Kshatriya style of leadership, his definition of dharma as the nonviolent pursuit of "truth," and his assimilationist conception of the Indian nation, which he saw as a brotherhood or a confederation of communities. Kurtakoti, Sankaracharya (a Hindu spiritual guide) of Karvir peeth, implored Hindus to return to the militancy advocated by Tilak, Vivekananda, and Gose (Anderson and Damle, 1987: 20).

The Equality Question Among the Revivalists

As a result of the intensification of Hindu-Muslim tension between 1921 and 1923, the dormant Hindu Mahasabha, formed in 1915 as a forum for a variety of Hindu interests (e.g., cow protection, Hindi in the Devanagiri script, caste reforms, etc.), was revitalized. It is in this setting of "Hinduism in danger" that a new, more influential Hindu militant organization known as the Rashtriya Swayamsevak Sangh (RSS) was established in 1925 by Keshab Baliram Hedgewar, who was deeply influenced by Tilak. The RSS claims to defend Hinduism against its so-called antagonists. Its avowed objective is the unification of the Hindu community and the inculcation of a militant awareness of its common heritage and destiny. One of the most influential books in the development of Hindu nationalist ideology was the treatise on *Hindutva* by V. D. Savarkar, a close associate of Tilak. *Hindutva* refers to a people united by a common country, blood, history, religion, culture, and language. This idea became the foundation and basis of the RSS's activities. Members of all castes are welcomed into the RSS if they conform to behavioral standards considered proper by the RSS leaders. Those standards continue to reflect, to a larger extent, the Maharashtrian Brahmin cultural values of the founders of the RSS.

According to M. R. Golwalkar, who succeeded Hedgewar as the chief of the RSS, at the heart of Hindu culture is Hindu religion, and at the heart of Hindu religion are the noble ideas of the Vedas. He also asserted that the diverse languages of India are the offshoots of Sanskrit, the dialect of the gods and the enlightened Aryans (Golwalkar, 1947). Golwalkar regretted the fall of the Brahmin in Hindu society, which, according to him, was deliberately brought about by the British. Thus he presents what may be called the Golwalkar notion of social structure in these terms: The unique feature of our society is its diverse functional groups (castes). The present-day mind, accustomed to viewing through foreign "isms" and their high-sounding slogans of equality, has failed to grasp this unique feature and talks of classless society. The glorious main feature that once distinguished our society was the *varna vyavastha,* which, he says, "is being dubbed as casteism and scoffed at." There are some who never tired of propagating the idea that the caste system was responsible for our downfall. This is not true; the so-called caste-ridden society has remained intact and firm and alive and unconquerable, whereas the so-called casteless societies crumbled at the very outset before foreign conquests (Golwalkar, 1968: 89–120).

Gandhi's Approach to Caste and *Varna*

Hindu reformers, including Gandhi, were of the opinion that the Untouchables could maintain a Hindu as well as a Vankar or Malliga identity without the stigma of being Untouchables. The Hindu reformers delinked the problem of untouchability from the caste system. Untouchability, according to them, was not an essential part of Hinduism or, for that matter, of the caste system. It resulted from a violation of the basic spirit of Hinduism. "Varnashram, Gandhi asserted, was for the preservation of harmony and growth of soul" (Shah, 1995: 28). Gandhi repeatedly harped on the evils of untouchability. He himself adopted a Dalit girl as his daughter. He voluntarily decided to live with the Untouchables to become one with them. He symbolically called Untouchables Harijans, that is, "people of God." He started the Harijan Sevak Sangh to launch programs. It is in this context of Hindu revivalism and the Gandhian approach to caste and *varna* that one has to view the ideas and visions of non-Brahmin leaders like Periyar and Ambedkar.

Periyar's Vision for Justice

E. V. Ramaswamy Naicker, known as Periyar (Great Sage), was born in 1879 in Erode into a respectable middle-class family of artisans. He married at the age of thirteen, but after six years he became a sannyasi, traveling as a religious mendicant over the whole of India. In his visits to pilgrim centers, he gained an intimate knowledge of the evils of popular Hinduism and also of the exploitation of the masses by Brahmin priests. Periyar became convinced that casteism and Hinduism were one and the same. He wanted Hinduism, as he saw it, to be removed altogether. His movement took a turn toward racial consciousness and became a "Dravidian" movement, seeking to defend the rights of the Dravidians against Aryan domination. It blamed the Aryans for introducing an unjust and oppressive social system in the country (see Hardgrave, 1965: 17). Periyar realized that the important feature of all new ideologies of the elite was the "Aryan view of race." The Aryan view was adopted enthusiastically by the Indian elite as a new model for understanding caste. That is, Brahmins, Kshatriyas, and Vaishyas were held almost as a matter of definition to be the descendants of invading Aryans, whereas Shudras and Untouchables were those of the native conquered inhabitants. In this new language of caste and race, to claim Aryan descent was equivalent to claiming "twice-born" status, but to say "Dravidian" or "non-Aryan" was almost equivalent to saying "Shudra."

The high-caste elite of India began to take Aryan and Sanskritic culture as the basis of "Indian nationality," but in so doing they were in fact taking a part—the culture of the upper castes and roughly more northern groups—for the whole. Periyar's movement sought to defend the rights of the Dravidians against Aryan domination. He saw in the Brahmins the representatives of Hindu arrogance and the stronghold of social injustice (see Devanandan, 1960).

Periyar quit the Indian National Congress and attacked it as a tool of Brahmin domination. In 1925, he organized the "Self-Respect Movement," designed as a way to uplift Dravidians, seeking to expose Brahmin tyranny and the deceptive methods by which they controlled all spheres of Hindu life. He publicly ridiculed the *Puranas* as fairy tales, not only imaginary and irrational but grossly immoral as well. Periyar attacked the Hindu religion as the tool of Brahmin domination.

Under the Congress ministry of C. Rajagopalachari in 1937, Hindi was introduced to the south as a compulsory subject in schools. Taking this as an affront to Tamil culture and its rich literary tradition, Tamil patriots like Annadurai, Karunanithi, and others under the leadership of Periyar reacted with violent protest. He saw the imposition of Hindi as a step toward subjugation of the Tamil peoples by the north Indian Aryans. The Hindu religion was denounced as an opiate by which the Brahmins had dulled and controlled the masses: "A Hindu in the present concept may be a Dravidian, but a Dravidian in the real sense of the term cannot and shall not to be a Hindu" (A. S. Venu, cited in Harrison, 1960: 127). Pains were taken to destroy images of Hindu deities such as Rama and Ganesha. According to Periyar, "Rama and Sita are despicable characters, not worthy of imitation or admiration even by the lowest of fourth-rate humans." Ravana, on the other hand, is depicted as a Dravidian of "excellent character." In his preface to *The Ramayana: A True Reading,* he states that "the veneration of the story any longer in Tamil Nad is injurious and ignominious to the self-respect of the community and of the country" (Naicker, 1959: iii–iv).

On the eve of independence, Periyar called upon the Dravidian people of south India "to guard against the transfer of power from the British to the Aryans" (*The Hindu,* 11 February 1946). Fearing Brahmin dominance under Aryan "imperialism," he called for the formation of a separate southern Indian state, Dravidasthan. Today, the several Dravidian political parties in Tamil Nadu trace back their inspiration to Periyar in their program to build a Dravidian civilization on the Indian subcontinent.

Ambedkar, a Revolutionary

It is indeed impossible to understand the contemporary Dalit revolt without understanding the ideas of Bhimrao Ramji Ambedkar. For a growing number of young Dalits across India, many born after his death in 1956, he has become a symbol of a vision that can be achieved, a vision of freedom from social and economic injustice. Ambedkar attacked two central features of the Indian order: culturally enforced inequality and economic inequality. Throughout his writings and actions there is one common thread, that is, socioeconomic transformation in India requires a cultural revolution, one that will not only destroy the culture of the past but also build something of value in its place.

Ambedkar was inspired and guided by the noble example set by Mahatma Jotirao Phule. His example had an indelible imprint on Ambedkar's mind. He was determined to complete the work started by Jotirao, and it is not surprising that it became his life's mission (Rajasekhariah, 1971: 18–19; see also Keer, 1974: vii). Ambedkar led the fight against untouchability, Hinduism, and the Brahmin caste. He was convinced that the caste system was not only unjust but also immoral. He established a new dispensation, a new religion (neo-Buddhism) whose foundation is its unequivocal rejection of Hinduism. Ambedkar criticized the caste system vehemently. For him, the fight against casteism and untouchability was central, at the heart of his agenda. Hence, he was very critical of the two contemporary approaches to reform of the caste system, namely Dayananda Sarasvati's and Gandhi's (see Baxi, 1994). According to him, neither could bring about a real solution to casteism. He held that society should be based on the three fundamental principles of liberty, equality, and fraternity. If caste was to be destroyed, he said, then its religious foundation in the Vedas and *Shastras* must also be destroyed. Faith in these scriptures was nothing more than a legalized class ethic favoring the Brahmins: "If you wish to bring about a breach in the system, then you have got to apply the dynamite to the Vedas and the Shastras, which deny any part to reason, to the Vedas and Shastras, which deny any part to morality. You must destroy the Religion of the Smritis" (Ambedkar, 1945a: 70).

Ambedkar also rejected the position of Gandhi with regard to caste and its reform. Gandhi felt that the ancient Hindus had already achieved an ideal social system with *varna vyavastha*. According to Gandhi, "The law of *varna* means that everyone will follow as a matter of *dharma*-duty the hereditary calling of his forefathers. . . . he will earn his livelihood by following that calling" (Zelliot, 1992: 154). In contrast, Ambedkar believed that an ideal society had yet to be achieved in India. For him, the priority was not making Hinduism or Hindu society "shine forth" but building a new, equal, free, open, nonhierarchical, modern India. According to Ambedkar, "It is wrong to say that the problem of the Untouchables is a social problem. . . . the problem of the Untouchables is fundamentally a political problem (of minority versus majority groups)" (Ambedkar, 1945b: 190). Hence, he launched his revolutionary movement for the liberation and advancement of the Dalits. On 20 July 1942, he declared the following at Nagpur:

> With justice on our side, I do not see how we can lose our battle. The battle to me is a matter of full joy. The battle is in the fullest sense spiritual. There is nothing material or sordid in it. For our struggle is our freedom. It is a battle for the reclamation of human respectability which has been suppressed and mutilated by the Hindu social system and will continue to be suppressed and mutilated if in the political struggle the Hindus win and we lose. My final word of advice to you is, "educate, organise and agitate"; have faith in yourselves and never lose hope. (Das and Massey, 1995: viii)

Thus Ambedkar was able to put the untouchability issue on the center stage of Indian politics (see Shashi, 1992).

Ambedkar realized the painful truth that within Hinduism the Untouchables would never be able to get equal status and receive just treatment. He was also convinced that individual and group mobility was difficult for the Untouchables within the Hindu social system. In this context, he saw two possibilities for social emancipation: the political unity of Untouchables or an en masse conversion. Hence, in 1936 he talked of conversion to another religion: "Though I have been born a Hindu, I shall not die as a Hindu" (31 May 1936, Bombay). He had already made a first mention of conversion at the Yeola Conference of 1935.

Ambedkar's conversion call disturbed the Hindu leadership very much. Several leaders tried to persuade him not to go ahead. Ambedkar expressed surprise that the caste-Hindus, who had never shown any fellow feeling for the Untouchables, were suddenly beseeching them to stay within Hinduism. Since Untouchables had been for centuries ill-treated and humiliated by caste-Hindus, why did they suddenly take such an interest in keeping them within the Hindu fold?

On 14 October 1956, after long deliberation and a conscious choice in favor of Buddhism, Ambedkar took his *diksha* at Nagpur at 9:30 A.M. Assembled were about five lakh Mahars, who all converted to Buddhism on that day. Ambedkar's embrace of Buddhism was a strong protest against all that the Hindus had failed to do. For him *swaraj* did not mean anything if it did not also put an end to the slavery of the Untouchables (Gore, 1993: 144). Ambedkar's legacy at the time of his death included a large body of writings; a political party for all oppressed Indians, the Republican Party; a nascent Buddhist conversion movement; a system of higher education begun with Siddharth College in Bombay that was spreading to other cities; a host of reserved places for Scheduled Castes in education, administration, and legislative bodies; and a critical mass of awakened ex-Untouchables (Zelliot, 1996: 12).

Phule began and Periyar and Ambedkar continued the tradition of constructing an alternative identity of the people, based on non-Aryan and low-caste perspectives, that was critical not only of the oppressiveness of the dominant Hindu caste society but also of its claims to antiquity and to being the dominant Indian tradition (see Omvedt, 1994; 1995).

Politics of Numbers in Independent India

With the growth of democratic institutions and the "politics of numbers" in contemporary India, the Dalits began to assume some importance in national politics. The Dalit leaders in different political parties, in order to take advantage of the situation and bring about their liberation, began to mobilize forces.

Fighting untouchability, which was spread throughout the country and was deeply rooted in the minds of the people, was not a simple task. First, the Dalit leaders had to lift their brothers and sisters from their ignorance, to teach them to agitate against injustice, and to organize them into a pulsating force. The response was at first weak, clumsy, and slow, but later it became positive and healthy. Second, the leaders had to stand up to the reactionary caste-Hindus. Every step toward the liberation of the Dalits was followed by a sharp reaction from the caste-Hindus in the form of boycotts, atrocities, arson, and other crimes. In all such critical situations, the Dalit leaders had to stand by their poor brethren, raise their morale, and help them wage a peaceful and legal battle against the forces of reactionaries. Third, the Dalit leadership had to convince the government to accept their demands of human rights.

An Unfinished Revolution

All those things, certainly, have had an impact on the socioeconomic and cultural life of the Dalits. Economic development in general as well as the reservation policy and the special component plan have led to some improvement in the educational and economic status of the Dalits. Their literacy rate increased from 10.2 percent in 1961 to 37.41 percent in 1991, and their enrollment in schools doubled between 1981 and 1991. The reservation policy has also had a positive impact. The number of Dalit employees in government service has risen from 212,000 in 1956 to 604,000 in 1992, and those employed in public sector undertakings have increased in number from 40,000 in 1970 to 369,000 in 1992 (see S. K. Thorat, 1996: 1). These and other positive trends led to some decline in the percentage of poor Dalits. In rural areas the percentage of the poor among the Dalits declined from 58.07 percent in 1983–1984 to 50 percent in 1987–1988, and in urban areas this percentage went from 56.52 percent to 46.95 percent during the same period (see S. K. Thorat, 1996: 1).

Despite these improvements, Dalits still lag far behind other groups in Indian society. Their literacy rate is now 37 percent; that of non-Dalits is 57 percent. In rural areas, where most Dalits live, their economic base continues to be weak. In the late 1980s, 63 percent of the Dalit households were landless or near landless wage laborers, but only 31 percent of non-Dalit households were. Only a fraction of Dalits owned land, and 73 percent of those who did were marginal farmers with too little to live on. The cumulative result has been a high incidence of poverty among Dalits, 50 percent as compared with 37 percent among non-Dalits in 1987–1988. Meanwhile, civil rights violations and atrocities against Dalits continued to increase. In 1966–1976 there were 40,000 such atrocity cases, or 4,000 per year; in 1976–1978 there were 17,000, or 8,500 per year; in 1981–1986 there were 91,097, or 18,000 per year (S. K. Thorat, 1996: 4). The government admitted in parliament on 22 April 1994 that there were 62,113 cases of atrocities against Dalits and tribals between 1991 and 1993. The annual report of the Ministry of Welfare for 1995–1996 shows that the number of crimes committed against members of Scheduled Castes (SCs) and Scheduled Tribes (STs) by members of other groups has shown a continuous increase, with the number of cases rising from 25,352 in 1992 to 38,926 in 1994. The increase in crimes against SCs and STs in 1994, as compared with crimes in the preceding year, was as high as 36 and 27.4 percent, respectively (Godbole, 1997: 14). Studies indicate that atrocities were committed over land disputes and minimum wages as well as to prevent Dalits from securing justice under civil rights laws.

With regard to Dalit women, in all respects, they are at the lowest level of the socioeconomic and educational hierarchy. Dalit women tend to be concentrated in areas of work in which wages are lowest and regular employment least certain. In 1991, about 74 percent of them were agricultural laborers, whereas only 43 percent of the non-Dalit women were agricultural laborers. Even in urban areas, 28 percent of Dalit women were employed as agricultural labor, as compared with only 5 percent of the non-Dalit women (Vimal Thorat, 1997: 1).

The New Economic Policy also affects the Dalits adversely. After the new reforms were implemented in 1990, both unemployment and poverty levels increased. The poverty ratio increased from 38 percent to 48 percent in 1992. Since Dalits constitute the bulk of the poor and unemployed, they have suffered most. The number of Dalit employees in government service declined from 628,000 in 1991 to 604,000 in 1992, whereas those in the public sector dropped from 432,000 in 1990 to 369,000 in 1992 (see S. K. Thorat, 1996: 4). What is most disturbing is that most of this decline has occurred in the lower-level posts. Thus, the burden of the New Economic Policy has fallen most heavily upon the poor.

The persistence of poverty and caste injustice remain a shameful blot on Indian society. Over the past ten years, an emerging Dalit identity and social consciousness have created a new political consciousness among poor rural Dalits, which then spread beyond the Scheduled Castes to a much broader spectrum of the oppressed and hitherto excluded social strata. It is based on an attempted, though by no means yet realized, solidarity of the poor and the oppressed classes of people.

Today's political scene in India cannot be understood without taking into consideration the phenomenon of the upsurge in self-consciousness among Dalits and Other Backward Castes that has spread from the south and the west to the north. Among the northern states, the meteoric rise of the Bahujan Samaj Party in Uttar Pradesh since the 1980s is almost unprecedented. Of late, it has also made significant inroads in Punjab and Madhya Pradesh. The desecration of an Ambedkar statue in Mumbai on 11 July 1997 resulted not only in several deaths from police firings but caused widespread protests and *bandhs* (strikes and lockouts) throughout Maharashtra and Gujarat. The new spirit of independence among Dalits is not confined to economically developed western states of India but is a countrywide phenomenon and, together with the logic of fresh realignments of political parties, has made the Dalits the new pivotal players in Indian politics. The Dalits and the backward castes hold immense political potential, if they could be united into a powerful force. They would bring about a true social revolution for equality and justice.

There are some signs of such change today. The Dalits are asserting themselves much more than before (Vanaik, 1997: 323–326). They have decided that they will not call themselves "Harijans," simply because it is a paternalistic expression. There are numerous small and large organizations of Dalits all over the country, such as the Dalit Sangharsh Samiti in Karnataka; the Indian Dalit Federation in Kerala; the Dalit Maha Sabha in Andhra Pradesh; the Bahujan Samaj Party in Uttar Pradesh, Bihar, and other northern states; and Dalits Sena consisting of Dalits from several states. The Dalits are trying to form a well-coordinated political movement with an all-India organization and all-India leadership that can challenge the established sociopolitical order. This aim is inspired by their resentment against the existing social system, which expresses itself through various forms of agitation and struggle and is bound to acquire the momentum of a national movement in the years to come (Ayrookuzhel, 1990: 14–23).

However, the movement is always opposed by external and sometimes by internal forces. Every move of Dalit mobilization is virtually followed by a counter upper-caste assemblage. The ongoing controversy centered around Ambedkar and his detractors is an example (see Shourie, 1997). The Phule-Ambedkar ideology has challenged the very legitimacy of Hindutva/Brahminism as a social order or religion. While there is a concerted attempt by the Brahminical forces to co-opt Jotirao Phule and Ambedkar as "Hindu reformers," a sustained attack has also been launched by Hindutva/Brahminical ideologues like Arun Shourie to denigrate and malign these great Dalit-Bahujan personalities. In reality this controversy centered around Ambedkar and his detractors should be analyzed in the broader perspective of the emerging sociopolitical trends in the country. As discussed earlier, the social justice movement has become one of the most remarkable and relevant sociopolitical movements of modern India and is evolving into a democratic, empowering, and assertive mass movement against the Brahminical social order. Ambedkar is of central relevance to the growing human rights movement and is fast emerging as the pan-Indian leader, symbol of the Dalits and other oppressed masses. Precisely because of this, Ambedkar has been chosen as a prime target since he best symbolizes the aspirations of the Dalit-Bahujan masses.

Unfortunately, Dalits are also divided among themselves, and their leadership too is riven with both confusion and schism. The Dalit movement is beset by the virus of endemic co-option—from the old days of the Scheduled Caste Federation and the Republican Party to the Dalit Panthers to the various antireservation movements to the recent controversy over Arun Shourie's book on Ambedkar (Shourie, 1997). In spite of this experience of continuing letdowns and reactions, there are also signs of new hope emerging, namely the Dalit-Bahujan alliance of Scheduled Castes and Other Backward Castes, groups couched not only in terms of achieving social justice but also capturing political power (see Kothari, 1997: 439–458). There is also no shortage of sensitive and committed people in the Dalit movement to take forward the vision of Phule, Periyar, and Ambedkar. Hence, what is required is a strong unity among the poor, the marginalized, and the outcastes. Achieving unity will not be an easy task because these groups are internally divided into several castes and subcastes, externally scattered throughout the vast country, and prone to fall prey to divisive forces. Therefore, the Dalit leadership has to strive constantly for bringing about unity among the Dalits and other oppressed groups to fight against their common foes and enemies (see Kshirsagar, 1994).

Conclusion

The pioneers who worked for the liberation of the Dalits and other backward castes, like Phule, Periyar, and Ambedkar, propagated the idea of the need for a cultural revolution or a total transformation of Indian society. They rejected the vision of the upper castes, which identified the Indian nation as basically Hindu, deriving from Vedic times, and fundamentally a creation of the Aryan people. While rejecting the ideals of the upper-caste notion of Indian society based on the ideas and values of Manu and *varna vyavastha*, they propagated the principles of equality, justice, liberty, and rationality. This broad-based standpoint is widely accepted among the Dalits.

There is, however, much discussion and dispute on the means of attaining these ideals of social justice. This problem is worsened by the multiple divisions existing in the Dalit ranks; for example, the Dalits are divided among themselves along subcaste lines and, like the proverbial crabs, keep clawing at each other, pulling down those who move up, so that all of them remain in their lowly position. They are also hindered by the present political climate in which the upper castes are trying to establish a unified Hindu cultural nationalism.

All the same, it is true that if the goals of a movement are clearly outlined and well-defined and if it finds active support, first in its own ranks and second in those of others likely to be sympathetic to its cause, the movement will become an organic, living entity. What is needed is good and able leadership. If the cause is right and the leadership is good, then the movement will certainly grow even if faced with antagonism and hostility. Every step ahead will encourage the Dalits to move forward toward final victory.

References

Ambedkar, B. R. 1945a. *Annihilation of Caste*. Bangalore: Dalit Sahitya Akademy.
———. 1945b. *What Congress and Gandhi Have Done to the Untouchables*. Bombay: Thacker.
Anderson, W. K., and S. D. Damle. 1987. *The Brotherhood in Saffron: The Rashtriya Swayamsevak Sangh and Hindu Revivalism*. New Delhi: Vistaar Publications.

Ayrookuzhel, Abraham, A. M. 1990. "The Ideological Nature of the Emerging Dalit Consciousness," *Religion and Society* 37 (3), September: 14–23.
Babb, Lawrence, A. 1975. *The Divine Hierarchy: Popular Hinduism in Central India*. New York: Columbia University Press.
Baxi, Upendra. 1994. "Emancipation as Justice: Babasaheb Ambedkar's Legacy and Vision," in *Ambedkar and Social Justice*, Vol. 1. Edited and published by Ministry of Information and Broadcasting, Government of India, Delhi.
Damle, Y. B., and Jacob Aikara. 1982. *Caste, Religion and Politics in India*. New Delhi: Oxford and IBH Publishing Co.
Das, Bhagwan, and James Massey. 1995. *Dalit Solidarity*. Delhi: The Indian Society for Promoting Christian Knowledge (ISPCK).
Devanandan, P. D. 1960. *The Dravida Kazagham: A Revolt Against Brahmanism*. Bangalore: Christian Institute for the Study of Religion and Society.
Gandhi, M. K. 1949. *Communal Unity*. Ahmedabad: Navajivan.
Godbole, Madhav. 1997. "Crime and Punishment: Trying Times for Tribal Peoples," *The Times of India*, 14 February, p. 14 (Mumbai).
Golwalkar, M. S. 1947. *We or Our Nationhood Defined* (4th edition). Nagpur: Bharat Prakashan.
———. 1968. *Bunch of Thoughts*. Bangalore: Bharat Prakashan.
Gore, M. S. 1993. *The Social Context of an Ideology: Ambedkar's Political and Social Thought*. New Delhi: Sage Publications.
Hardgrave, Robert L., Jr. 1965. *The Dravidian Movement*. Bombay: Popular Prakashan.
Harrison, Selıng. 1960. *India: The Most Dangerous Decades*. Princeton: Princeton University Press.
Irudayaraj, Xavier (ed.). 1990. *Emerging Dalit Theology*. Madras: Jesuit Theological Secretariat.
Keer, Dhananjay. 1964. *Mahatma Jotirao Phooley, Father of Indian Social Revolution*. Bombay: Popular Prakashan.
———. 1974. *Dr. Ambedkar: Life and Mission*. Bombay: Popular Prakashan.
Kejariwal, O. P. 1988. *The Asiatic Society of Bengal and the Discovery of India's Past*. Delhi: Oxford University Press.
Kothari, Rajni. 1988. "Integration and Exclusion in Indian Politics," *Economic and Political Weekly* 23 (43), 22 October: 2223–2229.
———. 1997. "Rise of the Dalits and the Renewed Debate on Caste," in Partha Chatterjee (ed.), *State and Politics in India*. New Delhi: Oxford.
Kshirsagar, R. K. 1994. *Dalit-Movement in India and Its Leaders*. New Delhi: M. D. Publications.
Marshall, P. J. 1970. *The British Discovery of Hinduism in the Eighteenth Century*. Cambridge: Cambridge University Press.
Massey, James. 1990. "Christian Dalits in India: An Analysis," *Religion and Society* 27 (3), September: 40–53.
Michael, S. M. 1986. "Politicization of Ganapathi Festival," *Social Compass* 23 (2–3): 185–197.
Naicker, Ramaswamy, E. V. 1959. *The Ramayana: A True Reading*. Madras: Rationalist Publications.
O'Hanlon, Rosalind. 1985. *Caste, Conflict and Ideology: Mahatma Jotirao Phule and Low Caste Protest in Nineteenth-Century Western India*. Cambridge: Cambridge University Press, in association with Orient Longman Ltd.
Omvedt, Gail. 1976. *Cultural Revolt in a Colonial Society: The Non-Brahmin Movement in Western India, 1873 to 1930*. Pune: Scientific Socialist Education Trust.

———. 1994. *Dalits and the Democratic Revolution: Dr. Ambedkar and the Dalit Movement in Colonial India.* New Delhi: Sage Publications.
———. 1995. *Dalit Visions: The Anti-Caste Movement and the Construction of an Indian Identity.* New Delhi: Orient Longman.
Parvate, T. V. 1959. *Gopal Krishna Gokhale.* Ahmedabad: Navjivan Publishing House.
Prabhakar, M. E. 1990. "Developing a Common Ideology for Dalilts of Christian and Other Faiths," *Religion and Society* 27 (3), September: 24–39.
Rajasekhariah, A. M. 1971. *B. R. Ambedkar: The Politics of Emancipation.* Bombay: Sindhu Publications.
Shah, Ghanshyam. 1995. "Dalit Movements and Search for Identity," in Manorama Savur and Indra Munshi (eds.), *Contradictions in Indian Society.* Jaipur: Rawat Publications, pp. 23–45.
Shashi, S. S. (ed.). 1992. *Ambedkar and Social Justice.* New Delhi: Government of India.
Shourie, Arun. 1997. *Worshipping False Gods: Ambedkar and the Facts Which Have Been Erased.* New Delhi: ASA Publications.
Smith, Donald Eugene. 1963. *India as a Secular State.* London: Princeton University Press.
Smith, William Roy. 1938. *Nationalism and Reform in India.* London: Yale University Press.
Thorat, S. K. 1996. "Dalits and the New Economic Policy," *Dalit International Newsletter* (2): 1, 4.
Thorat, Vimal. 1997. "Dalit Women," *Dalit International Newsletter* (1): 1, 10.
Vanaik, Achin. 1997. *Communalism Contested: Religion, Modernity and Secularisation.* New Delhi: Vistaar.
Weber, Max. 1958. *The Religion of India.* Hans H. Gerth and Don Martindale, eds. and trans. New York: Free Press.
Zelliot, Eleanor. 1992. *From Untouchable to Dalit: Essays on the Ambedkar Movement.* Delhi: Manohar.
———. 1996. "The Dalit Movement," *Dalit International Newsletter* 1 (1): 1, 4.

3

Phule's Critique of Brahmin Power

Mahesh Gavaskar

Nowadays, British colonialism is loaded with every possible sin. The cause of every malaise in contemporary postcolonial India is sought in policies initiated by the British. So much so that the malaise of caste reservation and its recent manifestation in the form of the Mandal Commission is traced to the colonial method of mapping the Indian populace according to their caste identities in the government censuses and gazetteers. That such a codification had a role to play in the emergence of various caste associations and caste-based politics in the early decades of this century is not to be denied. But to emphasize the colonial authorities' ascribing rigidity to caste identities while overlooking the denial of basic civil rights in precolonial times on the basis of those very identities is lopsided. If it were not, there would have been no need for Jotirao Phule to throw open the well in his courtyard to the Shudras and Ati-Shudras in 1869.

The Phule-Ambedkarian discourse draws attention to the fact that just as India went through a phase of British colonialism, it had previously passed at various stages of its history through "Brahminical colonialism," and that the British colonialism inadvertently made available certain normative and cognitive tools with which to fight Brahminical colonialism.

Brahminical colonialism has its roots in certain Hindu scriptures that provide divine justification for caste-based discrimination and domination. In times of resurgence of orthodoxy, in the pre-British days, caste-based communitarian rules strictly guided the daily life of the populace. Economic exploitation was implicit in caste communities but was legitimized on extra-economic grounds. British colonialism, in contrast, was a child of capitalist global expansion. Yet, the epoch-making contributions of the Enlightenment had given birth to the notion of civil society, though the colonial state was often to violate the norms of civil society during its hold over India. Nevertheless, civil society was the contradiction of the colonial state at an ideational level and led to the latter's ultimate demise. Phule locates himself in this space of civil society to develop a critique of Brahminical colonialism, which apparently was devoid of such a notion.

This chapter is a textual reading of Phule's corpus and attempts to argue that the normative ground for Phule's favorable attitude toward British rule stems from his identification of the British with the forces of enlightenment, which aimed to reconstitute intrahuman and human-divinity relationships on a higher level of egalitarianism.

Situating Phule

The political economy of pre-British days granted many bodies, extending from the tillers of the land to the topmost political authority, rights in the agricultural produce. The produce was expropriated by power holders beyond the ambit of the village, and within the confines of the village the produce was distributed according to the customary practice of *balutedari* prevalent in Maharashtra in those days. Thus, an interlinked two-tier structure reigned before the advent of the Britishers—first, a hierarchy that included *deshmukhs, mansabdars, jagirdars,* and the Mughal emperor (or the Peshwa, the regional ruler of the Deccan) standing above the village system and, second, the *balutedari* pattern determining the intravillage relationships. In a long process spanning the latter half of the eighteenth century through the first half of the nineteenth century, the British knocked off the top half of this two-tier structure and in its place either institutionalized the *zamindari* system to collect land revenue or, as in the Deccan, inaugurated the *ryotwari* system, wherein the cultivator paid revenue directly to the state (Fuller, 1989). The *ryotwari* system, besides doing away with a host of intermediaries between the state and the cultivator, introduced private ownership of land into the village economy.[1] Land was no longer owned by the village community as a whole but by individual *meerasdars*. Firmly tied to their piece of land and with no obligations to the village community, they were bound to develop a worldview that saw previous interdependencies of the *balutedari* as parasitical upon agricultural produce.

The new bureaucratic setup of the British administration, accompanied by the development of communication infrastructure, opened up new avenues of employment in the colonial period. This resulted in increased labor migration between cities and their hinterlands. A handful rising from the lower sections of semirural society took advantage of the various schemes of development initiated by the British and in the process came in contact with the urban environment.

> The process of "development," i.e. of building the roads, railroads and buildings that linked Maharashtrian agriculture to the world economy,

also required labour and its organisation. The business of contracting for these development projects which grew in importance after 1850, was an important source of wealth . . . at lower levels of the contracting process many non-Brahmans would rise to a fair degree of wealth; these were not usually old aristocratic landlords or wealthier peasants, but often poor and rising men. (Omvedt, 1976: 75)[2]

But this social mobility also made these upcoming men from the lower strata painfully aware of the need for acquisition of literacy skills to secure employment. Since, within Hindu society, the Brahmins traditionally enjoyed the privilege of learning, they were able, in spite of the downfall of the Peshwai, to make a smooth transition to the new order and corner almost all the job opportunities. At the village level, because of the introduction of a new legal system, the traditional role of the *patil* (village headman) as maintainer of law and order became redundant, and it was the Brahmin *kulkarni* (village accountant) who gained in importance. Thus, the colonial transition foregrounded the Brahmin in two ways. First, the gradual demise of the *balutedar* and the increasing penetration by a monetary economy brought to the forefront the *joshi* (village priest–astrologer) at his unproductive parasitical best. Second, in the new expanding economy too, the Brahmins, with a virtual monopoly over jobs, were an overwhelming presence.

Reality Redefined

Phule, who was born in Pune into a Mali (gardener) household of comparative stability a decade after the collapse of Peshwa rule, was to occupy in his later years the strategic socioeconomic position of a member of the rising, independent yeomanry, which placed him at the center of the changing times. Besides his exposure to new intellectual currents after coming in contact with Christian missionaries in his early formative years, Jotirao's agricultural activities drew him into a widening market circuit of rural-urban interlinkages. Govind Ganapat Kale, a younger contemporary of Phule, recalls that in the 1870s Phule owned 60 acres of land at Manjri on the outskirts of Pune.

> Besides the farm at Manjri, the main income earning activities of Jotirao were contracts of construction works, a shop vending *Mushi* and an agency to sell vegetables. . . . The tunnel at Katraj on Pune-Satara road was completed shortly before my birth. Jotirao had taken sub-contract for this scheme. Further, he had taken a sub-contract of supplying stones, cement for the construction of a dam on Mula-Mutha and a bridge Yervada. (Kale, n.d.: 12)

Transactions at these sites provided Phule with firsthand experience of Brahmin nepotism and corruption at the lower and intermediate rungs of the colonial bureaucracy. The recent past of Peshwai where the Brahmins (especially, the *chitpawan* or *kokanastha* Brahmin whom Phule consistently addresses in his writings as "Bhat") controlled economic, administrative, and cultural functions raised for Phule an ominous specter of the persistence of Brahmin domination into the future. Thus, when Phule launched a scathing attack on Brahmins for their privileged positions in both the decaying and the emerging economies, the particular historical background of Peshwai together with a couple of significant events in his life was crucial in formulating his critique.

The rule of Bajirao II (1796–1818), the last Peshwa, besides being a period of sheer wastage of wealth on decadent practices and utter chaos in administration, was the period when Brahminical orthodoxy attained its zenith. As Narayan Vishnu Joshi notes:

> In those days the brahmins of Poona had grown supercilious and purity pollution was strictly observed. Mahars, mangs, chambhars, bhangi, dheds were not even allowed to spit on roads. They should walk with earthern pots tied to their waists. If a brahmin is noticed on the road [they] should immediately sit down for shadow not fall [on the brahmins]. Such was their misery. (Joshi, 1868: 61)

The amount of money that was distributed as *dakshina* for the Brahmins got enormously inflated in Bajirao II's regime, and a five-day spectacle of Ramana used to be held annually in Pune. Brahmins, all and sundry from Kashi in the north to Kumbhakonam in the south, used to flock to attend the "Ramana." This dependence on *dakshina* made them lazy, ignorant, and greedy. They were chiefly interested in "Brahman-Bhojan" and considered the British to be residents of an island named Calcutta (Joshi, 1868: 69). The Brahmins of the late Peshwai boasted of their superiority, recounting that only two *varnas*—Brahmins and Shudras—remained in the *kalyug* after Parashuram completely annihilated the Kshatriyas. Such being the common notions of those days, it is not surprising to read that when Govindrao Phule sent his son Jotirao to a village school near Pune, a Brahmin clerk insisted that Govindrao withdraw his son from the school since learning was not the dharma of a Shudra. It was later, after a Muslim teacher, Gaffar Beg Munshi, and a British administrator, Mr. Liggit, prevailed on Govindrao's behalf, that Jotirao was admitted to a Scottish mission school run by Murray Mitchell.[3]

Another incident occurred when Phule was twenty years of age. He was upbraided for joining the marriage procession of his Brahmin friend and thus considering himself equal to the Brahmins. In those days, Phule and his Brahmin friends used to take lessons in *dandapatta* under the tutelage of Lahuji Mang. The body-building exercises and training in martial skills were aimed at accumulating strength to drive away the British.[4] But Phule's experiences of discrimination in his life convinced him that far more important than fomenting anti-British hatred was the need to cleanse the minds of his fellow men and women of the outdated belief system that denied equal status to all human beings. It was this conviction that prompted Phule to extend normative support to British rule, which, Phule expected, would unleash the forces of enlightenment to root out the Brahminical religion that legitimized evil customs and practices.

(Re)Entry into History

Phule locates the beginnings of Brahminical tyranny in the usurpation by the Brahmins of a privileged position for themselves in the form of Bhudev. This not only helped them justify asymmetrical application of justice in mundane matters but appropriated to them a position more exalted than a god's. The following conversation between a Brahmin priest and an illiterate Kunbi woman from *Tritya Ratna*, a play Phule wrote for the Dakshina Prize Committee in 1855, brings out the Brahmin's claim to omnipotence. The *joshi* informs the Kunbi woman that the child of her neighbor died because

> Joshi: . . . had she satisfied me [by giving ample *bhiksha*] then certainly I would have removed all the evils [*pidda*] on her son and she would have bore a son, isn't so? . . . .
> Bai: I can't understand what evils prevailed over her son, why don't you tell me?
> Joshi: Don't you know the evil forces of planet? O, where a god like Mahadev had to hide under waters fearing him and who has escaped from his clutches? (Phule, 1991: 6)

It is because of his sway over destiny, his power of making and breaking others' futures, that he should be fed properly, claims the Brahmin. Phule denounces this parasitical livelihood.

> To ashes go your living
> Fresh food without toil. (Phule, 1991: 97)

With the use of well-chosen phrases like "*arranging* the horoscope" (*rashichakra mandun*), "*laying out* the planets" (*graha yojuniya*), "*plotting* in mind, *inventing* planets" (*mani yojun, graha dhundun*), Phule unveils the concoctedness of the Brahmin world. The Brahmins make merry by defrauding ignorant folk who, as a result, sink into absolute misery. Phule argues that the laboring masses, by being trapped in notions of *daiva* (fate), *sanchit* (accumulated demerits of previous births), and *prarabdha* (predestination), have lost their dialectical relationship with the world and have become *dasa* to external forces. Hence, Phule exhorts that British rule is the appropriate moment to recollect their glorious heritage and liberate themselves from the thralldom of the Brahmins.

> It's god's grace that the Britishers have come and denounced the bhats totally, How aryas became masters, shudras slave. This is the time to inquire the fraud. (Phule, 1991: 557)

Tale of a Prisonhouse

> Narratives are always told from someone's point of view. . . . Narrative does not therefore aspire to be a universal form of discourse. It draws lines, distributes people. . . . Narratives are not for all to hear, for all to participate in to an equal degree. It has a self in which it originates, a self which tell the story. (Kaviraj, 1992: 44, 59)

To grasp the narrative structure of *Gulamgiri,* especially Phule's vituperation of some Hindu myths, the theological underpinnings of Phule's vision need to be first understood. Keeping company with Christian missionaries, Phule came to accept the deist conception of the universe wherein God—Phule calls him *Nirmik,* the creator—after creating the world, no longer intervenes, allowing the world to operate according to the laws of reason. Says Phule:

> The creator has produced all things. After working day and night by contemplating on where and how to utilise each object [one will realise] the *unfathomable power, unfathomable skill and unfathomable splendour* of the creator. (Phule, 1991: 445; emphasis in original)

This implies a radical transcendentalization of God, a separation of the superhuman from the human world, of myth from history. From this perspective, Hindu myths, which display the immanence of supernatural forces in the human world, are rendered highly problematic. *Gulamgiri,* by situating itself in chronological time as against mythical time, narrates a sequence of dramatic events, a history of conflict extending back 3,000 years between alien Aryan invaders and indigenous Shudra–Ati-Shudras. It dispels the sacred aura bestowed by Hindu myths on its deities of great and little traditions and reveals them in human form. Thus, Narasimha, Vaman, Parashuram, and others no more appear as incarnations of the same "Lord" Vishnu but as successive chiefs of an army waging war against the aborigines. Similarly, on the indigenous side, Khandoba, Jotiba, Mhasoba, and others are no longer "deities" of a little tradition in the Hindu pantheon but regional chiefs in the regime of King Bali. Phule coins his own etymology to explain the origins of their names. For instance, "Khandoba" emerged because Bali made his lieutenant chief of nine provinces (*khands*) of his kingdom, and "Mhasoba" is a corruption of the original *mahasuba* (large province) (Phule, 1991: 150–151). Phule's construction of the "Aryabhats" as Satanic forces has its roots in his acceptance of Christian theology.[5] The Christian theology that conceived of God, the creator of the universe, as essentially good attributed the sufferings in the mundane realm to the evils inherent in man himself. Thus, Phule says:

> The implicit accusation against God is turned around to become an explicit accusation against man. In this curious reversal the problem of theodicy is made to disappear and in its turn appears a problem of anthropodicy. (Berger, 1969: 74)

Employing "the form of a catechism," Jotiba informs his pupil, Dhondiba, about the essential evil nature of the Aryabhats.

> Dhondiba: How was Narasimha by nature?
> Jotiba: Narasimha was greedy, deceiving, treacherous, cunning, heartless and cruel. . . .
> Dhondiba: How was Parashuram by nature?
> Jotiba: Parashuram was reckless, adventurous, wicked, pitiless, stupid and mean. . . . (Phule, 1991: 160)

Thus, Phule's historiography presents a Manichaean world with a ceaseless battle between the forces of good and evil. If in the ancient times the opposite camp had villains ranging from Matsyas and Varahas to Narasimha and Parashuram, on his side, Phule narrates, were heroes like Shankhasur, Hiranyakashapu, and Bali. It was in this period that the most savage violence, aggression, looting, and plundering took place. It was after Parashuram annihilated the Kshatriyas that the age of coercion ended and the age of domination started. *Smritis, Samhitas,* and *Shastras* were compiled to establish hegemony; diacritical markers like *Gayatri mantra* and sacred thread[6] were invented to legitimize superiority; and Shankaracharya, Mukundraj, Dnyaneshwar, and Ramdas philosophized to reinforce the Brahminical view of the world (Phule, 1991: 156–167). In recent times, according to the divine plan, the Muslims were entrusted with the mission of freeing the lame Shudra–Ati-Shudra from the slavery of crafty Aryabhats, but they failed to execute their task because they became engrossed in aristocratic pleasures (Phule, 1991: 457).[7] Now it was upon the British to rescue the subject populace from Brahminical oppression. Phule reorients the cyclical notion of *yuga* to suit his eschatology. If the orthodox Brahmins of his times were lamenting, "Kalyug aale, vidya shudragharigeli" (*Kalyug* has descended; knowledge is passed on to the Shudras), Phule inversely hails the coming of the British as *satyayug:*

> With the dawn of truth, wisdom of vedas stunts . . .
> By giving knowledge to shudra, bhudev is put to shame. (Phule, 1991: 422–423)

Yet the struggle against the evil forces is not over, cautions Phule. Brahmins in new incarnations of *kulkarni* and *bhatkamagar* are maintaining day-and-night vigils over their interests in villages and urban centers and poisoning the minds of the British against the Shudras. In *Brah-manache Kasab* (Priestcraft exposed), by depicting the omnipresence of Brahmins in the roles of a priest, a schoolteacher, a *kulkarni*, a *mamlatdar*, a reformer, a clerk in the public works, and a reporter in the vernacular press, Phule builds a demonology of *gramrakshas* (village demons) and *Kalamkasais* (wielders of pen) out to gobble up the ignorant Shudras. Behind this demonology lays Phule's sharp grasp of power relations that made him boldly state:

> We know perfectly well that the Brahmin will not descend from his self-raised high pedestal and meet his Coonbee [*sic*] and low caste brethren on an equal footing without a struggle. (Phule, 1991: 125)

And it was this acumen that drove him to search for an alternative center of power that would overthrow the inegalitarian social setup of his times.

Recuperating "Balistan"

Phule also discerned that power had been transferred from the sword to the pen and hence that any transformation in power relations meant establishing command over the new skill. Convinced that the Brahmin *pantoji* (schoolteacher) would never step forward to disseminate knowledge among the lower orders, Phule beseeches, pleads, advises, and warns the British to exert their state apparatus to educate the downtrodden. Yet, to his chagrin, Phule notices that the colonial education system, instead of addressing the needs of the downtrodden, is bent upon prioritizing higher education, which ultimately serves the interests of the upper castes. Phule graphically depicts the drain of wealth within the country wherein the taxes paid by the laboring classes go into educating the sons of Brahmins:

> He who owns goods suffers the most
> goes the Pathan saying,
> children of queer people study;
> Mali, Kunbi slog in the fields to pay taxes,
> don't have enough to clothe. (Phule, 1991: 77)

He demands, "How long should the shudras pay funds, to feed aryas, says Joti" (Phule, 1991: 568). What most alarms Phule is that although times have changed, the Brahmins still continue to function as middlemen, albeit in a different way. If in pre-British days the *purohit* used to withhold knowledge from the masses, in contemporary times, the *pantojis* deny access to education to the downtrodden. Hence, it is with great apprehension that Phule observes the political developments of the later years of his life. The formation of the Sarvajanik Sabha in 1870 and the Indian National Congress in 1885 are seen as Brahmin ploys to oust the British.[8] These Brahminical moves, intended to give them a decisive role in politics, provoke Phule to question their claim to represent the whole of India. Phule debunks the absolutist claim of the nationalist by reminding them of their culture based on *bhed:*

> Listen, crafty aryabhat brahmins following the mischievous, self-serving religion of the aryas consider the shudras inferior. . . . Moreover, besides themselves, crafty, excessively puritan aryabhats imposed ban on intermarriage and inter-dining amongst all shudra-atishudra because of which their different lifestyles, habits, customs do not merge. How is it possible [to accept] that the crisp "kadbole" born out of a unity of such eighteen varieties be a "ekmaya lok," a "Nation" [*sic*]? (Phule, 1991: 494)

It is against this *bhedniti* (ethic of discrimination) of the Aryabhats, which ghettoizes communities into programmed behavior, that Phule posits his Satya Shodhak Samaj based on universal brotherhood. Phule stresses fraternity as a distinctive characteristic of his future society so as to sharply distinguish its *jagbhandu* (universal pattern) from the *jatbhau* (kinship pattern) of the Aryabhats. Further, even though the relationship between the *Nirmik* and earthly creatures is that of parent and child (not a blood relationship but one based on faith), the transcendentalization of God makes "him" remote and in a way foregrounds the fraternal aspect among the residents of the earth. Says Phule, "Hug brotherly Christians, Muslims, Mangs, Brahmins" (Phule, 1991: 537). Nonetheless, Phule's *Nirmik,* being transcendental and unitary, like the sun, the moon, and the wind, is equally available to all (Phule, 1991: 536). It is in this sense of empirical confirmation that Phule's *Nirmik* is *sarvajanik* and not esoteric and hidden as the gods of the Aryabhats are in the Vedas. Moreover, Phule's *Nirmik,* by being nonexclusive, that is, by being accessible to all at any particular moment, does not have any chosen people and chosen language through which to reveal itself. In fact, Phule views Brahminical mystification as an outcome of the withdrawal of the Brahmins—either in the form of renunciation or of their ideas about purity and pollution—from any engagement with the empirical world. This has goaded them to despise natural functions of human organs and deluded them into believing that self-mortification will reveal "Brahma" (Phule, 1991: 564–565). Nowhere does Phule's eulogization of labor as value come out as strongly as in his thirteen-stanza poem on a Kunbi woman entitled "Kulumbin." If the early Phule predominantly portrays the reified labor of toiling masses as a tool of Brahmin exploitation, the later Phule, by attaching positive value to productive labor, symbolically undermines the Brahmin lifestyle by speaking about it consistently in negative terms.[9] Thus, in "Kulumbin," the labor of the Kunbi woman, near the hearth and in the fields, becomes the point of reference. Whereas her labor nourishes and sustains the whole of humankind, including the "Brahmin beggar," the *bhatin* (Brahmin woman) "doesn't look after shudra children, doesn't kiss them" (Phule, 1991: 485).

Like labor, reciprocity is another normative site defining human relations in Phule's schemata, which is opposed to the hierarchical notions of Aryans.[10] The myth of the dispossession of Baliraja by Vaman is read politically by Phule as the destruction of the egalitarian, agrarian community of Bali and the establishment of a hierarchical society of Aryabhats. Phule, by identifying the present-day Shudra–Ati-Shudras as descendants of Bali, legitimizes the claim that they are the primordial inhabitants of this land.[11] Thus, by providing contestatory renditions of history, education, politics, and religion and morals, Phule repoliticized diverse arenas of public discourse. In a combative mood, he challenges, "Brahmananache Ved Maidani Aana na" (bring the Vedas of the Brahmins out into the open).

"Productive" Power

There is, however, a theological inconsistency in Phule's worldview. If Phule means his *Nirmik* to be transcendental, devoid of human attributes, then it is surprising to find him saying that *Nirmik* was enraged at the intemperance of the Muslims and dispossessed them of their glory. Thereafter,

> he raised the Englishmen in an extremely barbarous country, and making them brave, *deliberately* sent them *to this country to liberate* the lame shudra-atishudra from the *slavery* of crafty aryabhats. (Phule, 1991: 457; emphasis in original)

Thus, Phule's "God" reveals human passions and motivations. Yet, politically, Phule is consistent. Throughout his "conjectural reconstruction of [the] past" Phule searches for those forces that at a normative level espoused the cause of egalitarianism. Seen from this perspective, Phule's *Nirmik* is his imagining of an absolutist power center that works in his favor.[12] In a way, Phule recognizes that power is essential, even to establishing egalitarianism.[13]

Though Phule's attribution of egalitarian purpose to the pre-British state(s) is open to question, his similar expectation from the British colonial state is not exaggerated. For the first time in the history of India, the state, as established by the British colonialists, was poised to do away with its "traditional marginality" that had inhibited it from restructuring social relations on a large scale.[14] The British colonial state in the first half of the nineteenth century, buoyed by the evangelical and utilitarian zeal of a "civilizing mission," certainly articulated such ambitions.[15] But the resistance of traditional, entrenched power centers in India forced the British colonial administrators to take a negotiating stand (a position that made Phule impatient with British rule) and, later, as the exploitative political economy of colonialism became all too evident, to abandon its self-imposed role altogether. If Phule's acuteness is seen in his excavating of the Brahminical self-interest in the maintainence of a hierarchical society, its shortcoming is that he overlooked the vested interests of the British as a colonial power. Though it is true that he severely admonished the British rulers for neglecting the welfare of the downtrodden and in his later years for formulating policies that were detrimental to the interests of the toiling masses, it was always from the point of view of reminding them of their historic duty and cautioning them against succumbing to the guile of the Brahmins.[16] Phule's understanding missed the point that there might be—in fact, was—a need on the part of the British rulers themselves to enter into nexus with the Brahmins (and other power-wielding sections of society) so as to legitimize their entry into the political domain of India. The complete deletion of the colonial rulers' intentions to dominate is a serious lacuna in Phule's historiography.[17] Yet, given the powerless site from which Phule was articulating his radical critique of inegalitarian society, it was inevitable that he side with one of the two power centers—the British or the burgeoning nationalist assertion of Brahmins[18]—to render his reality meaningful.[19] Ernest Gellner, commenting on the dilemma of Diaspora nationalism, says:

> Those [entropy inhibitions] which are not due to mere communication failures and are remedial neither by assimilation into the dominant pool, nor by the creation of a new independent pool using the native medium of the entrants, are correspondingly more tragic. (Gellner, 1983: 67)

Phule's case exemplifies this predicament, though Phule attempted vigorously to create "a new independent pool using the native medium."

Notes

This paper was presented at the Cultural Studies Workshop jointly organized by the Centre for Studies in Social Sciences, Calcutta, and International Development Studies, Roskilde University, Denmark, on 19–23 November 1995 in Mysore. I thank all the participants present at the workshop for their comments on the paper. The translations of Phule's writings into English in this text are mine.

1. The removal of intermediaries between the state and the cultivator under the *ryotwari* system runs parallel to Phule's insistence of removal of middlemen between God and the laity. Phule also looked upon the British state as *maibaap* and directly addressed his grievances to it, without recourse to the Brahmins.

2. The bulk of the early members of the Satyashodhak Samaj belonged to this upcoming economic stratum: "A high proportion of the most prominent members were engaged in commerce as merchants and contractors, and often formed business connections in addition to their ideological commitments. A considerable number were also employed in local government administration, or had a profession" (O'Hanlon, 1985: 246).

3. The central characters—the *padri*, the husband of the Kunbi woman, and the *vidhushak*—in Phule's first literary production, *Tritya Ratna,* seemed to have evolved from a mix of real-life personalities of Murray Mitchell, Gaffar Beg Munshi, and Phule himself.

4. It is interesting that the Rashtriya Swayamsevak Sangh was formed in 1925 with similar emphasis on martial skills "to organize Hindus."

5. At one point Phule clearly addresses the Brahmins in these terms: "[Brahmin] is the true descendant of demon brahma, a son of devil, says Joti" (Phule, 1991: 558).

6. Phule on other occasions mockingly calls the sacred thread "pandhra dora" (white thread) to contrast with the black thread that the Untouchables were forced to wear during the Peshwa regime. Significantly, unlike the Arya Samaj, which sought to make Vedas accessible to Hindu women and Shudras, Phule does not seek democratization of the Brahminical marks of difference. He insists on the overthrow of the Brahminical framework and instead demands democratization of the British educational system.

7. If Phule considers that aggression, violence, and annihilation by the Aryabhats ultimately led to the subjugation of the Shudra–Ati-Shudras, he also blames the excessive indulgence of the native chiefs as leading to the downfall. His disdain for the "hollow splendour" of the aristocratic sardars of his times emerges from his appreciation for a life of honest labor as an antidote against sloth.

8. Phule derisively calls the National Sabha "Naradachi Subha," province of Narad, the Brahmin emissary from the heavens.

9. Cohen (1985) talks about "tactical and symbolic reverses," a recent strategy among the disadvantaged groups, to render positive their very stigma and thus destigmatize it. The most eloquent example was the "Black Is Beautiful" movement that swept the United States in the late 1960s.

10. Phule is radically egalitarian in gender relations too. In the context of *sati,* Phule asks, "Has anyone heard of a man having done 'sata' out of sorrow for her

[deceased wife]?" (Phule, 1991: 447). Phule wrote *Satsaar* in defense of Pandita Ramabai when the latter was reviled for conversion to Christianity. Tarabai Shinde, who wrote *Stree-Purush Tulna* in the 1880s, found inspiration in Phule's work.

11. Smith (1986) considers "association with specific territories" as one of the dimensions of ethnic claim. The others are a collective name, a common myth of descent, a shared history, a distinctive shared culture, and a sense of solidarity (Smith, 1986: 23–31).

12. Chatterjee (1994) labels the form of history writing of Mrityunjay Vidyalankar, the early nineteenth-century Brahmin scholar of Bengal, as "puranic history" wherein the divine element plays the omnipotent role of directing the course of history. It would not be out of place to characterize Phule's history writing too as puranic history, only with the difference that whereas Phule saw the advent of the British as a transition form *kaliyug* to *satyayug*, Vidyalankar saw it otherwise.

13. See Dirks, Eley, and Ortner (1994), especially "Introduction," for a recent commentary on the Foucauldian concept of power.

14. See Kaviraj (1991) for his two notions, "ceremonial eminence" and "traditional marginality," describing the place of the state in traditional Indian society.

15. See Stokes (1989) for an account of the mental makeup of the British colonial administrators in the early nineteenth century.

16. In *Shetkaryacha Asud,* Phule sarcastically comments: "While assessing after every thirty years land of such ignorant farmers, the European servants who pray, keeping our pious government in darkness, do not get up saying 'Amen' [*sic*] unless they have slightly raised the burden of taxes on the farmers" (Phule, 1991: 275).

17. In the present context, Sharad Joshi of Shetkari Sanghatana wholeheartedly welcomes the globalization process, calling Dunkel the *muktidata* (liberator) of Indian farmers. Though Sharad Joshi may position himself as a modern-day Phule, contemporary geopolitics is vastly different from Phule's times.

18. Besides the Indian National Congress, Phule was equally harsh toward the attempts made by some contemporary Brahmins, especially people like Vasudev Balwant Phadke, to stage a revolt against British rule by recruiting youth from the Bhil, Ramoshi, and other communities. Phule advises "our righteous government . . . to finalise a reasonable tax on the lands of the illiterate farmers [and] to educate them in agricultural matters so that they won't lose life by following treacherous rebellious Brahmins like the Peshwa, Tope, Khajgiwale, Patwardhan, Phadke and others" (Phule, 1991: 293).

19. Later on, Ambedkar too took a collaborationist stand vis-à-vis the British, though on pragmatic rather than normative grounds. That is, giving topmost priority to the welfare of the Dalits, Ambedkar extended his cooperation to the Britishers after taking due cognizance of the prevalent balance of power. Nevertheless, he never lost sight of the exploitative nature of British colonialism and its lack of seriousness toward abolition of untouchability.

References

Berger, Peter L. 1969. *The Sacred Canopy: Elements of a Sociological Theory of Religion.* New York: Anchor Books, Doubleday and Company.
Chatterjee, Partha. 1994. "History and Nationalisation of Hinduism," in Preben Kaarsholm and Jan Hultin (eds.), *Inventions and Boundaries: Historical and*

Anthropological Approaches to the Study of Ethnicity and Nationalism. Roskilde: International Development Studies, Roskilde University.
Cohen, Anthony P. 1985. *The Symbolic Construction of Community*. London: Tavistock Publications.
Dirks, Nicholas, Geoff Eley, and Sherry B. Ortner (eds.). 1994. *Culture/Power/History: A Reader in Contemporary Social Theory*. New Jersey: Princeton University Press.
Fuller, Chris. 1989. "British India or Traditional India? Land, Caste and Power," in Hamza Alavi and John Harriss (eds.), *Sociology of Developing Societies: South Asia*. London: Macmillan Press.
Gellner, Ernest. 1983. *Nations and Nationalism*. Oxford: Basil Blackwell Publishers Ltd.
Joshi, Narayan Vishnu. 1868. *Pune Shaharache Varnan*. Mumbai: Sahitya Shahakar Sangha Prakashan.
Kale, Govind Ganapat. n.d. *Mahatma Phuleyanchya Aprakashit Athavani*. Pune: Raghuvanshi Prakashan.
Kaviraj, Sudipta. 1991. "On State, Society and Discourse in India," in James Manor (ed.), *Rethinking Third World Politics*. London: Longman Group UK Ltd.
———. 1992. "The Imaginary Institution of India," in Preben Kaarsholm (ed.), *Modernisation of Culture and the Development of Political Discourse in the Third World*. Denmark: International Development Studies, Roskilde University.
O'Hanlon, Rosalind. 1985. *Caste, Conflict and Ideology: Mahatma Jotirao Phule and the Low Caste Protest in Nineteenth-Century Western India*. Cambridge: Cambridge University Press, in association with Orient Longman Ltd.
Omvedt, Gail. 1976. *Cultural Revolt in a Colonial Society: The Non-Brahman Movement in Western India, 1873 to 1930*. Pune: Scientific Socialist Education Trust.
Phule, Jotirao. 1991. *Mahatma Phule Samagra Vangmaya (MPSV)*. Edited by Yeshwant Dinaker Phadke. Mumbai: Maharashtra Rajya Sahitya ani Sanskriti Mandal.
Smith, Anthony D. 1986. *Ethnic Origins of Nations*. New York: Basil Blackwell.
Stokes, Eric. 1989. *The English Utilitarians and India*. Delhi: Oxford University Press.

4

Ambedkar, Buddhism, and the Concept of Religion

Timothy Fitzgerald

The leader of the Untouchables movement from the 1920s until his death in 1956 was not Mohandas Gandhi but B. R. Ambedkar, himself an Untouchable and one of the great men of modern world history, though one would rarely find his name mentioned in religious studies books. It is notable that in books published within the religion genre one rarely, if ever, finds any analysis of the rituals of untouchability or bonded labor. Instead, one finds idealized accounts of gods and goddesses, *varnasramadharma,* the various theological schools, the great high-caste Hindu reformers, and of course the satyagraha and vegetarianism of Gandhi. I have never seen a religious studies book that gave a proper account of why Untouchables generally despise the paternalistic Gandhian word "Harijan," or an account of Ambedkar's detailed critique of Gandhi's high-caste reformism. Generally speaking, religion books give the high-caste view of the ecumenical construct "Hinduism," and it is a view that facilitates a rapprochement between the elites of the colonizers and the colonized.

In this chapter I have two aims. The first is to discuss the different concepts of religion found in Ambedkar's writings. The second is to suggest why, for the researcher, "religion" has become a fairly useless concept. These aims are connected. Ambedkar was a highly educated and intellectually brilliant man who mastered the law to such an extent that he was able to chair the Constitutional Committee of the new republic. He was also able to write penetrating analyses of Indian society that reflected a sophisticated anthropological understanding. But the center of his life was his devotion to the liberation of the backward classes, and he struggled to find a satisfactory ideological expression for that liberation. Though he talked a great deal about "religion," I believe he really went beyond that concept (see Ambedkar, 1957: 225). His evolving ideas about religion suggested to me why we could abandon the word without any real loss.

I will try to place different concepts of religion found in Ambedkar's writings in a theoretical context that illustrates wider social and cultural issues affecting the Scheduled Castes. I have in mind particularly the modern coexistence in India of an egalitarian constitution (for which Ambedkar was largely responsible) and caste hierarchy. Ambedkar himself offers a striking example of the subjective aspect of this institutional dichotomy by his identity as a middle-class barrister and political activist on the one hand and a member of an Untouchable caste on the other. We seem to have a direct conflict of fundamental principles or values, and passages in the *Annihilation of Caste* (Ambedkar, 1936: 123–128) suggest that for Ambedkar this conflict could be expressed as being between different religions. He referred to these respectively as "the Religion of Rules" (by which he meant essentially caste hierarchy) and "the Religion of Principles" (by which he meant essentially democratic egalitarianism, though not the extreme individualism of the West). Ambedkar has the insight here that principles or values that are normally referred to as "secular" are as sacred as those conventionally referred to as "religious," for example, those found in Hindu texts like *Manusmriti*. Furthermore, the so-called secular values—unlike those found in *Manusmriti*—are universal and thus make possible what he calls a "True Religion" (1936: 126). But I will show that in other texts such as *The Buddha and the Future of His Religion* (Ambedkar, 1950), his concept of religion changes again, until eventually in *The Buddha and His Dhamma* he concludes that it is "an indefinite word with no fixed meaning" (Ambedkar, 1957: 225).

Though Ambedkar certainly believed in the liberation of the individual, he saw clearly that in the modern world the priority must be *institutional* liberation. The struggle for liberation, traditionally symbolized by the solitary renouncer in the forest, or by Gautama Buddha sitting alone beneath the *bodhi* tree, had to be transformed into a struggle against *institutionalized* bondage. I use the word "bondage" here deliberately because even today there is bonded labor in parts of Maharashtra such as Marathawada (Pandit, 1990; Fitzgerald, 1994). Thus, for Ambedkar, "fetters" were not only those karmic hindrances that conditioned the individual's consciousness from one lifetime to another. They were also institutionalized realities that required a political solution.[1]

Ambedkar studied anthropology at Colombia University in New York, where he received a Ph.D. in 1916. He also qualified as a barrister in the Inns of Court in London. But though a great scholar, his main goal in life was to help create a peaceful revolution in India that would liberate the Untouchables and the backward classes generally from caste oppression. Much of his writing is polemical. It is not surprising, therefore, if his uses of the word "religion" should be as varied and imprecise as those of many other scholars. But in fact, as with so much in his writing, Ambedkar had insights into the nature of religion that help us to disentangle some of the different meanings that make it an inherently confused concept. In his desire to formulate a new consciousness for people who are now called Dalits and Buddhists, he raised many important issues that we can try to develop.

The "Religion of Rules" and the "Religion of Principles"

In some of his most famous writings, such as *Annihilation of Caste* (1936), *The Buddha and the Future of His Religion* (1950), and *The Buddha and His Dhamma* (1957), Ambedkar tried to develop a coherent account of the nature of religion and its relation to politics and power. In *Annihilation of Caste* he argues that Hinduism is a religion of rules, a compendium of ritual regulations that are based on the caste ideology of hierarchy and untouchability. For him, caste is the central fact of Hinduism, and untouchability is a defining characteristic of caste. He argues that you cannot reform caste because untouchability is an inherent feature. This was one fundamental reason that he strongly opposed Gandhi's reformism.

Annihilation of Caste was originally written as a speech that he had been invited to deliver by the Jat Pat Todak Mandal of Lahore, a high-caste reform group. When they read it they found it too dangerous, so they canceled the speech. Consequently, Ambedkar published it as a pamphlet instead. The second edition includes a preface, a prologue, including the correspondence between him and the Mandal, and two appendices, which include Gandhi's review and Ambedkar's reply to Gandhi.

The published correspondence makes it clear that the reason the Mandal canceled the speech was that Ambedkar refused to cut what he considered to be the essential point of his argument, but which they variously found to be either irrelevant or too dangerous, that "the real method of breaking up the Caste System was not to bring about inter-caste dinners and inter-caste marriages but to destroy the religious notions on which caste is founded" (1936: 49).

The religious notions he was referring to were, of course, the traditional Hindu ideology of rank based on purity and untouchability, which manifested itself in caste, ritualism, and the suppression of autonomous individuality. He was not thinking primarily of the tradition of renunciation, of sannyas. On the contrary, in a footnote he suggested that the *Upanishads* contain ideas about equality and freedom.[2] At this stage Ambedkar's focus was the pervasive hierarchical ritualism that was given its most potent codification in the religious principles in *Manusmriti*, a text of fundamental importance in orthodox thinking, which he burnt in a public protest at the Mahad Satyagraha, 25 December 1927 (see Ahir, 1991a: 15).

A Summary of Ambedkar's Argument

Political and constitutional reform cannot succeed unless it is preceded by social reform aimed at the eradication of untouchability. But social reform can only mean abolition of caste because untouchability is a *defining feature* of caste. In reality, caste cannot be *reformed* (contrary to Gandhi's hope), only annihilated. And the annihilation of caste implies the abolition of Hindu ideology particularly as it is formulated in the *Shastras* and *Smritis*. Caste is fundamentally "a state of mind" (Ambedkar meant this both collectively and individually) that is systematized in these scriptures, and although endogamy is what he calls the "mechanism" of caste, it is religious dogma that prohibits intermarriage, and therefore ultimately it is the religious values that must be destroyed: "it must be recognised that the Hindus observe caste not because they are inhuman or wrong-headed. They observe caste because they are deeply religious . . . the enemy you must grapple with is not the people who observe caste, but the Shastras that teach them this religion of caste" (1936: 111). Ambedkar's insistence that political reform could not succeed unless preceded by social reform (and therefore by a revolution in the sphere of values) may, in retrospect, appear to contradict his own achievement as India's first law minister in piloting through the constitution that made untouchability illegal. More likely, though, it will prove his point, since making untouchability unconstitutional has not in fact abolished it. This demonstrated something that Ambedkar was painfully aware of: that modern law (which implies equality and which was introduced by the British) is subordinated to ritual hierarchy.[3] In contrast, at around this time Gandhi did not want to abolish caste as such but to reform it according to an ideal model. True, his views changed over the years (Zelliot, 1972; 6ff.). But Ambedkar severely criticized Gandhi for his view that caste was essentially a division of labor and that inequality and untouchability were extraneous distortions.

Ambedkar wished to replace the Religion of Rules with True Religion, the Religion of Principles, which is the basis for civic government. These principles, liberty, equality, and fraternity (1936: 9, 128), are True Religion. He says, "True Religion is the foundation of society." He was perfectly well aware that these were the principles of the American and French revolutions. However, he wanted to bring this alternative (non-Indian) tradition into line with traditional Indian ways of thinking, which in effect meant identifying a strand of his own indigenous culture that could legitimately be presented as a critique of Hindu ritual orthodoxy. This was the connection with the sannyasi tradition mentioned before; near the end of the *Annihilation of Caste*, he suggested in a footnote that this ideology of liberty, equality, and fraternity could be found in the *Upanishads*, though he does not pursue this tantalizing statement. Later, he found it in Buddhism.

In both cases it is the religion of the renouncer in which he finds the universal values that can replace the Hindu ritual system. However, though there is a sense in which renunciation remained important in Ambedkar's thinking about religion, his modernizing tendency transformed the renouncer into a socially engaged and politically committed individual. I return to this point later.

Putting the issue of renunciation to one side for the moment, so far I have identified two concepts of religion, one a religion essentially characterized by caste hierarchy, and the other a religion essentially characterized by individual freedom and equality. The religion of caste hierarchy described by Ambedkar reveals an opposition between Brahmin purity and dominance, on the one hand, and Untouchable impurity and subservience, on the other. These ritual values permeate traditional Hindu society and are most clearly codified in texts such as the *Manusmriti*. The other concept of religion is similar to and perhaps initially derived from Western democratic principles and institutions, based on the belief in the formal equality of all individuals, equal rights under the law, the abolition of hereditary status, and personal freedom to choose one's own occupation and to develop one's own individual talents. These were the principles that he was to build into the constitution. These sacred principles are what Westerners generally like to think of as the secular or the nonreligious but what Ambedkar suggests are the basis for a concept of True Religion (1936: 126). This is one reason Ambedkar's view of religion is interesting. For him, the bases of religion are *values,* the values that hold a society together. Concepts of the supernatural were not essential for Ambedkar. Indeed, he came to see supernaturalism as irrational and irrelevant to true religion.

Thus the concept of religion implied in this kind of analysis is not essentially about supernatural beings, transcendental worlds, or spiritual salvation in a life after death. It is about the fundamental values that make possible different kinds of social institutions, in one case the institution of caste that is based on the sacred Brahminical principles codified in the *Smritis,* and in the other case the institutions of democracy that are based on the sacred principles of liberty, equality, and fraternity.

However, one significant way in which these sets of values differ from each other is that for Ambedkar, the democratic values are universalist in the sense that they apply equally to everyone in principle, for all humans are individuals and all humans have equal rights and obligations and all humans deserve the opportunity to discover their own true talents. In contrast, the Hindu values are particularistic. There is one set of rules for Brahmins, one for Marathas, one for Mahars, and one for Mangs. In a democratic world, anybody can in principle become president, get a good education, marry the partner of his or her choice regardless of caste (and presumably of nationality), live in the preferred neighborhood, and be respected for what he or she is or does rather than for inherited status. But in the case of the caste system in India, rules apply to particular people in particular situations. Different categories of people must marry only into a specific subcaste, have different occupations, live in different parts of the village, wear different clothes, and so on.

In a democratic society, freedom of the individual implies a new kind of freedom, the freedom to choose one's religion. But here we have a different concept of religion emerging. Here religion is conceived as a body of doctrines about salvation that the individual can choose to adhere to because he or she finds it the best, the most rational, the most suitable for his or her personal needs. The religious principles of equality, liberty, and fraternity make possible (paradoxically) a "secular" society in which religion becomes a matter of personal commitment and choice. This different concept of religion is implied in Ambedkar's *The Buddha and the Future of His Religion,* where he does a comparative analysis of the rationality and ethical principles of Buddhism, Christianity, Islam, and Hinduism and concludes in favor of Buddhism. I do not want to claim that the distinction between these different concepts of religion is clearly and consciously demarcated, but I believe it is there. Indeed, I would argue that it is inevitably there because the emergence of what in the West and elsewhere is referred to as secular society, but which Ambedkar (in my view very perceptively) calls a religion, has historically also produced a concept of religion that is a private affair, a matter of personal choice and commitment, something one gets converted to. In a caste society, you do not get converted to Brahminical hierarchy. It is not something anybody chooses.

According to Ambedkar's understanding, *Buddha Dhamma* is essentially *morality.* By morality he means compassion, caring for one's fellow human and for the natural world, feeling a sense responsibility and commitment, being actively committed to the well-being of the world. Morality, unlike ritual obligation, springs from the heart of the individual and is based on a sense of brotherhood and sisterhood. Thus Buddhism, in this line of reasoning, becomes the basis of the new egalitarian society, the structural equivalent of hierarchy as the basis of Hindu society. For this is not a traditional sectarian dispute about which is the true path to liberation—a dispute that takes for granted a whole structure of shared assumptions. This is a questioning of the basis of the structure itself.

Undoubtedly, this very notion that one can change one's religion, that one can move from one religion to another, that one can look around for a more suitable religion than that which one has at present, is itself a modern idea. Regarding this concept, Buddhism is one of a number of religions that, in *Buddha and the Future of His Religion,* Ambedkar compares with Christianity, Islam, and Hinduism. Buddhism is the best of these because it is the most rational, the most scientific in its principles, the most moral. It is therefore the religion that Ambedkar advocates and that he seeks to persuade others to adopt. But this concept of religion as being a matter of private choice itself involves another political principle, the Freedom of Religion that is guaranteed by the constitution. Buddhism is thus intended both as the fundamental basis of the new social order and as the most rational choice for the individual. So his Buddhism is a highly rational blend of individualism with sociopolitical commitment, a Buddhist modernism with a crucial element of liberation theology, but intended to be the basis of the new social order.

Ambedkar's own analysis of Hindu ideology sometimes sounds more like a kind of Marxist revolutionary sociology when he says, "The problem of Untouchability is a matter of class struggle" (B. R. Ambedkar, quoted in Ahir, 1991a: 21). But this surely is as much an appeal for class-consciousness as an analysis, a revolutionary desire to transform the traditional inertia of untouchability into a politically conscious movement cutting across caste lines. In fact, Ambedkar was not a Marxist in one sense because he did not believe in violent revolution. But he seems to have believed that the emergence of politically conscious classes might act as an agent for fundamental change in Indian society. He was a socialist in the sense that he believed that the redistribution of wealth and opportunity in a society needed some direct government intervention, such as the nationalization of key industries. He also wanted separate electorates as a way around the problem of electoral intimidation and a guaranteed number of seats for backward classes, and he wanted an employment and educational policy that actively countered the discriminatory tendencies of traditional caste loyalties. But his long-term aim was the creation of a society of morally free and responsible individuals.

From as early as 1935, Ambedkar indicated the fundamental importance of religion by publicly declaring untouchability to be an inseparable part of Hinduism and his own intention to convert to Buddhism (Ahir, 1991b: 20ff.). There is no doubt that Ambedkar was an intensely religious man, in the sense of a deep commitment to values and principles such as compassion, justice, and equality. But he needed a religion that made a difference in this world, a religion that could change society and empower the backward classes. Therefore, his interpretation of Buddhism has some modernist features. As a *soteriology* (doctrine of salvation), Buddhism has always been concerned with the fate of the individual, but in the sense of release (nirvana) from this world (samsara) through the self-discipline of the four noble truths and the eightfold path. Ambedkar was critical of the Theravada Sangha of South and Southeast Asia for its tendency toward detachment from the world. For Ambedkar, soteriology has a strong social and political component. *Bhikshus* (monks) should be socially and politically committed to justice. He was more attracted by the Mahayana concept of the Bodhisattva, who delays his own liberation out of compassion for less fortunate or less advanced beings. Furthermore, the Bodhisattva ideal lends itself more easily to modern concepts of democracy, human rights, and social justice, for it can easily be seen as a compassionate activity in favor of the oppressed and the fight against social and political injustice. Salvation is conceived in terms of the struggle for emancipation and dignity of the oppressed classes of Hindu society. And the individual is in *some* respects more like the autonomous individual of Protestant Christianity, committed to rational action in this world, than the renouncer who turns his or her back on the world.

In this sense I find it illuminating that on all Buddhist shrines in Maharashtra one finds two pictures. One is of the Buddha sitting cross-legged in the rags of the renouncer meditating beneath the *bodhi* tree and achieving enlightenment. In the other one sees Ambedkar, dressed in a modern blue business suit, wearing heavy-rimmed glasses, and holding a large book that represents literacy, education, and also perhaps the egalitarian constitution of India, which he wrote and which is reputed to be one of the most advanced constitutions in the world. These are the ancient and modern conceptions of liberation side-by-side (see Tartakov, 1990).

In his posthumously published *The Buddha and His Dhamma* (1957), Ambedkar wanted to revive what he took to be the main principles of original Buddhism. In this book he says that "dharma" and "religion" are entirely different (1957: 225), which is another shift of meaning. His interpretation of Buddhism here is strongly flavored with "scientific" materialism. It has to be remembered that this book was not completed before he died, he had written some notes while he was ill, and the editors had the task of putting it together afterward. The end result is a book that tends to emphasize an interpretation of Buddhist liberation as a social and political liberation rather than as traditional enlightenment. For example, he equates nirvana (the Buddhist concept of the transcendent) to the Eightfold Path (which in traditional Buddhism is the way, the practice, by which to obtain nirvana). He said "Nibbana is naught but that 8-Fold Path" (1957: 288), and the Eightfold Path's most important aspect, "Right Outlook," is in turn defined as the recognition of cause and effect (1957: 291). Logically, therefore, this is almost like saying that nirvana is equivalent to scientific rationality. In this way, Ambedkar attempts to present traditional Indian Buddhism as fully consistent with materialism; with scientific rationality; with parliamentary democracy; and with the principles of equality, fraternity, and liberty. To do this he asserts that Buddhism has no place for belief in the supernatural, that the doctrine of karma is a theory of causation only, that *prajna* (wisdom) means the ability to think rationally and without superstition, that *karuna* (compassion) means the ability to love one's fellow humans and to work for social justice, and that the *bhikshu* (monk) is not (or should not be) merely an ascetic intent on his own enlightenment but a social worker dedicated to the betterment of human welfare. In his account, enlightenment seems much closer to the enlightenment of the French philosophies of the eighteenth century than to the nirvana of the Buddha. In short, he has almost nothing to say about the central Buddhist soteriology concerning nirvana, meditation, and the ending of karma and rebirth. This does not mean that he was not concerned about the traditional concept of *pratitya samutpada* (conditioned origination), only that his goal was conceived in terms of *institutional* liberation (liberation from the institution of untouchability and ritual pollution) as a necessary precondition to any personal freedom.

Ritual, Politics, and Soteriology

I have suggested that Ambedkar uses religion in different ways to mean (1) the system of caste hierarchy; (2) traditional asceticism, that is, release from this world through meditation and self-discipline, as found in the *Upanishads* and traditional forms of Buddhism; (3) democratic society (usually referred to as secular society in the West) based on the sacred values of liberty, equality, and fraternity; and (4) the religions such as Christianity, Islam, Hinduism, and Buddhism, which in a free society the individual should choose on a personal basis. One point to note is that so much is included in these different uses that one might as well abandon the word altogether and find different terms that make more precise distinctions.

This idea in fact coincides with my own research on Buddhism in Maharashtra. I have not found the concept of religion very useful as an analytical concept for understanding the situation of the Ambedkar Buddhists. If I were a "comparative religionist," meaning someone who believes that there are many religions in the world and all one has to do is go out and find them, probably the first thing I would notice if I visited the communities at all would be their temples and their *puja* performed to pictures of Gautama Buddha and Ambedkar side-by-side on the shrines. And there is no doubt that many Buddhists conceive of Buddha and Ambedkar (who is considered a Bodhisattva) as supernatural beings who can bring benefits. In this sense they fulfill the same function as some Hindu deities.

The concept of Ambedkar as a Bodhisattva or enlightened being who brings liberation to all backward classes is widespread among Buddhists. However, Ambedkar himself was entirely against supernaturalism, seeing it as a form of dependency induced by the traditional oppression of Hindu caste culture. And the dominant understanding of present-day Buddhists, especially more educated Buddhists, is explicitly against the idea that

Ambedkar is a supernatural being. Some Buddhists believe Ambedkar was enlightened or partially enlightened in a way similar to traditional Theravada interpretations of Gautama Buddha's enlightenment, which stress his humanity and refrain from turning him into a god. Indeed, in the traditional stories the god Brahma is depicted as asking Buddha to show him the way to liberation. When such Buddhists perform *puja*, they are recalling Gautama Buddha's and Ambedkar's outstanding lives and examples. Many educated Buddhists interpret Ambedkar's enlightenment not in a transcendental way but as the product of education and the full realization of his potential as a human being.

The concept of religion either as a traditional soteriology or as interaction with superhuman beings is patently inadequate for dealing with the realities of the situation. This is true even though transcendentalist or supernaturalist aspects of the movement exist. And when one realizes that the vast majority of Buddhists are members of the same Untouchable caste, then it becomes obvious that caste hierarchy must be a fundamental part of the analysis. This reflects Ambedkar's focus on liberation as an *institutional* problem in the first place.

I have developed a typology of ritual, politics, and soteriology to make sense of my fieldwork. Here I can do no more than summarize my published research in order to clarify why the concept of "religion" is in my view analytically redundant.

Ritual

Ambedkar's analysis of Indian (Hindu) society was that it is fundamentally a ritualistic (rather than moral) system and that caste, untouchability, and supernaturalism were its main institutional expressions. Though he did advocate some simple Buddhist rituals such as *puja* and simple Buddhist wedding and funeral rites, he believed that these should be cheap (to avoid dowry problems), transparent, and nonmystifying. Ritual, as referred to in this category, is the whole spectrum of ritualistic practices that Ambedkar condemned, ranging from worship of the supernatural, exorcism, possession states, caste ritualism such as endogamy and dowry, or rituals of purity and pollution. This would include the ritual location of the Untouchable quarter in the villages (previously called Maharwada, now Buddhawada) and the ritually defined duties of scavenging and night soil removal. As I have shown above, Ambedkar himself analyzed "Hinduism" as a ritual system encoded in texts such as the *Manusmriti*, which gave ideological justification for untouchability.

Ideologically, when we identify the form of life indicated by ritual, we are not really talking about Buddhism here (certainly not Ambedkar's understanding of Buddhism) but about a de facto lifestyle that many people who are proud to identify themselves as Buddhists do (by default) practice. For example, subcaste endogamy is widespread among all categories of Buddhists, at least in certain areas such as Nagpur and Marathawada,[4] including highly educated academics with a sophisticated understanding of Ambedkar's teaching. It is therefore part and parcel of contemporary Buddhist identity, even though Buddhists themselves deplore it. Another example is that Buddhists who have proved their commitment and courage by exposing themselves to the dangers of high-caste anger by refusing to perform some ritual services such as scavenging may still be themselves practicing untouchability against other Untouchable castes like Mang and Holar, or be involved in the worship of the goddess Mariai, or may be worshipping Buddha and Ambedkar as though they were Hindu gods. The importance of this element of ritual is that, though logically it is incompatible with Ambedkar's teaching, it is to some variable degree part of the actual situation and identity of Buddhists and consequently has to be investigated as such.

Politics

"Secular" rationalism and social democracy are central to Ambedkar's understanding of Buddhism, and again, this kind of interpretation is to some variable extent identifiable in the thinking of most Buddhist groups in Maharashtra, whether they be Dalits, academics, village teachers, community spokesmen, local urban activists who sometimes lead *puja* in the local temple, or even monks and *dharmacharis*.[5] I believe that "politics," in the sense of social activism directed toward the exercise of political power for the purpose of peaceful social revolution, may be the best single word to encapsulate this element of Ambedkar's Buddhism. This notion of politics is not arbitrary, for it is closely linked with the fundamental principles of a democratic constitution, a modern judicial system based on the value of equality before the law, and the legitimate pursuit of power through constitutional means.[6]

Soteriology

Soteriology is traditionally a doctrine of spiritual salvation or liberation from the world of suffering and evil. Traditional Theravada Buddhism is a soteriology par excellence because it provides the analysis of suffering, the means for its eradication, and the transcendental goal. It is particularly a doctrine concerned with the individual, for it is the individual consciousness that is put together through the karmic factors of suffering, and it is the individual who practices moral restraint, social concern, and meditation along the path to enlightenment. However, in Ambedkar's writing, social concern is given a distinctively political emphasis. The institution of caste hierarchy and its ritualistic mechanism are particularly identified as major causes of suffering. The concept of individual liberation is very closely linked with sociopolitical liberation, and the factors of suffering are identified more broadly with institutionalized exploitation, particularly caste and untouchability. Therefore, in Ambedkar's writing, soteriology and politics are closely identified, politics being understood as the pursuit of power within the jurisdiction of a democratic constitution and soteriology as liberation from inequality and exploitation.

Nevertheless, many Buddhists hold strongly that soteriology is not *only* political and social activism in Ambedkar's thinking but has an important spiritual or transcendental element as well, which is pursued through reading Buddhist texts, practicing meditation, and going on retreats. Sociopolitical activism and a more "spiritual" understanding of liberation are often (though not always) seen as complementary and even dialectically implicated.[7] One highly organized expression of this idea of soteriology is the Trilokya Bauddha Mahasangha (TBMSG), which has developed a sophisticated interpretation of Buddhist soteriological doctrine based on both Ambedkar's teaching and the scholarly writing of the Venerable Sangharakshita. This teaching holds social revolutionary and transcendental goals as complementary. To what degree any particular Buddhist group in Maharashtra does or does not exemplify these elements is an empirical issue. My point is that, when we talk about Buddhism in Maharashtra, we are talking about different combinations of and oppositions between these qualities. Buddhists want liberation from their ritual status as Untouchables, but the dilemma is that they are defined by that status in the predominant caste ideology. I suppose ritual, politics, and soteriology could all be defined as "religion," but then I cannot see that the word picks out anything distinctive.

My own ethnography of Buddhism is based on three broadly distinctive categories within the Buddhist community: (1) Buddhists living in villages, in this case in Marathawada, a remote and backward area of Maharashtra; (2) middle-class Buddhists, in this case academics living in Nagpur; and (3) Buddhists who have actually renounced ordinary lay life and become monks or something equivalent,[8] in a community that is explicitly concerned with traditional Buddhist practices such as meditation, in this case the TBMSG in Pune, which is arguably the most effective of the agencies for propagating soteriological Buddhism of a transcendentalist kind. However, this agency is deeply committed to social work, and though it is nonpolitical, it certainly sees individual liberation as being strongly connected with peaceful social revolution. It would not do justice to the reality of the situation to present one of these emphases out of context.

This is not an exhaustive classification of all the varied occupations and lifestyles of Buddhists. Many Buddhists are poor urban factory workers. There is a strong element of political activism both in the formal political parties such as the Republican Party (founded by Ambedkar, but now factionalized) and also in the Dalit movement, which is a general backward classes militant movement dominated by the Buddhists. There are Buddhist novelists and poets writing in Marathi (see Zelliot, 1992). Nevertheless, the groups that I have interviewed do, in fact, tend to reveal the predominance in one way or another of these different factors.

Conclusion: Hierarchy and Egalitarianism as Values

What is notable about all these different categories of Buddhists is the high degree of consciousness that exists of Ambedkar's writings and his political and soteriological goals, in short, of the meaning of Ambedkar's Buddhism. In my view, the fundamental value of Ambedkar's Buddhism is egalitarianism understood as the ethical autonomy of the individual but with the political realism to acknowledge that dominant institutions such as caste can only be changed through the agency of alternative institutions, such as courts of law and antidiscrimination policies of governments. Ambedkar is sometimes described as a socialist, and he certainly wanted to use the power of the state to bring about social reform and redistribute wealth. But his concept of liberation through social revolution is based to a significant extent on an appeal to the ethical autonomy of individuals and their ability to transform themselves and their society through collective action.

And this understanding is widely understood among present-day Buddhists. This is true despite the fact that the Buddhist movement is almost completely confined to one Untouchable caste of about four million people.[9] Though Buddhists apparently continue to practice untouchability against other Untouchable castes, there is also simultaneously widespread conscious and bitter rejection of these notions.[10] Buddhists are thus caught in a contradiction, much as a committed British communist is caught in a contradiction when he puts his house on the market and tries to get the best price. If one is living within a system, one is to some degree forced to conform to it unless alternative institutions grow strong enough to legitimate an alternative lifestyle. Not only is there no consensus with the dominant ideology, but there is conflict within the minds of Buddhists when, for example, they simultaneously decry caste endogamy but in fact practice it.[11]

Notes

1. This raises an interesting philosophical problem of explanation in Buddhism. It would be difficult to argue that institutionalized inequalities can be adequately explained simply as the sum of individual karmas. For example, could one really explain the invasion of Tibet by the Chinese and the consequent creation of a Tibetan Diaspora in terms of individual karmas?
2. He had not found Buddhism yet, though he was soon to develop an interest in it.
3. My own research on Buddhism in Pune, Nagpur, and Marathawada suggests that this is still largely the case, though there is no space to present this ethnography here.
4. I am told by Eleanor Zelliot and Dharmachari Lokamitra that this is not the case in Pune.
5. *Dharmacharis* (and *dharmacharinis*) are fully committed members of the Buddhist organization Trilokya Bauddha Mahasangha (TBMSG), which I discuss later in this chapter.
6. Ambedkar was himself a barrister (trained at the Inns of Court in London) and spent a great deal of his enormous energy defending the rights of Untouchables against the oppressive goals of high-caste Hindus during the British Raj.
7. There are committed Buddhists, especially some Dalits, who see the transcendental element as a form of mystification that is alien to Ambedkar's revolutionary understanding of liberation (*moksa*). There is thus a split within the movement on this issue. See, for example, Guru (1991).
8. These are men and women called *dharmacharis* and *dharmacharinis*. They may marry, or they may make a vow of celibacy if they choose.
9. This is not entirely true because some Buddhists come from other castes, though overall their numbers are small. There is also another Untouchable caste in Uttar Pradesh called Chamars, who are Buddhists.
10. I found evidence of this in the Parbhani district in Marathawada.
11. I dispute, for example, the claim by Michael Moffatt that Untouchables are in deep conformity with the caste system, even though it is true that high-caste notions of purity and pollution get replicated to some extent in the Untouchable subsector (Moffatt, 1979).

References

Ahir, D. C. 1989. *The Pioneers of Buddhist Revival in India*. Delhi: Sri Sat Guru Publications.
———. 1991a. *The Legacy of Dr. Ambedkar*. Delhi: BR Publishing Corpn.
———. 1991b. *Buddhism in Modern India*. Delhi: Sri Satguru Publications.
Ambedkar, B. R. 1916 (1936). "Castes in India: Their Mechanism, Genesis and Development," in B. R. Ambedkar, *Annihilation of Caste*. Jallandhar City: Bheema Patrika Publications.
———. 1936. *Annihilation of Caste*. Jallandhar City: Bheema Patrika Publications.
———. 1950. *The Buddha and the Future of His Religion*. Jallandhar City: Bheema Patrika Publications.
———. 1957. *The Buddha and His Dhamma*. Bombay: People's Education Society.
———. 1994. "Sangha and Social Change: Lokamitra, Dhammachari," in A. K.

Narain and D. C. Ahir (eds.), *Dr. Ambedkar, Buddhism and Social Change*. Delhi: B. R. Publishing Corporation, pp. 49–65.

Fitzgerald, T. 1994. "Buddhism in Maharashtra: A Tripartite Analysis," in A. K. Narain and D. C. Ahir (eds.), *Dr. Ambedkar, Buddhism and Social Change*. Delhi: B. R. Publishing Corporation.

———. 1996. "From Structure to Substance: Ambedkar, Dumont and Orientalism," *Contributions to Indian Sociology* 30 (2): 273–288.

Guru, Gopal. 1991. "The Hinduisation of Ambedkar," *Economic and Political Weekly* 26 (7): 339–341.

Moffatt, M. 1979. *An Untouchable Community in South India: Structure and Consensus*. Princeton: Princeton University Press.

Narain, A. K., and D. C. Ahir (eds.). 1994. *Dr. Ambedkar, Buddhism and Social Change*. Delhi: B. R. Publishing Corporation.

Pandit, Vivek. 1990. *Report of the Campaign for Human Rights*. Bombay: Vidhayak Sansad.

Tartakov, G. M. 1990. "Art and Identity: The Rise of a New Buddhist Imagery," *Art Journal*, winter: 409–416.

Zelliot, E. 1972. "Gandhi and Ambedkar: A Study in Leadership," in J. M. Mahar (ed.), *The Untouchables in Contemporary India*. Arizona: University of Arizona Press.

———. 1992. *From Untouchable to Dalit: Essays on the Ambedkar Movement*. New Delhi: Manohar.

Part 2

POSITIONING DALITS

5

Representing Hinduism

S. Selvam

Hindu society is historically marked by a rigid form of social stratification based on the *varna-jati* model of social organization, in which the Brahminical religious principle, namely purity and pollution, played a central role in defining social hierarchy and separation. This led to a variety of social inequalities characterized by social oppression and economic exploitation. However, caste as a social fact is now fast losing its significance in many areas of social life. Traditional meanings, especially, are slowly changing. The association of individual castes with specific occupations has to a great extent broken down. Significantly, the system of production and structures of authority and power have detached themselves from the ideology of caste under which they were for centuries subsumed. In other words, the individual's position in the system of production and structures of power is no longer tied to caste as in the past. A steadily rising awareness among the members of lower castes, especially the Dalits, and their aspiration for equality in every sphere of social life have led to a continued questioning of the fundamental principles of the caste system and its practices. The idiom of caste is invoked today by the oppressed for the purpose of political and social mobilization to challenge the traditional oppressive institutions and oppressors. But, in spite of these changes in the public domain, the idea of caste continues to be an important factor in Indian private and domestic life. Against this backdrop, this chapter presents a critique of two important and dominant trends in the study of India and Hinduism, set in motion by two eminent sociologists: M. N. Srinivas and Louis Dumont. Although their scholarship has made insightful contributions to the understanding of the Hindu society and Hinduism, their concepts and theoretical formulations beg for reconsideration. I focus on their key concepts and general theoretical formulation, for it is beyond the scope of this chapter to cover all their writings. It is also important to state at the outset that the discussion here confines itself to Hinduism and Hindu society. In the course of this critique, an attempt is also made to propose a method for the study of the complex nature of Hinduism and society in India.

Society and Religion

Religion, as a system of beliefs and practice, is eminently social, and its representations are collective. Worship is a specific human behavior that arises in the context of religiously linked social groups forming a community of worshippers. Acts of worship "excite, maintain and recreate certain mental states in these groups" (Durkheim, 1964: 10). Religion unites the worshippers into "one single moral community called a church, all those who adhere to them" (Durkheim, 1964: 47). It is important to note that places of worship like the temple, church, and mosque bring worshippers into some kind of solidarity that may vary from religion to religion.

Another aspect of religion that is a subject of much controversy is its relationship with economic factors. A much debated question has been whether and to what extent religion is shaped by these factors. In the Marxist scheme, the economic base in the ultimate analysis determines various components of superstructure, including religion. Without entering into the debate over this, we state that religion has a relative autonomy that may be located in the link between religion and social structures. It is important to stress that economic factors certainly influence religious institutions and sometimes do so substantially. In other words, religious institutions have an economic function too. In his writings, Max Weber combines both the material circumstances that entail interest and the guiding power of ideas in governing individual and group actions. He states: "Not ideas, but material and ideal interests, directly govern men's conduct" (Weber, 1965a: 34).

I show later in this section that in India, religious institutions like temples had, in the past, an active role in the structures of authority and power. This was facilitated, though not in a strict sense, by economic factors but also by the ideas governing the notions of caste, God, and salvation. A religion that lays emphasis on salvation might have its origin within socially privileged groups. However, in the course of time, as the relationship of such a religion with privileged groups changes, the underprivileged are also incorporated into it. This transformation in the religion of the privileged with an intellectual leadership has to accommodate the lay groups for whom "intellectualism is both economically and socially inaccessible" (Weber, 1965b: 102).

Religion also constitutes, among other things, an elaborate system of symbols and myths that capture the popular imagination and keep worshippers under its spell. Religion thus viewed is "a system of symbols which acts to establish powerful, pervasive and long lasting moods and motivations in men by formulating conceptions of a general order of existence and clothing these conceptions with such an aura of factuality that the moods and motivations are seen uniquely realistic" (Geertz, 1973: 90). Let us now look at Hinduism in this light.

Hinduism, unlike Islam or Christianity, is a religion that comprises many traditions, denominations, gods, and temples. Central to Hinduism is the Vedic-Brahminic religious tradition, which was for centuries a hegemonic religious system incorporating and, at times, influencing or adjusting to and coexisting with local and regional traditions. (I shall return to the hegemonic nature of Brahminic Hinduism later. Hereafter the Vedic-Brahminic religious tradition is referred to as Brahminic Hinduism.) The structural basis of Hinduism and traditional Hindu society was the caste system as prescribed by the Brahmins. But the caste system, besides its religious and ideological dimensions, has an important material basis in the economic and social division of functions. The *varna-jati* model of social organization prescribed by Brahminical Hinduism incorporated various occupational groups into its fold, with hierarchy and separation based on the notions of purity and pollution as organizing principles. The whole internal coherence of Hindu social organization is sustained by the ideology governing the caste system.

According to Brahminical Hinduism, the idea of dharma is "the sociocosmic order which organises the empirical world" (Biardeau, 1989: 41). "Dharma is therefore that all encompassing order that goes so far as to include even that which denies it [and] which consists in the well-balanced hierarchy of the four goals of man as well as in a respect for the hierarchy and proper definition of the four varnas" (Biardeau, 1989: 42).

Three cardinal components of Brahminical ideology are the samsara belief in the transmigration of souls, the karma doctrine of compensation, and the *varna-jati* model of society. The doctrine of karma transforms the empirical world into a strictly rational and ethically determined cosmos. In this doctrine, order and rank of the *varna-jati* model are eternal. The karma doctrine and the *varna-jati* system together place the individual within a clear circle of duties. They also offer him or her a well-shaped, metaphysically satisfying conception of the world and the self. It is indeed the ideological basis of Brahminical Hinduism that made order and rank into something divine and permanent, for membership is by birth.

Functionalist Method

Studies that provide insight into various aspects of religion and society in India are diverse, covering both Indological as well as social anthropological studies. Whereas the former attempt to construct Indian society or an aspect of it through the study of Sanskrit textual sources (Karve, 1953; Singer, 1959; Singer and Cohn, 1968; Biardeau, 1989), the latter place the fieldwork orientation and participant observation as central to their method (Srinivas, 1952, 1955; Marriott, 1955; Gough, 1955; Béteille, 1965; Moffatt, 1979; Fuller, 1984). It is to his credit that it was Srinivas who brought the anthropological approach to the forefront to challenge the Indological construction of Indian society.

Srinivas (1952), by placing religious beliefs and practices in their social context, presents a sociological insight into Hindu religion and society. In his efforts to explore the nature of diversity and uniformity in Hinduism, he follows Radcliffe-Brown's holistic structural functionalism, which posits that every part of society is functionally integrated in order to maintain the solidarity of the society. Srinivas divides Hinduism into four levels, namely, all-India Hinduism, peninsular Hinduism, regional Hinduism, and local Hinduism (1952: 213). He identifies all-India and local Hinduism with Sanskritic and non-Sanskritic Hinduism while granting some amount of intermixing of these two levels in peninsular and regional Hinduism, stating: "Regional Hinduism often contains some Sanskritic elements in which case it directly stresses Regional ties and indirectly all-India ties" (Srinivas, 1952: 217–218). However, he underplays traditions like the bhakti Hinduism of Tamil Nadu, which has its own characteristics.

Srinivas uses the concept of Sanskritization to explain the four levels of Hinduism and its unity and diversity. For Srinivas, "All India Hinduism is Hinduism with an all India spread and this is chiefly Sanskritic in character" (Srinivas, 1952: 213). The term "spread," used by Srinivas to indicate the extent of the influence of Sanskritization that had taken place both vertically and horizontally, suggests that the process is automatic and desired by everybody. It does not provide a coherent picture of the historical and social change that he attempts to unravel. To what extent the cultural process has been harmonious and conflict-free is a question that remains to be answered. It is, however, important to mention that the process of Sanskritization has now been largely rejected by the members of the lower castes, as the process of Dalitization, a counterforce, has in recent times been on a constant rise, leading to an increasing self-awareness, self-confidence, and sense of dignity among the people of lower castes and also the emergence of a new assertive identity as Dalits.

For Srinivas, all-India Hinduism has been spread all over India by the upper-caste people, particularly the Brahmins. He describes the other levels of Hinduism in terms of geographical area and the extent of Sanskritic elements found in the ritual and cultural life of the people. Srinivas's approach locates the unity of Hinduism "in a set of normative standards in belief and ritual and suggests a process whereby these standards have been adopted by an ever increasing number of groups" (Singer, 1972: 44). Therefore, by constructing all-India Hinduism, which is based on a body of Sanskrit scriptures, and identifying it mainly with the ritual practices prescribed by Brahminical Hinduism, one of the traditions in Hinduism, Srinivas offers the Brahminical tradition as an ideal standard-bearer for personal and social life. In other words, the Brahminical tradition is privileged above other traditions. This is an ideological construct that needs to be decoded and decanonized.

Because of his Brahmino-centric approach, Srinivas is unable to explore and explain convincingly the ways by which people were made to worship the "Sanskritic deities" with ritual practices. Nor does he provide a clear picture of the process of the "greater Sanskritization" of the rituals and beliefs of various groups that together form Hinduism. Changes and intermixing of beliefs and practices over a long period of time make it difficult to categorize present-day Hindu religious practices either as Sanskritic Hinduism or non-Sanskritic Hinduism. This is particularly true of religion in Tamil Nadu. The "Brahminical" temples in Tamil Nadu are in fact Brahminized temples in which a synthesis of both "native" bhakti and Brahminical ideas and practices was in existence for centuries. Srinivas states that "every caste tended to imitate the customs and rituals of the top most caste and this was responsible for the spread of sanskritisation. When the process is viewed on a continental scale over a period of at least 2500 years, it is easy to see how Sanskritic ideas and beliefs penetrated the remotest hill tribes in such as manner as not to do violence to their traditional beliefs" (1952: 31). He uses this notion of Sanskritization to study the cultural processes taking place ever since Vedic Aryans established their supremacy in India (Srinivas, 1989: 56).

Srinivas's analysis lacks historical insight. Though it advances to some extent our understanding of the fluid nature of the social hierarchy among the Hindus, Srinivas does not explain how the fluidity existed in spite of the rigid social order. He considers it in terms of status arising out of the caste to which an individual or a group of persons belonged. Though he admits in a later study that economic or political conditions should be taken into consideration (Srinivas, 1962: 56–57), his analysis is based mainly on cultural elements and does not provide an insight into the origin, sustenance, and hegemony of this specific cultural process that placed a group of castes above the rest and made their cultural practices influential. In fact, Srinivas does not fully recognize the political function of the Brahminical rituals and ideology (Hardiman, 1984: 212–214), and though he has attempted to combine history, his analysis makes this cultural process appear as though it takes place outside the realm of ideology, politics, and economy. One is made to believe that the goal toward which everyone is expected to strive is that of Brahminical purity (Hardiman, 1984: 214), which is obviously not always true. In fact, the cultural process Srinivas designates as Sanskritization is indeed an important hegemonic process that requires a deeper study.

Srinivas subsequently expands the scope of his concept "Sanskritization" by redefining it as "a process by which a low Hindu caste or tribal or other group changes its customs, ritual, ideology and way of life in the direction of a high, frequently twice born caste. Generally such changes are followed by a claim to a higher position in the caste hierarchy than that traditionally conceded to the claimant caste by the local community" (Srinivas, 1966: 6). He describes three models of Sanskritization, namely the Brahminical, Kshatriya, and Vaishya models.

The texts written in Sanskrit to which Srinivas refers embody a tradition providing a social, religious, and cosmic framework, a tradition to which a Brahmin, considered to be the universal self, and Brahminism as an ideology, are central. Srinivas does not take this ideological dimension seriously since he takes the preeminence of Brahminical beliefs and practices for granted. However, the reality is very different. As T. F. Staal puts it: "the material to which sanskritisation is applied consists of non-Sanskritic deities and non-Sanskritic rituals and beliefs—for example, the worship of village deities, ancestors, trees, rivers and mountains and local cults in general. Sanskritisation takes place 'at the expense' of these non-Sanskritic elements" (1963: 262). Staal stresses the point that the Sanskritic tradition itself is not as monolithic either in the use of language or in the matter of culture as made out by Srinivas. In Staal's view, the language of Sanskrit and Sanskritic culture owe much to the vernacular language and native non-Sanskritic cultural traditions. He says: "There is much evidence to show that origins of the great tradition in India lie often in little traditions and that these origins generally remain visible in the later stages. The new does not replace the old but the old continues to exist side by side with the new" (Staal, 1963: 269). Staal suggests that the process could only add Sanskritic elements to non-Sanskritic ones.

M. S. A. Rao rightly points out that the emphasis on imitative processes of change does not take into account the aspects of alienation and conflict resulting at times in protest movements:

> The ideology of these movements based on relative deprivation conceived both religious and secular axes of mobility on the same structural (conceptual) level. Both were expressions of egalitarianism and the language of mobility was protest, confrontation, agitation, aggression, conflict and in some cases violence. The basic spirit behind articulating the demands was to attack the monopolistic rights, privileges and possessions of high status, symbols, goods and services of Brahmins and other upper castes. (Rao, 1979: 235–236)

Both the bhakti movement led by the Basavanna (1106–1168) in Karnataka (Ramanujam, 1972) and the recent Self-Respect Movement led by E. V. Ramaswamy Naicker (1879–1973) in Tamil Nadu (Barnett, 1976; Ryerson, 1988) questioned the Brahminical monopoly in various aspects of social life. Therefore, in making emulation by choice the mode of Sanskritization, Srinivas fails to take into consideration conflicts among various caste groups, making it seem instead that Sanskritization is a built-in, self-propelling process (see Hardiman, 1984: 214).

For Srinivas (1977: 42), "Brahmanisation is subsumed in the wider process of sanskritisation though at some points Brahmanisation and sanskritisation are at variance with each other." Srinivas prefers the term "Sanskritization" to "Brahminization" because certain Vedic rites are confined to the Brahmins (Srinivas, 1952: 30). Since he derives the concept of Brahminization from the top category of the *varna-jati* model (the Brahmins), he finds the term narrow and therefore uses a common term to cover other categories of the twice-born (the Kshatriyas and the Vaishyas).

However, I derive the concept of Brahminization not from the category of Brahmins but from the ideology of Brahminism, which, as stated earlier, prescribes models for social and religious/cosmic orders. Since it is Brahminical ideology that determines the position of each caste category in the social hierarchy and their respective duties, I give primacy to the ideology rather than to the Brahmins themselves, though their role as carriers of this ideology is important.

Srinivas notes the transmission of theological ideas embodied in the Sanskritic texts:

> sanskritisation means not only the adoption of new customs and habits but also exposure to new ideas and values which have found frequent expression in the vast body of Sanskritic literature, sacred as well as secular. *Karma, dharma, papa, maya, samsara* and *moksha* are examples of some of the most common theological ideas and when people become sanskritised these words occur frequently in their talk. (Srinivas, 1977: 48)

In fact, these ideas are part of the ideology of Brahminism. Hence, all three models of Sanskritization offered by Srinivas are squarely Brahminism-centered since the reference groups he identifies for emulation are the castes grouped only under the first three twice-born *varna*s. For me, Brahminization is a process by which the Brahminical ideology and practices affect and influence the "native" social institutions such as religion, caste, politics, and economy.

In his attempt to explain the ways by which a village is articulated with the universe of Indian civilization, M. Marriott (1955) argues that the village extends itself to form part of a wider society and system of relationship. His concepts of parochialization and universalization provide insight into historical transformation and the ways by which transmission of religious values and practices takes place from one tradition to another (Marriott, 1955: 211–218). Marriott provides illuminating evidence to show that Sanskritization has not replaced any aspect of the "little tradition" by the "great tradition." According to Marriott, "while elements of the great tradition have become parts of local festivals, they do not appear to have entered village festival custom at the expense of much that is or was the little tradition" (Marriott, 1955: 208). Thus, instead of one replacing the other, Sanskritic elements coexist with native, vernacular elements to a large extent. This view indeed contradicts that of Srinivas.

Structuralist Holism

Dumont's (1988) holistic view seeks to place the system of Brahminic Hindu beliefs and practices as central to his analysis of religion and society in India. His structuralist approach is shaped by his emphasis on religious beliefs and values. For Dumont (1970, 1986, 1988), the basic institution of Indian society is caste. He constructs the caste system in terms of values of hierarchy and separation based on the ideology of purity and pollution. The level of purity is the sole criterion for ranking of occupations and caste groups.

In Dumont's structural model, what matters most is the extent or degree to which a particular caste occupation is pure and not the wealth or income it yields. As a result, for him, the politicoeconomic dimensions are unimportant or secondary aspects of the caste system. This is amply exhibited in his remark that "just as a religion in a way encompasses politics, so politics encompasses economics within itself. The difference is that the politico-economic domain is separated, named in a subordinate position as against religion whilst economics remain undifferentiated within politics" (1988: 165).

In his efforts to conceptualize the caste system from Indian sources and ideas, Dumont has failed to consider diverse textual sources and sociological and anthropological studies. As a consequence, in Dumont's holistic view a specific set of religious beliefs and values becomes central as a source and ideology. What Dumont calls the ideology of purity and pollution or impurity is nothing but the criteria set out by an ideology based on a body of beliefs and values embodied in the classical Sanskrit texts. I agree with G. D. Berreman's critique that apart from its being a distorted version of the caste system, Dumont's conception of caste is based upon "the limited, biased, albeit scholarly sources of evidence" (Berreman, 1979: 162).

I do not underestimate the role of the system of ideas constituting purity and impurity in sustaining the caste system. But it is not realistic to reduce the perpetuation of the caste system to these ideas alone by giving them a central place, without being aware of the institutional framework within which such ideas and practices flourish. It is important to place the caste system in a wider socioeconomic and political context than the narrow religious ideas of purity and impurity in order to reveal the ramifications of the whole system.

Dumont's explanation is not convincing as to how those numerous castes in the middle rung of the hierarchy occupy a specific rank, whereas the lower castes, considered permanently polluted and hence impure, are destined to remove the temporary pollution of higher castes. He, in fact, avoids the problem by stating that caste as an institution, by encompassing power within status, accommodates itself to power. Thus, Dumont overlooks other essentials of the caste system, which are mainly shaped and sustained by politicoeconomic factors (Tanaka, 1991: 6).

Dumont regards Sanskrit texts as sources embodying the indigenous ideas concerning the caste system. Though I do not dispute the fact that the dichotomous notion of purity and impurity is derived from indigenous ideas, it is pertinent to ask whose ideas these are and how they are produced, sustained, and reproduced in society throughout history. Since the indigenous ideas Dumont refers to and relies on are mainly drawn from Sanskrit sources, his conception of the caste system restricts the scope of his sociological/anthropological method to a segment of ideas that led him to perceive a large number of castes, as well as gods, as merely adjuncts, when they are in fact essential to the formation and functioning of the whole system.

In my opinion, caste ranking is a function of power relations and is a form of social inequality. Interdependence among various caste groups cannot be seen as a harmonious condition free of the conflicts prevailing in society. I consider the "harmony" among people of a village to be a consequence of the control of upper caste(s) over the economy and economic activities. It is the control over resources, not just the caste strictures, that plays a crucial role in ranking and maintaining the caste system (Gough, 1955). Oscar Lewis (1955: 151) states: "In the past the potential contradictions between the interests of the farm and non-farm populations in the village were held in check by the power of the landholders and by lack of alternatives for the untouchable and other low caste people."

Placing the caste system in an economic context as opposed to Dumont's religious interpretation produces a different conclusion. As I. Habib (1986: 38–39) puts it, because

> the menial castes were deprived of any pretension to setting up as tillers of land themselves, they could, therefore, form a vast reservoir of landless labour with exceptionally depressed wages. This would in turn correspondingly enlarge the surplus that the ruling class could derive from the

peasant. At the same time that share in the surplus could obtain for the ruling class a larger return in terms of goods and services because of the larger productivity from "special skill" transmitted through the system of hereditary occupation while wages could be further depressed owing to the low station assigned to artisan castes.

T. O. Beidelman argues that the caste system entails inequality in the distribution of power. He too considers land as the major integrative factor around which the caste and village system operate: "Although castes are separated, dependence upon land unites castes about *jajmans* by means of this coerced dependence. Such coercive integration is supported and reaffirmed by ritual and ceremonies which *jajmans* hold both to emphasize the *jajman-kamin* relationship and to enhance or affirm their status" (Beidelman, 1959: 75).

However, Dumont argues that Beidelman confuses inequality with exploitation, stating that Beidelman "failed to see that the system assures subsistence to each proportionately to his status" (1988: 32). I entirely agree with Berreman's criticism of Dumont on this count:

> It also assures life, comfort, health, self-respect, food, shelter, learning, pleasure, society, education, legal redress, rewards in the next life and all of the other necessary and valued things proportionately to status. And that is what exploitation is, that is what oppression is: providing for those at the top "proportionately to status" and at the expense of those at the bottom. This does not distinguish inequality from exploitation, it identifies the common characteristics, and caste systems in India and elsewhere epitomize this relationship. That the relationship is described as paternalism, that it is rationalised as being for the benefit of all—is universal and hardly surprising since such descriptions are purveyed by the beneficiaries of the system who arrogate themselves the role of spokesmen for it. (Berreman, 1979: 159–160)

Thus, though the Brahmins and their traditions played a central role in shaping Hinduism, it is important to place it in a wider context. As M. Biardeau puts it: "Orthodox Brahmanism, which is closer to the Revelation, is not the ancestor of modern Hinduism: it is its permanent heart, the implicit model for or/and against which Bhakti, Tantric and all their sects have been constituted" (1989: 15). In my view, it is the hegemonic nature of orthodox Brahminical ideology that holds the key to understanding social and cultural processes in India.

Toward a Marxist Method: The Concept of Hegemony

The Marxist formulation in general regards the reality of base, primarily economic relations as being reflected or reproduced directly in the superstructure, which is considered to be the realm of all ideological and cultural activities. I regard this as inadequate to explain the complex nature of Indian social and cultural realities and processes, which are not a mere reflection of primary economic activities. It is very important to recognize the relative autonomy of the various components of the superstructure. This autonomy is not a mere separation from the base but a fluid dynamic condition in which "homologous structures" are in existence.

Antonio Gramsci's (1975) concept of hegemony helps in understanding the role of the Brahminical ideology in influencing and shaping various sociocultural processes in India. The concept of hegemony refers to an active and continuing process, not to a static condition. Gramsci points out that a class sustains its dominance not just by an organization of force but with a moral and intellectual leadership. He also lays emphasis on the fact that compromises are made with a variety of allies who are unified as a social bloc of forces. This bloc manifests and articulates a basis of consent for a certain social order, and in this social order the hegemony of a dominant class is created, sustained, and re-created in the web of various institutions and social relations. The implied consent is not always achieved through force but by various other means. It is therefore important to situate the study of society and religion in India in a wider context in which institutions are developed, modified, or transformed into something different and new.

Religion in Tamil Nadu, for example, is a distinct variant of Hinduism in which both the *bhakti* and Brahminical traditions are present. In bhakti Hinduism the *Agamas* and *Saiva Siddantha* form a scriptural basis. Bhakti Hinduism evolved and was shaped throughout the medieval period. It emerged in a context in which an active alliance between the kings, Brahmins, and upper-caste non-Brahmins existed. It has historically been centered around what are now known as Brahminical temples devoted to Lord Siva and Lord Vishnu. Hence, these "Brahminical" temples display a very strong regional character with vernacular and regional traditions. It is very evident that in the evolution of the synthesis comprising mythological elements from the classical *Puranas* and epics such as the *Mahabharata* and *Ramayana* and local/native materials with Tamil origin, orientation experiences provided the ideological foundation for the temples in Tamil Nadu. For instance, Sthalapuranam among the "Brahminical" temples reveals the process of localization of the universal deities such as Lord Siva. This process, which took place at the time of the bhakti movement with the active support of the dominant sections of the then society, fashioned the evolution of religion and society in Tamil-speaking areas (Shulman, 1980: 3–7). The Brahminical temples indeed grew into an institution with a specialized priestly community during and after the bhakti movement (sixth to ninth centuries A.D.), when the huge temples were established and the *Agamas,* the scriptural base of the "Brahminical" temples, were introduced. The scriptural and mythical base not only supported the temples as institutions but also sustained the dominant social groups, which enjoyed a privileged status and complete access to the temples and their endowments. In this way, the Brahminical temples as an ideological institution legitimized the then social structure, which was marked by a rigid social hierarchy, oppression, and exploitation.

A brief consideration of the evolution of the bhakti Hinduism centered around the Brahminical temples in Tamil Nadu will reveal the manner in which the Brahminical tradition attained dominance by incorporating the bhakti traditions. The historical context, the establishment of the dominance of the peasantry of the plains and their culture over that of the non-peasant warrior tribes of the hills and forests, created a need for a cohesive ideology. This was provided by the long-associated Brahmin groups, who were able to offer an ideology because of their monopoly over the maintenance, development, and transmission of Sanskritic religious knowledge. This unique ideology of the bhakti schools accorded a legitimate and a high place in the Brahminical religion to the non-Brahmins as well as to popular folk traditions. It helped the Brahmins to receive extensive material support and enjoy some measure of autonomy from state control in return for according a high status to the dominant non-Brahmin peasantry. The Brahmins were motivated to enter into this "alliance" by the great strides Buddhism and Jainism had made in southern India around this period, which seriously threatened their position and privilege (Stein, 1980: 72–89).

This alliance between the Brahmins and the dominant peasantry continued till about the twelfth century A.D., by which time a new social base of power comprising a combination of the dominant peasantry and local traditional artisan groups began to develop. Concomitant with this came other developments like growth of towns, increased Brahminization of the non-Brahmin population, and its participation in the Brahminical religious institutions such as temples and monasteries. The bhakti religion undoubtedly contributed to these developments since it opened the doors of the classical Brahminical religion to the large non-Brahmin householder population, especially its upper stratum. Stein vividly demonstrates that for a period spanning the sixth to the sixteenth centuries A.D., groups and classes rising to economic and political dominance acquired higher status by making gifts like land to Brahmins and temples. In return, Brahmins legitimized the claims of these classes. This alliance between Brahmins, upper non-Brahmin castes, and kings existed throughout medieval southern India. Brahmins and sectarian leaders helped to legitimize the political authority of kings and dominance of upper castes, who in turn extended material support and respect to the Brahmins (Stein, 1980).

During the medieval period, temples functioned as a principal power center along with the palaces from where the kings reigned. The state and the temples reinforced each other, with temples legitimizing the political authority while the state or the kings supported temples and their functionaries with land grants and other resources, kings and the local rich thus acting as protectors and patrons of the temples. The relationship of temples with structures of power was unambiguous. It was regarded as a shared sovereignty between gods and humans.

In spite of the absence of any centralized authority to link the temples of all denominations during the pre-British period, the way in which the medieval state exercised its control over numerous temples demonstrates the close association that existed between the temples, denominations (or sects), and kings. A. Appadurai's model provides an insight into the process by which the king, through endowments, placed himself in an active relationship with the deity who was contexualized in a distributive system. This enabled the king to receive honor as well as perform his "dharmic" duty as protector of his subjects and various institutions, including temples. The king's mandatory function in resolving conflicts by arbitration had wide acceptance. The affiliation or association of the king with his agents (or ministers), local assemblies, "sectarian" groups and leaders, temple functionaries, and worshippers was not established and sustained in the line of the Weberian model of bureaucracy based on legal-rational principles (Weber, 1965a). Instead, this association, which was articulated through power relations, provided a human framework that was sustained by the king. In turn, the king received active support from the former. It may be added here that the human framework or social bases of these temples, including the "sectarian" (or denominational) groups and their leaders, formed the immediate support base of the king's authority (Appadurai, 1977: 50–55; 1981: 68–74).

Throughout the medieval period the alliance continued to be dominant in exercising religious, intellectual, and political authority and leadership. Acceptance by the majority of the lower caste governed by the principle of ritual pollution was achieved not by coercion but by a process of hegemony in which the consent was secured through the ideology of Brahminism. Thus, not simply political force succeeded in making people believe in the institution of caste, but the theory of karma and of the cycle of rebirth. In the process, hierarchy and separation became important organizing principles. Ideas of karma and dharma brought about a passive endorsement of the religious principle of pollution governing certain forms of social inequalities in India. It was this social and political milieu in which the Dalits were ideologically separated as Untouchables and excluded from certain social as well as religious spheres.

The social bloc that had exclusive rights over the temples for centuries began to disintegrate slowly with British intervention in temple affairs. The efforts of the British government to root out the corruption among the traditional trustees and other administrators of the temples were resisted. The temple entry proclamation in 1930 was opposed vehemently. Opening of temples to Untouchables and other lower non-Brahmin castes was contested on the ground that their entry would destroy the sanctity of the holy temples. An enormous amount of conflict arose between the state and various groups and individuals involved in temple affairs. This conflict, arising out of changes brought about by governments both before and after independence, demonstrates the extent of opposition from those who enjoyed power and status derived from their traditional monopoly over the affairs of temples. The temple priests and traditional trustees, especially, challenged various reform measures in courts of law (Appadurai, 1981; Fuller, 1984; Good, 1989). These court cases, especially after independence, meant that the secular constitution and other modern laws, not the religious texts, became the basis of the interpretation of certain practices in the realm of temples (Baird, 1976). As a result, courts began to view certain aspects of the temples as secular, although the basic character of the temple was accepted as religious.

The principal purpose of state intervention in the affairs of the temples both before and after independence was to remove corruption among trustees and mismanagement of resources, including temple funds and endowments attached to temples in the form of large estates. The alleged extortion and lack of *Agamic* knowledge of the priests and their consequent incompetence in organization and performance of worship accentuated the demands of the reformists and the efforts of successive governments since independence in Tamil Nadu (Mudaliar, 1975; Kennedy, 1974; Fuller, 1984). It is adequate to state here that the British government had established the foundation for the bureaucratic control of the temples by instituting the Hindu Religious Endowment Board in 1925. With subsequent modifications in the relevant act that legalized bureaucratic control, the department of Hindu Religious and Charitable Endowments (HRCE) was established on a firm footing during the postindependence period. In the light of the growing influence of the Dravidian ideology and its political success in 1967, the pace of change was accelerated. The complementary functioning of temples and state during the pre-British period has now been reversed by the modern state by universalizing Hindu temples. There is indeed a process of dehegemonization of the temples at one level and of society at another, for upper-caste monopoly in various areas of social life is also in constant decline.

I have used the concept of hegemony to help reveal the diverse nature of Indian society and religion. It certainly explains the process by which modes of dominance and subordination unfolded over time in India: the manner in which caste-class relations, centered around the ownership of means of production such as land, existed in the past, and the way human labor was married to the ideology of caste, determining the social hierarchy and legitimizing oppression and exploitation.

That the principle of purity and pollution and social hierarchy existed even among the members of lower castes indicates the powerful influence of Brahminical ideology on the one hand and the acceptance of the caste ideology by the lower castes on the other. To unravel the ways in which first the Dalits and then the tribals have been incorporated into the Brahminical social organization and religious pantheon now termed as Hinduism, studies will have to be undertaken at micro, regional, and macro levels. Reinterpretation of cultural symbols that embody the ideological elements drawn from Brahminism is most important. For a large section of Dalits, caste and the principle of purity and pollution are a reality offered by God from which they cannot escape. A change in this belief system of the Dalits, which is modeled on Brahminical ideology, holds the key to a major social transformation bringing about social equality.

References

Appadurai. A. 1977. "Kings, Sects and Temples in South India, 1350–1700 A.D.," *The Indian Economic and Social History Review* 14 (1): 47–73.
———. 1981. *Worship and Conflict Under Colonial Rule: A South Indian Case.* Cambridge: Cambridge University Press.
Baird, R. D. 1976. "Religion and the Secular: Categories for Religious Conflict and Religious Change in Independent India," in B. L. Smith (ed.), *Religion and Social Conflict in South Asia.* Leiden: E. J. Brill.
Baker, C. J. 1976. *The Politics of South India 1920–1937.* Cambridge: Cambridge University Press.
Baker, C. J., and D. A. Washbrook. 1975. *South India: Political Institutions and Political Change 1880–1940.* New Delhi: Vikas.
Barnett, M. R. 1976. *The Politics of Cultural Nationalism in South India.* Princeton: Princeton University Press.
Beidelman, T. O. 1959. *A Comparative Analysis of the Jajmani System.* New York: J. J. Augustin.
Berreman, G. D. 1979. *Caste and Other Inequities: Essays on Inequality.* Meerut: Folklore Institute.
Béteille, André. 1965. *Caste, Class and Power: Changing Patterns of Stratification in a Tanjore Village.* Berkeley: University of California Press.
Biardeau, M. 1989. *Hinduism.* Delhi: Oxford University Press.
Dumont, L. 1970. *Religion, Politics and History in India.* Paris: Mouton.
———. 1986. *A South Indian Subcaste: Social Organisation and Religion of the Pramalai Kallar.* Delhi: Oxford University Press.
———. 1988. *Homo Hierarchicus: The Caste System and Its Implications.* Delhi: Oxford University Press.
Durkheim, Emile. 1964. *Elementary Forms of the Religious Life.* London: Allen and Unwin.

Fuller, C. J. 1984. *Servants of the Goddess: The Priests of a South Indian Temple.* Cambridge: Cambridge University Press.
———. 1988. "The Hindu Temple and Indian Society," in M. V. Fox (ed.), *Temple in Society.* Winona Lake: Eisenbrauns.
Geertz, C. 1973. *The Interpretation of Cultures.* New York: Basic Books.
Good, A. 1989. "Law, Legitimacy, and the Hereditary Rights of Tamil Temple Priests," *Modern Asian Studies* 23: 233–257.
Gopalkrishnan, S. 1981. *Political Movements in South India 1914–1929.* Madras: New Era Publications.
Gough, K. 1955. "The Social Structure of a Tanjore Village," in M. Marriott (ed.), *Village India: Studies in Little Community.* Bombay: Asia Publishing House.
Gramsci, A. 1975. *Selections from the Prison Notebooks.* New York: International Publishers.
Habib, I. 1986. "Theories of Social Change in South Asia," *The Journal of Social Studies* 33: 34–54.
Hardiman, D. 1984. "Adivasi Assertion in South Gujarat: The Devi Movement of 1922–3," in Ranajit Guha (ed.), *Subaltern Studies III: Writings on South Asian History and Society.* Delhi: Oxford University Press.
Karve, I. 1953. *Kinship Organisation in India.* Poona: Deccan College.
Kennedy, R. 1974. "Status and Control of Temples in Tamil Nadu," *The Indian Economic and Social History Review* 11 (4): 260–290.
Leavitt, J. 1992. "Cultural Holism in the Anthropology of South Asia: The Challenge of Regional Traditions," *Contributions to Indian Sociology* (n.s.) 26: 13–49.
Lewis, Oscar. 1955. *Village Life in Northern India.* New York: Vintage Books.
Moffatt, M. 1979. *An Untouchable Community in South India: Structure and Consensus.* Princeton: University Press.
Marriott, M. 1955. "Little Communities in an Indigenous Civilisation," in M. Marriott (ed.), *Village India: Studies in Little Community.* Bombay: Asia Publishing House.
Mudaliar, Chandra. 1975. *State and Religious Endowments in Madras.* Madras: University Press.
Ramanujam, A. K. 1972. *Speaking of Siva.* Harmondsworth: Penguin Books.
Rao, M. S. A. 1979. *Social Movements and Social Transformation: A Study of Two Backward Classes Movements in India.* Delhi: Macmillan.
Ryerson, C. 1988. *Regionalism and Religion: The Tamil Renaissance and Popular Hinduism.* Bangalore: The Christian Literature Society.
Sastri, K. A. N. 1955. *History of South India.* London: Oxford University Press.
———. 1963. *Development of Religion in South India.* Bombay: Orient Longman.
Sharma, U. 1970. "The Problem of Village Hinduism: Fragmentation and Integration," *Contributions to Indian Sociology* (n.s.) 4: 1–21.
Shulman, D. D. 1980. *Tamil Temple Myths: Sacrifice and Divine Marriage in the South Indian Saiva Tradition.* Princeton: Princeton University Press.
Singer, M. 1959. *Traditional India: Structure and Change.* Philadelphia: American Folklore Society.
———. 1972. *When a Great Tradition Modernizes.* Delhi: Vikas Publishing House.
Singer, M., and B. S. Cohn (eds.). 1968. *Structure and Change in Indian Society.* Chicago: Aldine Publishing Company.
Srinivas, M. N. 1952. *Religion and Society Among the Coorgs of South India.* Oxford: Clarendon Press.
———. 1955. "The Social System of a Mysore Village," in M. Marriott (ed.), *Village India.* Chicago: Chicago University Press.

———. 1962. *Caste in Modern India and Other Essays.* Bombay: Asia Publishing House.
———. 1966. *Social Change in Modern India.* Bombay: Allied Publishers.
———. 1977. *The Cohesive Role of Sanskritization and Other Essays.* New Delhi: Oxford University Press.
———. 1984. "Some Reflections on the Nature of Caste Hierarchy," *Contributions to Indian Sociology* (n.s.) 18: 151–167.
———. 1989. *The Cohesive Role of Sanskritization and Other Essays.* Delhi: Oxford University Press.
Staal, T. F. 1963. "Sanskrit and Sanskritization," *Journal of Asian Studies* 22: 261–275.
Stein, Burton. 1980. *Peasant State and Society in Medieval South India.* Delhi: Oxford University Press.
Tanaka, M. 1991. *Patrons, Devotees and Goddesses: Ritual and Power Among the Tamil Fishermen of Sri Lanka.* Kyoto: Institute for Research in the Humanities.
Weber, Max. 1965a. *The Theory of Social and Economic Organisation.* New York: Free Press.
———. 1965b. *The Sociology of Religion.* London: Methuen and Co. Ltd.
Williams, R. 1980. *Problems in Materialism and Culture.* London: Verso.

6

Misrepresenting the Dalit Movement

Gopal Guru

The study of the Dalit movement has attracted some leading sociologists over the past two decades in India and abroad. The centenary year of B. R. Ambedkar's birth saw a plethora of publications, thus adding to the growing literature on Ambedkar, Dalit politics, and the Dalit movement. Among sociologists it is possible to discern a dominant ideological current that has bearings on the study of the Dalit movement. There is a "liberal" trend among a group of scholars, who believe that it is the ancient Hindu reactionary traditions and the deep-rooted prejudice of the upper castes against Dalits that has led to the protest of the latter. This trend views Dalit protest as a necessary outcome of an obscurantist Hindu tradition. This liberal view also has a strong tendency to assume that the Dalit movement is limited to achieving a partial advance in the socioeconomic, civic, and political fields within the existing social order; thus hardly any thought is expended on radical transformation in other respects. It is due to this ideological position that concepts like "social mobility," "reference group," and "relative deprivation" figure so prominently in liberal scholars' writings on the Dalit movement, and such concepts became a major frame of reference in studying the Dalit movement.

Among those notable scholars who fall into this liberal category is M. S. A. Rao, who has used similar concepts for understanding the emergence of the protest movement among the backward classes and the Dalits in India (1982: 4). Rao, taking a cue from Merton and Runciman, has argued that social mobility forms the major basis of the theory of relative deprivation (1982: 4). (Social conflict as a basis of relative deprivation finds mention in Rao's study but without much detailed discussion.) Rao further argues that the relative deprivation is connected with the moment of emulation of a positive reference group (1982: 194). Other scholars too have tried to link the emergence of the Dalit movement with the issue of relative deprivation, reference groups, and social mobility (Joshi, 1987; Issac,

1964; Lynch, 1974; Silverberg, 1968; Singer and Cohen, 1968; Sachchidananda, 1978; Bhat, 1971; Ram, 1988; Patwardhan, 1973). It is obvious from the works of these scholars that terms like "social mobility" and "relative deprivation" form the major frame of reference in discussions of the emergence of reform, protest, and movement among the Dalits.

In studying Dalit mobility, it has been suggested by some scholars that the process of Sanskritization could be a model; that is, certain Dalit groups or individuals could try to adopt either ritually or culturally higher groups or individuals in order to achieve a similar social position or try to adopt the values that promote the aspirations of an atomized individual in a civil society. According to this view, if the Dalits fail in their achievement of this imitation of the Sanskritization model of upper mobility, they then suffer from relative deprivation because at the social level their attempt to overcome relative deprivation is restricted by the upper-caste group, whom they cite as a reference group existing mostly in a pre–civil society situation that is still dominant in some parts of the country. At another level, the articulation of relative deprivation among the educated Dalits might take place when compared with the Westernized high caste. Thus, in the Indian case, as T. K. Oommen has pointed out, the deprivation is multifaceted (1990: 255).

Though inadequate in understanding the Dalit movement, studies establishing a link between the emergence of the Dalit movement and relative deprivation, social mobility, and reference group theory need to be supported on the following theoretical and strategic grounds. Both historically and dialectically, this concept of relative deprivation could capture social reality at a particular historical juncture when Indian society was trying to release itself from the feudal ethos that was facing an ever-increasing threat from the advancing civil society in India. In this transitional process, the Dalits, who were aspiring toward mobility of various kinds but were unable to achieve it due to the restrictions imposed by the feudal as well as colonial vested interests, felt deprived. This fact time and again prompted the Dalit movement (for example, in the 1930s in Maharashtra) to challenge feudal values through a process of emulation and Sanskritization (see Omvedt, 1994). This attempt to imitate the upper-caste values, particularly in the case of the Mahars of Maharashtra, certainly contributed to the development of a negative consciousness that, according to Antonio Gramsci, may not constitute a mature and fully evolved class consciousness but certainly is the first glimmer of such consciousness constituting the basic negative, polemical attitude (see Guha, 1983: 20). Gramsci further argues that the lower classes, historically on the defensive, can only achieve self-awareness by reacting against the identity and class limits of their enemy (Guha, 1983).

Taking a cue from Gramsci, Ranajit Guha tries to understand this consciousness of the insurgent peasantry in colonial India:

It was only by attacking the material symbols of governmental and landlords authority that the insurgents upset the established order. They did so by undermining its dominant semifeudal culture as well. Insofar as religion constituted the most expressive sign of this culture in many if its essential aspects, the peasants' defiance of the rural elite often involved an attempt to appropriate the dominant religion or to destroy it. To those who were high up in society the emulation of their culture by the lower strata seemed always fraught with danger. There have been occasions when, thanks to the stimuli given to casteism by British colonial policy, Sanskritising movements among the lower castes to upgrade themselves by adopting the rituals and religious idioms of their superiors were resisted by the latter and generated much social tension and even some actual violence. (1983: 20)[1]

In the same vein, the Dalit social protest of the 1930s under the leadership of Ambedkar focused its attention on entering the *savarna* temples and tried to improve the status of Dalits through the imitation of Hindu lifestyle by adopting gods and rituals of the upper castes, that is, through the process of Sanskritization (see Srinivas, 1962). Although the usual tendency is to view Sanskritization as a cultural process aimed at bringing about changes in the lifestyle of Dalits, because Dalits embraced it reluctantly and the upper castes invariably opposed it (see Oommen, 1990: 255), it fostered important structural changes such as a protest orientation and countermobilization. In addition, studies understanding the Dalit movement in terms of relative deprivation and social mobility helped to reveal the role of castes and inherited status that have for so long enabled the upper castes to monopolize the available jobs. It is in this context that studies establishing a connection between the Dalit movement and the above concepts bring out latent contradictions of a socioeconomic and political nature. Moreover, such studies also reveal that relative deprivation leading to socioeconomic mobility has, after all, a democratizing impact on the socioeconomic, political, and bureaucratic structure of India (Shah, 1991: 603).

Studies linking relative deprivation and social mobility with the Dalit movement assume importance for tactical and strategic reasons especially when the studies of these movements are denied their legitimate place in the academic world and are considered to be deviations from the mainstream and irrelevant in the Indian context (Oommen, 1990: 30). Oommen, while criticizing this approach as historical and biased, has argued that an adequate framework for the study of social movements should take into account the historicity, the elements of social structure, and the future vision of the society in which they originate and operate and that the dialectics between these provide the focal point for the analysis of social movements (Oommen, 1990: 30).

However, the present scenario, highlighted by three major developments—the total marginalization and annihilation of the rural Dalits, the

Hinduization of the Dalit masses, and the growing crisis of the Indian welfare state—seems to be questioning the theoretical validity of relative deprivation both as a concept and as a form of consciousness. Concepts of relative deprivation and also social mobility are quite inadequate to capture this reality at the theoretical level. Given the happenings in the rural areas where the upper castes or class forces are committing brutal atrocities on the Dalits and when the state's response is either callous or repressive, the Dalits do not feel a sense of relative deprivation so much as a total alienation and exclusion and the threat of physical liquidation. What one observes in rural Maharashtra and also in the rest of the country is the complete alienation of the Dalits from resources like land, water, and agricultural implements. Thus, the Dalits do not find sufficient access to either the natural or human resources and, therefore, feel totally marginalized in relation to the so-called decentralization of political power in rural India. Such a situation in which the Dalits are collectively and absolutely worse off questions the validity of the concept of relative deprivation, which primarily presupposes the perception of contrasting one's situation, even at the most trivial level, with that of others worse off than oneself (Runciman, 1966: 9). Moreover, it is this perception of total exclusion from the developmental processes that forces the Dalits to protest in the most militant way, ranging from radical reaction to physical retaliation in self-defense. This militancy is evident among the Dalits of Andhra Pradesh, Bihar, and Maharashtra.

In the urban setting in Maharashtra, however, the concept of relative deprivation and social mobility has some relevance to the newly educated, employed Dalit class that is emerging from among the Mahars and Mangs. It is true that the Mahars do feel relative deprivation at two levels. First, at the vertical level, the Mahars feel relatively deprived both socially and materially in comparison with the upwardly mobile upper castes. To assuage this feeling of deprivation, these Dalits, particularly officers, float some kinds of welfare associations to gain, among other things, more patronage from the system and to overcome their relative deprivation by raising the material and social status of the individual up to the level of those who are immediately above them. Thus, at the vertical level, the reference group for the Mahars is the upwardly mobile upper castes.

At the horizontal level, for the Mahars and the Mangs, the reference group is the emerging Mahar elites. The Mahars and even the Mangs in the urban setting seem to have developed a sense of relative deprivation often reflecting the feeling of hatred, contempt, and jealousy toward those Mahars who, according to the group under reference, are more fortunate in raising their material status. This feeling of relative deprivation among the less fortunate Mahars and Mangs is now being openly articulated—an articulation that can lead to the formation of a subgroup or a social category based on the region-specific identity of these Mahars. The Marathwada Mitra Mandal (the organization of the Dalit teachers from Marathwada University) is a case in point. It is alleged that the members of this group feel relatively deprived in comparison with the Dalits of northern Maharashtra and Vidarbha (see Jondhale, 1992). It is interesting to note here that this is true of the Dalits of Telangana, who feel relatively deprived in comparison with the Dalits of coastal Andhra Pradesh, particularly of the Guntur region, who, according to the former, are far ahead in terms of socioeconomic and educational achievements.

These feelings have important effects on the stability of the system. First, the feeling of relative deprivation, if assuaged successfully, has a built-in atomizing tendency that isolates the Dalits under reference from the larger Dalit community. Second, the concept of relative deprivation tends to prevent the formation of a critical consciousness involving a critique of the Indian state and its lopsided economic development. Instead, it fetters itself to the narrow contours of envy, contempt, and hatred against persons from the same social situation. For example, the Dalits (Mahars, Buddhists) of Marathwada, who, in educational and material terms, are relatively backward as compared with the Dalits of Vidarbha, consider this relative advance of their counterparts from Vidarbha as the major cause of their own backwardness. They do not consider their backwardness to be a result of the feudal ethos that dominated the socioeconomic life of Marathwada for 500 years.

Similarly, relative deprivation makes the Mangs overlook the connection between their backwardness and their traditional skilled occupation, which had bound them to the feudal agrarian structure. Due to the socioeconomic and technological changes in Indian agriculture and state intervention in the condition of the Dalits in general, the Mangs are now being displaced from the agrarian economy and are compelled to take to education and to the subsequent quest for jobs. This compulsion and displacement is a result of the replacement of the old agricultural implements that were made by the Mangs by the more sophisticated implements manufactured by the Garwares. In this situation, the Mangs are lagging behind the Mahars owing to the former's late response to the state, which, as we will see, seems to have lost the capacity to accommodate these latecomers in its rather obsolete network of patronage. Why do the Mangs not question the capacity of the Indian state and find fault with the market society that underlines and renews the structures of inequality? Why does their feeling of relative deprivation revolve around the relative advance of the microscopic section of Mahar elites?

The answer to this question lies in the politicization of relative deprivation, which finds expression among the Mang elites. These elites, though emerging on a very small scale, are now vocalizing the sense of relative deprivation of the common Mangs with the intention of sharing the spoils with the Mahars by forcing a bargain with the power centers.[2] This political expression of relative deprivation aimed at creating a constituency among the ignorant but innocent Mangs surfaced in one of the state-level conferences organized by the Mang elites in Maharashtra at Ichalkaranji in November 1991. It is interesting to note that in this particular conference the feeling of relative deprivation with a negative reference to the Mahars was articulated by the Mangs with the encouragement and patronage of the upper-caste political forces, which are alleged to be instrumental in fanning hostilities between the two communities for the electoral politics of the former in the state.[3] Needless to say, this feeling of relative deprivation suspends, if not eliminates completely, the possibility of the development of a homogeneous Dalit unity cutting across castes as well as regions. In addition, since relative deprivation underlines the quest for social mobility, this mobility syndrome of Dalits could diffuse the formation of social consciousness, leading to the isolation and independence of the Dalits from their community and pushing them away from the center of collective struggles to the periphery. By participating in the struggle by paying only lip service to the Dalit cause, these Dalits would bypass the assumption of historical responsibility that Ambedkar had rested on their shoulders for their emancipation and that of the common Dalits from their dehumanizing conditions.

The real damage that the concept of relative deprivation can cause to the Dalit movement today is that it obscures issues of power. This concept attempts to describe "what is" without linking it with "what can be" and thus results in an adequate description of social phenomena. It denies to sociology a critically subversive character while also denying an emancipatory consciousness to the groups under reference. It impels the Dalit groups to organize their thought and action not in their own authentic terms but in terms of those privileged sections whose hegemonic worldview underlines the structures of domination.

The state plays an extremely important role in keeping the sense of relative deprivation vital, by systematically and shrewdly transferring resources from the more privileged sections to the underprivileged sections as a part of its welfare strategies. In doing so, the state not only weakens the critical consciousness that had begun to articulate itself against the structure of domination but as a corollary also discredits the movement by co-opting the most vocal and assertive elements into the pacification structures built around the welfare state. For example, in the 1960s in Maharashtra, the state seems to have, time and again, effectively scattered Dalit consciousness. In Maharashtra this was exemplified by the state's treatment of Dadasaheb Gaikwad in the early 1960s in the Dalit movement. Later, there was an alliance of the Dalit Panthers with the left and democratic forces. However, the Dalit integrating consciousness become fragmented into at least a dozen small groups of the Republican Party of India (RPI) in Maharashtra. This diffusion was effected through the introduction of the Integrated Rural Development Programme (IRDP) and National Rural Employment Programme (NREP) packages, and the discrediting was achieved through the co-optation of important Dalit leaders, including Gaikwad, by the state.[4]

But scholars studying the Dalit movement have not focused much attention on such a vital aspect of the movement as the subversive role of the state. Oommen has tried to locate the state response to the Dalit movement, but he seems to have given a more formal and legalistic explanation of the state response to the Dalit movement or any other movement of the weaker sections of the population (Oommen, 1990: 187). For example, he tends to argue that the state either becomes repressive or discredits the movement because the latter defies its authority (Oommen, 1990: 187). But an emasculation of any movement, particularly the Dalit movement in Maharashtra in the late 1960s and early 1970s, was done by the state not solely because the Dalit movement had undermined its authority but more because this phase of the Dalit movement, which focused on the question of redistribution of land, seriously threatened the material interests of the rural rich by demanding government land and land declared surplus under the ceiling law.

Though the concepts of relative deprivation and social mobility play a diffusionist role as they render the formation of an integral Dalit consciousness difficult in the urban setting, they were relevant inasmuch as they could capture the social reality, although fractionally. However, it seems now that the growing crisis of the Indian welfare state, the systematic attempt by the Hindutva forces to Hinduize the Dalits, and the revitalizing of Buddhist culture among the Dalits all seem to have rendered the concept of relative deprivation too fragile to lead to new initiatives.

The levels of the feeling relating to relative deprivation and social mobility are conditioned by the capacity of the state to intervene in the conditions of the population sections concerned. This can be corroborated by citing W. Runciman, who observes that in Europe the welfare provisions of the interwar period helped to keep the level of relative deprivation lower than the actual hardships imposed by the depression might appear to warrant (1966: 70). But in the Indian context, the experience is quite contrary to that stated by Runciman because, in view of the absolute deprivation of the Dalits, it was politically imperative for the Indian state to shift resources (this includes various constitutional provisions and different welfare programs for the Dalits) from the more privileged sections, thus reducing absolute deprivation to relative deprivation.

In the last few years—particularly in the urban setting—developments in Maharashtra in the sphere of state and religion are conducive to reversing the process, from relative to absolute deprivation. This is so because the current fiscal crisis of the Indian state renders it difficult to shift resources from the privileged to the underprivileged; consequently the state withdraws from the social sphere. Two facts emplify the change in the state's role. First, according to a rough estimate, the budgetary provision for Dalit social welfare is 1 percent. In fact, the percentage outlay on the Scheduled Castes had increased only marginally from 0.35 percent in the First Five-Year Plan to 0.84 percent in the Fifth Five-Year Plan. Thus, we find that the Scheduled Castes, who constitute 15 percent of India's population and a much greater proportion of the poor, have been provided a disproportionately low share of the plan's resources. Second, the state's thrust toward privatization means practically a total marginalization of the Indian Dalits because the private sector would hardly be interested in accommodating them. This growing privatization and the resultant exclusion of the Dalits from the urban settings is also likely to lead toward an articulation of their critical consciousness as a collectivity.

As of today, however, such an articulation of corporate Dalit consciousness has not found any organized expression among urbanite Dalits. Unfortunately, the growing privatization of the Indian economy and the crisis of the welfare state in India did not figure at all in the state conference recently organized by the Backward, Adivasi, and Muslim Caste Federation at Nasik. In the 1930s, the sense of relative deprivation resulting from upper-caste restrictions on the Dalit adoption of certain high-caste social norms had led the Dalits to overcome it through collective mobilization. But today, the Hindutva forces are taking the initiative in accommodating the Dalits in the *savarna* culture. The notable example of this deceitful elevation of the Dalits was marked by the laying of bricks during the Ram Shilanyas at Ayodhya by two Dalits, who were pressed into the God Rama's service by the Bharatiya Janata Party–BJP-VHP combine a couple of years ago. This particular case certainly did not involve a genuine desire on the part of Hindus to overcome the relative deprivation of the Dalits. However, whatever the reasons, this accommodation certainly suspends the necessity for the Dalits to initiate movements toward Sanskritization. Further, since the concept of relative deprivation has meaning only in a hierarchical socioeconomic situation, it cannot explain the phenomenon of the Buddhist conversion movement in Maharashtra and of late in Andhra Pradesh.

By way of conclusion, it can be observed that if the critical function of the social sciences, and therefore of sociology, consists of an attempt to question its own theoretical assumptions in relation to the changing socioeconomic reality, then it becomes necessary to develop this critical function in order to understand any movement from below.

Notes

This paper is a revised version of an earlier draft presented in the seminar on "Dalit Movement in India" organized by Vikas Adhayan Kendra, Bombay, August 1992, and which subsequently appeared in *Economic and Political Weekly*, 3 April 1993, pp. 570–572.
   1. This is also borne out by Ambedkar's Chowdar Tank movement at Mahad in 1927 and temple entry movement in 1929 at Nasik.
   2. This was evident at the state-level conference organized by one of the important Mang leaders at Ichalkaranji in November 1991.
   3. During the Ichalkaranji conference, the Congress leaders from the state tried to instigate the Mangs against the Mahars by projecting the latter as prospering at the cost of the former.
   4. *Sugawa*, a special number on the theme "Ambedkar and Hindutvavadi," was published by Sugawa Publications at Pune in 1991 (in Marathi).

References

Bhat, Anil. 1971. "Politics and Social Mobility in India," *Contributions to Indian Sociology* 1, December: 105.
Guha, Ranajit. 1983. *Elementary Aspects of Peasant Insurgence in Colonial India*. London: Oxford.
Issac, Harold. 1964. *India's Ex-Untouchables*. Bombay: Asia Publishing House.
Jondhale, B. V. 1992. "A Report on Milind College," *Maharashtra Times*, July 6.
Joshi, Barbara. 1987. "Recent Developments in Inter-Regional Mobilisation of Dalit Protest in India," *South Asian Bulletin* 7: 112–135.
Lynch, Owen. 1974. *The Politics of Untouchability*. Delhi: National Publications.
Omvedt, Gail. 1994. *Dalits and the Democratic Revolution: Dr. Ambedkar and the Dalit Movement in Colonial India*. Delhi: Sage.
Oommen, T. K. 1990. *Protest and Change: Studies in Social Movements*. Delhi: Sage.
Patwardhan, Sunanda. 1973. *Change Among India's Harijans*. Delhi: Orient Longman.
Ram, Nandu. 1988. *The Mobile Scheduled Castes: Rise of a New Middle Class*. Delhi: Hindustan Publishing Corporation.
Rao, M. S. A. 1982. *Social Movements in India* (Vol. 1). Delhi: Manohar Publications.
Runciman, W. 1966. *Relative Deprivation*. London: Routledge and Kegan Paul.
Sachchidananda, S. 1978. *Harijan Elite*. Faridabad: Thomson Press.
Shah, Ghanshyam. 1991. "Social Backwardness and Politics of Reservation," *Economic and Political Weekly* Annual Number, March: 603.
Silverberg, James (ed.). 1968. *Social Mobility in the Caste System in India*. Mouten: The Hague.
Singer, M., and Bernard Cohen (eds.). 1968. *Structure and Change in Indian Society*. Chicago: Aldine.
Srinivas, M. N. 1962. "A Note on Sanskritization and Westernization," in M. N. Srinivas, *Caste in Modern India and Other Essays*. London: Asia Publishing House.

7

Becoming Hindu: *Adivasis* in South Gujarat

Arjun Patel

The Problem

Culture plays an important social role in every community, including the *adivasis*.[1] Accordingly, the changing social and cultural life of the *adivasis* has been the subject matter of studies by anthropologists and sociologists. J. Troisi (1979) has classified the study of *adivasi* religion into two major trends: evolutionist and functionalist. The evolutionists propounded a number of theories regarding the origin of religion. The common assumption among nineteenth-century evolutionists such as E. B. Tylor, Morgan, Spencer, and others was that primitive religion grew out of ignorance and intellectual inadequacy. They emphasized the social usefulness of various religions but looked at them as bodies of erroneous beliefs and illusory practices. The other approach was functionalist and was advocated by Emile Durkheim, A. R. Radcliffe-Brown, Malinowski, and Evans-Pritchard. They wanted to show that religion is essential to social cohesion and community feeling in society. According to Radcliffe-Brown, the existence and continuance of an orderly social life depended on the presence of collective sentiments in the minds of the individual members. Evans-Pritchard criticized the theories put forward to explain religion as fantasy or illusion as well as sociologists and anthropologists who imposed their own cultural criteria on quite incompatible subject matter. He advocated the importance of analyzing religious facts in relation to the whole institutional system of society.

The religious aspect of *adivasi* societies has been studied by many, mostly European travelers, missionaries, or historians. Broadly, these studies can be classified into four groups. The first group (Dehon, 1906; Roy, 1925; Ferreira, 1965; and others) gives ethnographic details about the religion of different *adivasi* groups. The second group of studies (Bose, 1941; Sahay, 1962; Sachchidananda, 1964, 1970; and others) tries to depict different cultural processes among *adivasis* such as assimilation, Sanskritization, the *adivasi*-caste continuum, Christianization, cultural changes, and the like. Various movements such as revitalization, Bhagats, and messianic movements form a third group of studies (Sen, 1968; Paul, 1919; Swain, 1969; Das, 1968-1969; and others). A fourth group (Radcliffe-Brown, 1964; Banerjee, 1968; Hajra, 1970; and others) describes relations between different *adivasi* religions and their social structure. All these groups focus on the process of cultural transactions, the contacts of "little traditions" with "great traditions."[2]

These four approaches have dominated the scene for years, but now efforts have been made to apply a different approach to the phenomenon of Hinduization of the *adivasis*. This new approach saw the light of day during the 1990s, particularly after the demolition of the Babari Musjid at Ram Janma Bhumi at Ayodhya. The antagonism between Hindus and Muslims has come to a head in recent years. In this context, researches on Hindu nationalism have become an important area of study (Bajaj, 1993; Graham, 1990; Iyer, 1991; Jayaprasad, 1991; Nandy et al., 1995; Panikkar, 1991; Rajkishore, 1995; Shourie, 1987). The rise of Hindutva and the Bharatiya Janata Party (BJP) has opened new areas of research for scholars. They have now begun to look into this matter and how it affects the Dalits and other marginalized groups in India. Politics and society have once again become a major focus of inquiry. Recently K. Yogendra Malik and V. B. Singh (1994) have made a praiseworthy study of this subject. In their book *Hindu Nationalists in India: The Rise of the Bharatiya Janata Party,* they have analyzed the circumstances leading to the emergence of the BJP as a major political force in the 1980s and 1990s. The study has shortcomings, however. For instance, it covers the subject in broad outline but does not deal with local groups and events or regional tendencies.

Achyut Yagnic (1995) has contributed an article titled "Hindutva as a Savrana Purana," in which he has made an attempt to describe the rise of communal feelings among the Hindus in Gujarat. Recently, a political scientist, Ghanshyam Shah (1991, 1992, 1993, 1994, 1995), has written articles on the rise of the BJP in Gujarat. In one of these articles (1994), he tries to analyze the rise of the BJP among backward classes. Gopal Guru (1991), another political scientist, has pointed out in an article why certain sections of the Dalit community are being attracted to the rightist movements and why and how these reactionary movements are coaxing Dalits into Hinduism and spiritualizing B. R. Ambedkar and his writings (Guru, 1991: 339).

Thus we have two conflicting views on the Hinduization of certain social groups. According to the first view, the process of integrating *adivasis* into Hinduism is a natural process. According to the second, it is not natural but something imposed on them from the outside by the Hindus. I find both viewpoints extreme. The reality lies somewhere in between these two.

In the present chapter I follow this line of approach: I describe how the *adivasis,* particularly of southern Gujarat, are Hinduized by Hindutva organizations, which have successfully exploited religious beliefs and emotions for political purposes in order to increase the Hindu vote. The term "Hinduization" in this chapter is given not only a religious but also a political meaning. Hinduization means that one group consciously manipulates others for its own material and political benefit. The manipulation is done in such a systematic way that the exploited group/section does not realize the intention and intricacies behind it. I also briefly highlight the possible consequences of Hinduization for the *adivasis.* The information herein is based on my long association with the *adivasis* of Gujarat; I have referred to secondary sources for necessary supplementary information.

The *Adivasis* of Southern Gujarat

As the name itself indicates, the *adivasis* are considered the original inhabitants of Gujarat. They constitute about 14 percent of the total population and are divided into seventeen groups, each of which is further subdivided into five or six subgroups. The main groups among the *adivasis* of southern Gujarat are Gamit, Chodhari, Dungari Bhil, Rathava, Tadvi, Vasava, Dhodiya, and Halpati (for details of such groups, see Satyakam Joshi, 1996; Lobo, 1996; Patel, 1996a, 1996b, 1996c; Pinto, 1996; S. P. Punalekar, 1996; D. S. Punalekar, 1996; Shah, 1994). There are also differences of status among them. Except for the Dublas, they are concentrated in certain areas on the eastern frontiers of the hilly tract of the Sahyadris and Satpuda ranges and hence have become a very politically significant group. The *adivasis* of southern Gujarat are concentrated in the eastern belt, which covers eight districts, namely, Dang, Valsad, Surat, Bharuch, Vadodara, Panchmahal, Banaskantha, and Sabarkantha.[3] Some *adivasi* regions (Kiran Desai, n.d.) are rather poor in infrastructure facilities as well as being agriculturally backward. The living conditions in Gujarat were so poor that the *adivasis* were not able to earn enough to survive throughout the year in their native place; hence they migrated to other areas (Patel and Desai, 1992). About 2.5 lakh *adivasis* migrated as seasonal workers. Poverty, illiteracy, bad health, unemployment, and lack of drinking water are urgent problems. Of course, a few *adivasis* have been fortunate enough to take advantage of government aid schemes since 1960 and find a place in the mainstream culture of Indian society. *Adivasis* were considered to be outside the Hindu social system, and they were not included in the governmental Scheduled Caste (SC) aid program because they did not have the stigma of untouchability. Ghurye (1963) considered *adivasis* to be backward Hindus.

Influence of Hinduization on *Adivasis*

The influence of Hindu religion on the *adivasi* community has early beginnings. Old *adivasis* in the interior villages of the Bharuch and Vadodara districts revealed in talks that their forefathers were often helpful in guiding pilgrims, who came for *parikrama* on the banks of the Narmada River. While visiting one shrine after another in the hills, the *adivasis* used to beat drums to scare away animals. The annual fairs and *hats* (weekly markets), considered an integral part of *adivasi* culture, were also important meeting places for *adivasis* and Hindus. There are several studies available that have brought to light how the *adivasis* have absorbed certain elements from the Hindu religion. K. S. Singh (1993), K. N. Sahay (1980, 1967), S. K. Srivastava (1958), and others have shown how some of the *adivasi* groups have been integrated into the Hindu social order. Although the impact of Hindu religion on the *adivasi* community has been great in the last decade or so, it did in fact begin a long time ago. Evidence is found in some of the temples, for instance, in Surpaneswer in Rajpipla *taluka* and Hafsewer in Chhotaudepur *taluka* in southern Gujarat, which points to the fact that the spread of Hindu gods and goddesses in the *adivasi* region has early beginnings. There are a few old Hindu shrines and temples from ancient times on the bank of the Narmada River. All these temples have been centers from which Vedic culture has spread in the *adivasi* region. The temples in the *adivasi* belt are living examples of the cultural synthesis between Hindu and *adivasi* traditions (Gazetteer of India, 1979).[4]

The Brahmin priest served as a model for the *adivasis,* and through him they learned to imitate the beliefs and lifestyle of the Hindus. Priests, however, do not take meat or alcoholic drinks, which is common among *adivasis*. The princes also encouraged Hindu religious activities. I was told that the Prince of Rajpipla attended the *mela* (fair) of Surpaneswer regularly around the beginning of the ninth century. Some of the temples in the *adivasi* belt are considered important *dhams*. There were many instances in which the local raja had contributed to the renovation of a temple from time to time before independence. In some places, the rajas employed Brahmins to perform regular worship in the temple and manage its affairs. In Hanfeswer I was told that land was given to the priest for the maintenance of the temple. In Hanf village, thousands of rupees had been invested for water supply in the village. Government officials, politicians, and social workers sometimes pay visits to the temple, and they always show a readiness to help in all possible ways.

After the middle of the nineteenth century, the process of Hinduization speeded up. As a result, certain procedures and regulations have increased the interactions of *adivasis* with others. The influx of moneylenders, traders, contractors, and non-*adivasi* peasants has further accelerated the process. Hinduization was given a fresh impetus in the nineteenth century with the new bhakti movements (Singh, 1993: 11). The great influence of these movements on the *adivasi* people has been one of the important instances of the interaction of the *adivasi* people with Hinduism.

The Hindu revival movement, or neo-Hinduism, which emerged in the first decade of the present century, is also part of the campaign to bring so-called lower social groups under the spiritual and social umbrella of Hinduism.[5] R. B. Lal (1977, 1982) has described Hindu movements in the southern Gujarat *adivasi* belt in the period 1920–1950. Recently, Lancy Lobo has studied the phenomenon, and he found sectarian movements in various *talukas* of Surat and the Bharuch districts. Some of the most prominent Hindu sects are Sanathan, Mokshmarg, Satkeval, Nairant, Ramand (belonging or relating to the Ramanuja sect), Kabir, Swadhyay, and Jaygurudev (for details about each sectarian movement and its spread, see Lancy Lobo, 1995, 1992). Groups who convert can rise in the social scale. This possibility fulfills the aspirations of many *adivasis*, particularly the ambitious ones, and it also gives them a new sense of identity. One of the aims of the new Hindu revival movement has been to prevent Christian influence on the *adivasis* and to purify them so that they become acceptable to upper-caste Hindus.[6]

Thus *adivasis*, particularly the educated ones, have joined different Hindu movements and are now emulating the Hindus in order to win acceptability and esteem among caste-Hindus (Lobo, 1992: 54). It must be noted here that the Gandhians have also implemented some welfare measures for the uplift of the *adivasis* and are trying to civilize them (I. P. Desai, 1982; Satyakam Joshi, 1996, 1992; S. P. Punalekar, 1993; Shah, 1995). Affiliation with such movements means cultural change, a new lifestyle (dress, decorum, rituals, customs, and practices), and a new sense of identity.

The interaction between *adivasis* and Hindus has been augmented in scope due to better communication and to the fact that *adivasis* have been constantly on the move as seasonal migrant workers. The district gazetteer for Vadodara noted that as a result of the intensive interactions of the *adivasi* people with the Hindus, they no longer remained isolated. Their religion, language, habits, and social customs are being greatly influenced by the Hindu community, to which they bear close linguistic and racial affinities (Gazetteer of India, 1979: 190–191).

Changes in *Adivasi* Culture

The *adivasis*, though rich in local culture, began to feel inferior to people of non-*adivasi* culture since the introduction of market economy by the caste-Hindus in this region from the middle of the nineteenth century. Since then, *adivasi* culture has greatly changed, and a mixture of Hindu and *adivasi* elements are found in their socioculture life. I observed during my stay in *adivasi* areas that the *bedevo* (the *adivasi* priest) was increasingly losing his importance in the cultural and ritual life in the community and is gradually being replaced by the Brahmin priest. Many *adivasis* have begun to believe that calling a Brahmin priest is a sign of progress. Now Brahmins are officiating at birth, marriage, and death rituals and ceremonies among *adivasis*. My neighbor in the village Vaghrali in Rajpipla *taluka*, where my institute, the Centre for Social Studies, has opened a field office for monitoring and evaluation work of the Narmada dam project, had no spare time because he was continuously busy in performing one or the other religious activities among the *adivasis*.

Today *adivasis* are gradually adopting the Brahminical value system. They have also started performing the *shraddha* and the *chhathi puja* ceremony. Their food habits are also changing in imitation of upper-caste Hindus. In this regard, the impact of Guru Vishvanath Maharaj among the Dhanka Tadvis, who are found in seventy-seven villages of Rajpipla *taluka*, is quite visible. Many Dhanka Tadvis have become vegetarians and teetotalers. *Adivasi* folk culture and traditional habits are changing under the cultural impact of upper-caste Hindus. The leaders among the *adivasis* are influenced by Brahminical ideas. Many *adivasi* groups today have crystallized into two socially different groups, identified as Bhagat and non-Bhagat among Dhanka Tadvis and Variela and Sariela among Chaudharas. The former group, which has adopted many Brahminical customs, believes itself to be more advanced in its sociocultural life than the latter group (Satyakam Joshi, 1995; Patel, 1996c; S. P. Punalekar, 1996; Shah and Patel, 1984). They also observe certain specific rules and procedures. For instance, the Bhagat Tadvi generally eat first when attending weddings among non-Bhagat Tadvi people. Their utensils and drinking pots are of brass metal.

Traditional *adivasi* culture is different from that of the Hindus. For example, the *adivasis* have no concept of temples such as the Hindus have. They generally have their own *devasthan*, in which they keep small clay horses and cows and stones painted red.[7] The *adivasis* offer goats, fowls, and liquor on social and cultural occasions. Liquor forms an integral part of *adivasi* life, which is altogether different from the customs of upper-caste Hindus. But now they have begun to worship gods and goddesses from the Hindu pantheon. In many *adivasi* houses, one will find photographs of Hindu gods and goddesses.

Stephen Fuchs (1973: 73) has pointed out that various Hindu deities like Vishnu and Shiva played an important part in the religious life of the early *adivasis*. The *panth* (a Hindu sectarian movement) has also played a major role in changing the lifestyle of *adivasis*, especially upper-class ones. It is well known that *adivasis* who are members of the Hindu *panth* have stopped worshipping their traditional *adivasi* gods; instead they now worship Hindu gods (Shah and Shah, 1993: 135). Something similar has taken place in the case of festivals. Ind and Kunvari are two of the original festivals of the *adivasis* in Gujarat, but now they have started celebrating Hindu festivals such as Diwali, Holi, Navratri, Ganesh Chaturthi, and Ram Navami. I was told that there is a big celebration of the Ganapati festival in Vansada *taluka* of Dharampur district. The Bania shopkeepers are providing the necessary financial means for these activities. During my stay in different *adivasi* villages, I noticed that *adivasis* are fully committed to Hindu beliefs and customs. Like Hindus, they believe in the existence of a divine spirit, theories of birth and rebirth, *pap* and *punya,* and so on.

The influence of the Hindu caste has been very strong on *adivasi* social structure. Like Hindus, *adivasis* also have caste characteristics such as social divisions, hierarchies, endogamy, and restrictions on food and drink. The notion of purity and pollution has become firmly entrenched, particularly among educated and middle-class *adivasis*. Many social anthropologists and sociologists such as N. K. Bose (1941) and B. Kalia (1961) have called attention to the fact that *adivasis* have borrowed ideas and institutions heavily from the Hindus.

Although the effect of Hinduization on *adivasis* can be easily seen, it is difficult to assess accurately the extent of its influence. Consulting the census report is one way of doing it. During the period 1921–1981, only 6 percent of the *adivasi* population identified themselves as *adivasis,* whereas 87 percent claimed that they were Hindus by religion, and 7 percent claimed to be Christians.[8] Scholars like K. S. Singh (1993) and J. Troisi (1979), however, believe that in spite of the fact that *adivasis* claim to be overwhelmingly Hindus or Christians, the *adivasi* religion has not disappeared, as many feared. According to Singh, a great many non-Brahminic rituals and ideas still survive.

Religious Practices in *Adivasi* Regions

Numerous religious activists and leaders of various movements have been campaigning among *adivasis* in order to propagate their ideas. Nath Panthi

Bhakta Parivar has been active in *adivasi* areas expounding its philosophy of religion. Its aim is to convince the *adivasis* that the ultimate goal of religion is to realize God. *Bhagvat Kathas* have been held at various places in the *adivasi*-dominated regions. Nath Panthi Bhakta Parivar's message was that through the medium of *katha* (storytelling), humans can attain the highest level of spiritual life. Saint Shri Laxmi Chand Bapu is propagating Hindu religion in Mahuva *taluka* through Ramdev Bapu Parivar Nainas Nath. He is achieving his ends through *satsang* (spiritual gathering), *gaashala,* and education. Yog Vedant Samiti is active in one of the most backward *taluka* areas, named Dharampur in southern Gujarat. Shri Sureshanandji, follower of Shri Asharam Bapu, is teaching a philosophy of life and advising people not to be too materialistic but to set apart some time for spiritual matters also. Gayatri Shaktipath is campaigning in *adivasi* areas in order to make people aware of the modern nature of *Bhartiya* Vedic *Shastras.* I came across a few *adivasis* who had learnt the Gayatri mantras by heart and who repeated them at social gatherings and ceremonies.

The efforts to spread Vedic *sanskriti* culture in *adivasi* areas has been made for many years. For instance, Pandit Satvalekar, who received the honor of Padma Bhushan, came to Killa Pardi near Vapi in 1948 and began his work through Swadhyay Mandal. He has also translated the Vedic texts and rituals for the use of the tribals of this area. His activities have been concentrated in the southern part of Gujarat. The Ram Sevak Samitis are working for Hindu *Jagran* in these areas.

The *Ram katha, Bhagvat katha,* and lecture series by various saints such as Morari Bapu, Praful Shukla, Chhote Morari Bapu, Swami Shri Viditatmanand Saraswatiji, and Nilesh Bapu have been organized at various places in the *adivasi* area of southern Gujarat.[9] The *adivasis,* who reside in the adjoining areas, took part in these activities and received them very well.[10] These religious leaders emphasize the importance of *Bhartiya sanskriti.* They also advise people to liberate themselves from the bad habits of drinking and smoking. They speak in favor of *lok seva, samaj seva, arogya seva, vidya dan,* and *sarva dharm sambhav.* Several saints have settled permanently in towns in the *adivasi* area and founded religious trusts such as Sitaram Seva trust and Sanskriti Parivar. They often attend religious programs and teach their philosophy.

The masterminds behind the Hindutva campaigns have realized that the mere existence of temples in the *adivasi* localities will not drastically change the situation in the long run. They constantly feel threatened by Christian missionaries.[11] The role of Arya Samajists in Gujarat is quite important in Hinduizing the lower social groups, including *adivasis.* The Arya Samajists have realized the mistakes of orthodox Hindu leaders long ago. They have come to see the seriousness of the situation and are aware of the possible threat to the Brahminical social order, which, it is feared, probably cannot survive if the age-old oppressive and inhuman practices toward Dalits are not changed into something more constructive. Swami Sachchidanand, an Arya Samajist, has become an advocate in books and speeches for a change in policy toward Dalits in Gujarat.[12]

To oppose the work of missionaries and to propagate Hindu ideology among *adivasis,* some of the campaigning Hindu movements such as the Swaminarayan have institutionalized their activities. They are opening schools and recreation centers in the *adivasi* region. They have purchased hundreds of acres of land in the *adivasi* areas at various *talukas,* namely, Chhotaudepur and Dediyapada. They have opened schools, dispensaries, hospitals, and welfare centers. The *adivasis* were easily won over because the state had failed to help them. The Hindu Sampradayas have started introducing Hindu ideas into the community, beginning by teaching *adivasi* boys at an early age. The saints have not confined their activities to religious pursuits but have also engaged in welfare work. For instance, Prafulbhai Shukla, a well-known saint in Gujarat, organized a *katha* in an *adivasi*-dominated village for the renovation of a school building and for introducing a science curriculum in the village high school.

Temple-building activities are quite visible in *adivasi* villages, and remote villages are not neglected.[13] Stany Pinto (1996) observed that over the past ten years there has been a steady increase in Hindu shrines and temples. He cited a follower and propagator of the Bhatiji movement as saying that 350 shrines have been built by this movement alone in the past five years in three *adivasi talukas.* Nowadays, almost every village has its own temple. Pinto (1995) has recorded one instance in which an *adivasi* god was replaced by a Hindu deity. This is rather common and has happened in other places in India also.[14]

Swadhyay Parivar is also an organization working in an *adivasi* area.[15] Founded by Shri Pandurang Shastri Athvale, it concentrates on community building that cuts across caste and class. He has initiated various programs, among which *Gharmandir* is one.[16] In traditional *adivasi* culture, there is no concept of a temple. Athvale found a remedy for that by consecrating *Gharmandir* and *Amrutlaya,* even in remote villages.[17] Athvale's seventy-second birthday was celebrated at the village of Umergao in an *adivasi* area. I was also present at this celebration, together with more than a million other participants, who came mostly from lower and middle castes, including *adivasis* and Harijans. The seventy-fifth anniversary of his birth was celebrated in several places. On 17–18 February 1995, a big celebration was planned at Vadodara, and hundreds of *adivasis* participated. Athvale took advantage of these opportunities and spoke in favor of Hinduism and the importance of the Bhagavad Gita.

Nowadays, one finds that different kinds of Hindu religious activities and new forms have been developed in *adivasi* Gujarat. There seems to be a keen competition in the celebration of *kathas,* festivals, and *yagnas* (fire sacrifices). Various Hindu movements and *sampradayas* (schools of thought or traditions) have also intensified their activities. The founding of religious trusts, the renovation of temples, and construction of Hindu temples are common events in the *adivasi* region.

Athvale has not confined himself to the devotional field but has also implemented programs that are economically helpful to the *adivasis.* He has opened technical training centers, locally known as "Manav Pratishtha Kendras." *Adivasi* children are given the benefits of practical training such as sewing, carpentry, electric motor rewinding, and repairing vehicles. The Swadhyay Parivar also gives interest-free loans to the trainees. The ideas of Athvale have fascinated some of the intellectuals of Gujarat. The families who have benefited from these programs have started performing *trikul sandhiya* (prayer performed three times a day—morning, midday, and evening), and they also regularly listen to discourses on the Bhagavad Gita (Dilip Shah, n.d.).

Religious institutions have launched other activities. Vanvasi Kalyan Parishad-Sidumbar in Dharampur *taluka* in Gujarat runs several schools, and Prafulbhai Shukla has been made trustee of some of the educational foundations. The president of Gayatri Parivar arranges multiple weddings free of cost at the temple of Bandar Road. The Gayatri Shaktipath runs a low-cost ayurvedic dispensary, Bal Mandir, Gayatri Yagna, and library service. Tailoring classes are given free of cost. The Gayatri Parivar has for the current year planned 1,001 *yagnas* in the villages of Navsari *taluka.*

The Rise of the BJP

The rise of the BJP has been phenomenal in the past decade. The election results show that the BJP has made rapid progress in winning seats at all levels. The BJP, which won two seats in the 1984 elections, emerged as the single largest party in the eleventh Lok Sabha. The number of *adivasi* members of parliament (MPs) was also higher in the BJP than in other political parties, including the Congress Party. In this parliament, the total number of *adivasi* MPs was forty-one. Out of that the BJP had eleven (the figure is based on Vajpayee's lecture in Parliament House). In fact, the BJP broadened its base in all pockets of Gujarat and became the ruling party in the state. In the Gujarat State Assembly, twenty-six seats were reserved for *adivasis,* out of which fourteen belonged to the BJP. The election result of the *panchayats* in 1995 showed that the BJP won 82 percent of the seats and came to power in eighteen out of nineteen districts in Gujarat, with a two-thirds majority in the *adivasi*-dominated districts such as Valsad, Bharuch, Surat, and Panchmahal. The trend was also visible in the election of *taluka panchayats,* where the BJP won forty-four out of fifty-four *taluka panchayats* in six *adivasi* districts of Gujarat (Satyakam Joshi, 1996).

Shah (1994) observes that the BJP is also gaining ground among the Dalits and *adivasis* in urban areas, which is something new and amazing because until now the *adivasis* used to back the Congress Party. The *adivasis* even remained with the Congress Party during non-Congress rule in the states. Until 1995 Congress had a monopoly in the districts and *taluka panchayats* in the *adivasi* areas. The question arises, how has the BJP managed to gain in influence among the *adivasis?* According to Prime Minister Atal Bihari Vajpayee, the BJP influence has not come about all of a sudden but is the result of systematic efforts over the past thirty years. The BJP has succeeded in undermining the growing solidarity among Scheduled Castes, Scheduled Tribes (STs), and Other Backward Castes (OBCs) and other minorities and instead replaced it by a loyalty to the upper castes. According to the followers of the Jotirao Phule–B. R. Ambedkar ideology, the Mandal Commission imposed a unity among the SCs, STs, and the OBCs, which in turn constituted a major threat to the Brahminical social order. The Congress Party failed to maintain upper-caste hegemony in Indian politics. The BJP made an ideological unity out of the resulting caste divisions, and the Hinduization of *adivasis* is one step in the policy for retaining the status quo in the Brahminical social order.

Wooing the *Adivasis*

Besides stirring up Hindutva feelings, the BJP has tried to win the people's confidence by organizing unique programs such as "Sarkar Prajana Dware" (government on the doorstep), Gokul Gram Yojana, Rojgar Mela, and Kuvar Bainu Memeru. In "Government on the Doorstep" campaigns, BJP ministers and other government officials visit the villages and try to solve their problems on the spot. The BJP has very cleverly used such tactics in order to improve the image of the party. The *adivasi* people like this style because they have had only bad experiences with government bureaucracy. Up to September 1995, the BJP has successfully carried through such campaigns in ten places in Surat and found solutions to about 3,000 problems that had remained unsolved for years.[18] Generally, the cases involved are related to roads, health, dams, electricity, irrigation, transportation, and drinking water. With such campaigns, the BJP has tried to win the people over by sanctioning on-the-spot projects up to crores of rupees. They responded to the demands of the people, and programs were initiated or halted as per the people's wishes. Another initiative provided jobs for unemployed youth. One such program was implemented in Gandevi *taluka* of Valsad district, where 678 unemployed were given jobs. The BJP deputy minister also distributed machines and tools for tailoring, wiring, and the like.

The BJP has also begun to arrange multiple weddings for *adivasis*.[19] At election time, the BJP also arranged several *sammelans* (gatherings), group meetings, and door-to-door campaigns in *adivasi* areas. In one campaign a BJP minister, assisted by local *adivasi* leaders, contacted around 400–500 Halpati families. Generally, BJP leaders used to announce projects to be implemented in the near future by the BJP government, such as the installation of electricity and hand pumps or the building of schools. Such occasions used to attract great numbers. At one time so many Halpatis turned up that one was led to believe that it was a Lok Darbar (people's court). The air rang with the slogans of "Bharat Mata ki Jai" (Hail, Mother India) and "Vandematram" (Bow to Mother India). The Halpatis have promised the BJP overwhelming support in the next election. The strategy of the BJP has been to expose the neglect and want of concern of previous governments toward the *adivasis* and then to present themselves as the only reliable alternative.

The *adivasis* of Rajpipla *taluka* have been demanding the regularization of forest land since 1956. The Congress Party promised to consider the question in 1974 but failed. The present BJP government, however, immediately passed a resolution to regularize 65,000 hectares of land as a concession to *adivasi* demands. In election speeches they first blacken the image of the Congress Party and then present the BJP as the true friend and sympathizer of the *adivasi* cause and the only party that is able to save Hindu dharma (i.e., Hindu *rashtra*) from outside attacks. During its 111 days in power, the BJP took numerous steps for improving the welfare of the people. The Gokul Gram scheme was meant to benefit 62 lakh *adivasis*. The poorest among the poor were to have been helped, for instance, the Kotvaliyas, which is one of the most backward *adivasi* tribes in Gujarat. Hopes were raised among the poor, and the image of the BJP has been greatly improved. The BJP used every platform, state or national, to spread the message that it is the only party that is fully committed to the *adivasi* cause. The party also succeeded in convincing the masses that it is the real guardian of national interests.[20]

Exploitation of *Adivasi* Emotions by the BJP

As mentioned earlier, in Gujarat many saints (Morari Bapu, Praful Chandra Shukla, Asharam Bapu, Pandurang Athvale, Swami Sachchidanand) are trying to rejuvenate the Hindu religion in order to bring different social groups to the Hindu fold. Though they may take different approaches, they have one thing in common: they work for Hindu unity by incorporating the tribals into the Hindu fold and equating Hinduism with Indian nationalism. The role of *sadhus* and saints has become crucial, particularly at the time of elections. A saint like Praful Shukla lives in an *adivasi* area, where he openly propagates BJP viewpoints, and others such as Morari Bapu, Pandurang Athvale, and Asharam Bapu advise people to vote for the party that works for preservation of Hindu *sanskriti*.

According to the followers of Phule and Ambedkar, all these saints aim at one and the same thing, that is, unity based on Hindu religion, but their style of persuasion may differ. Various religious and political leaders have been constantly drumming up religious and political feelings of fear and insecurity by repeating the idea that the Hindu religion is endangered; that unless they unite, Hindus will soon belong nowhere; and that their nation is in danger, its very existence threatened. Such propaganda created insecurity but also persuaded *adivasis* to unite on the basis of Hindutva.

Hindutva activists in most *taluka* headquarters have founded *shakhas* (branches of various Hindu organizations) such as Hindu Milan Mandir, Swaminarayana, Swadhyay, Ram Krishna, or Radha Krishna. There are also *shakhas* of the BJP, the Rashtriya Swayamsevak Sangh (RSS), and the Shiv Sena. They all aim at spreading Hinduism among *adivasis*. Helping them in many ways, these groups try to convince *adivasis* that they will benefit from Hinduism. They let them know that there is no harm in taking up arms in order to protect Hindus if the situation should demand such a course of action.

Adivasis have also been called upon to instigate communal riots against Muslims. Ghanshyam Shah (1994), Pinto (1995), and Lobo (1990) have described how *adivasis* have been communalized very systematically by the BSS, the RSS, the VHP, and the BJP and encouraged to turn against Muslims in post-Babari mosque incidents. There are many initiatives taken to Hinduize *adivasis*, the most important being the "the Ramshila Pujan," "Rathyatra" of Advani, "Ramjyoti," and "Kar Seva." During the Ramshila Pujan in 1984, according to Pinto, a token collection of 1.25 rupees was taken from *adivasis* with the question: "Are you Hindus? If you are, then prove it by contributing Rs 1.25 for Ramshila Pujan. If not, then prove that you have come from a Muslim womb!" (Pinto, 1995).

There are also a number of other initiatives, such as organizing celebrations of Hindu festivals, Independence Day, and Republic Day; blocking roads; and participating in destructive activities. The stickers that read *Vande Mataram* and *Garv se Kaho Ham Hindu Hain* (Hail, Mother India and Say with pride, we are Hindus) have become very popular among *adivasis*. Propaganda is spread to convey the message that the Sangh Parivar, political parties such as the BJP, the Shiv Sena, and saints and *sadhus* are the real protectors of India; others, especially the Congress Party, are portrayed as pro-Muslim and anti-Hindu. The Rathyatra campaign was successful in mobilizing the *adivasis* for a Hindu celebration (S. Yagnic, 1995). Many mini-Rathyatras have been organized by Hindutva groups in the *adivasi* regions of Gujarat.[21] *Adivasis* were encouraged to light the fire from Ramjyoti, which was carried by a mini-*rath*. Speeches were also given to instigate *adivasis* to drive out Muslims and Christians (Pinto, 1995). The *adivasi* youth have been especially influenced by the Hindutva campaign. They have openly attacked Muslims and have resorted to looting, arson, and assault. Communal riots have become a widespread phenomenon throughout the *adivasi* belt of Gujarat.[22] There have also been instances of attacks on Muslim *dargahs* (sacred places of Muslim saints) and shrines.

Political Strategies to Win Over the *Adivasis*

Religious leaders have played a major role in polarizing religious life in India. Activists from Hindu organizations like the VHP and the RSS have very systematically used *adivasi* politicians, Bhagats, Sarpanchs, police, and some primary schoolteachers for spreading their radical Hindu views and for instigating communal riots. Muslims are accused of destroying Hindu shrines, of being exploiters of *adivasis,* and of causing them many ills and much trouble. Expulsion and elimination of Muslims was proposed as a solution (Pinto, 1995: 2418). In all these campaigns, the tactics employed were to portray *adivasis* as Hindus and to depict Muslims as their enemies. An *adivasi* teacher told me that in these days feelings of communalism were so widespread that real ills like poverty, illiteracy, disease, exploitation, indebtedness, pauperism, and land alienation were nonexistent to the *adivasis*. For them the main problem was the Hindu-Muslim controversy, as it was for the majority of Hindus. Growing expectations, especially among the educated *adivasi* youth, have accelerated Hinduization and BJP influence among the *adivasis.*

Dipika Chikhaliya, a famous actress who played the role of Sita in a television serial on the *Ramayana,* made speeches at various places at election time in *adivasi* areas. In a meeting at Mandvi, she severely criticized the Congress Party and emphasized that the misrule of Congress in Gujarat was the root cause of all the evils. She spoke in favor of BJP rule in the state for the protection of Hindu *sanskriti*. BJP politicians at state as well as national levels have made the Congress Party responsible for poverty, unemployment, rising living costs, and corruption. Lal Krishna Advani, national president of the BJP, at mass meetings in two *adivasi*-dominated *talukas,* Vyara and Bardoli, pointed out that the nation had made no progress at all during the past four-and-a-half decades of Congress rule.

The BJP has also very skillfully made use of *adivasi* leaders in its campaigns. For instance, at Dholikui village in Mahuva *taluka,* a big *sammelan* (gathering) was organized under the chairmanship of Chandu-bhai Deshmukh, a BJP *adivasi* president of Gujarat. He didn't mince words, criticizing Congress for having allowed corruption to grow like cancer and for having neglected local needs related to roads, drinking water, electricity, and irrigation. He then highlighted the BJP programs, which were to be implemented out of a concern for *adivasi* needs, provided the party got sufficient support in the elections. He called attention to Congress corruption in shares, sugar, and Bofors; he mentioned the corruption case during the rule of the former chief minister Amarsingh Chaudhare and said that Congress has made no inquiries into the theft of rupees 25 crores in the Bharuch district and of rupees 14 crores in the Surat district. He concluded his speech with the question: "Are you going to vote for such a band? Are you going to support a party involved in so much racketeering?"

BJP supporters have visited most *adivasi* areas during election campaigns. The prestige of the Congress Party has diminished throughout the *adivasi* belt.[23] In remote villages, nobody knew the name BJP four or five years back, but now numerous followers are recruited there. The BJP has succeeded in nurturing feelings of hatred toward the Congress Party, especially among young people who have begun, rightly or wrongly, to accuse the Congress of having kept them backward with the ulterior motive of using them as a permanent vote bank. The question of identity has become important to many *adivasis,* and recognition as Hindus is the fulfillment of an aspiration for a larger identity now much in demand among *adivasis.*

The issue of a common civil code has also been raised and the fact that Hindus have suffered differential treatment in their own country has been criticized. Anti-Muslim feelings have been so vigorously propagated by Hindutva supporters that the average educated person does not remain unaffected. Congress Party influence has been further weakened by infighting among *adivasi* leaders: although few Congress politicians have criticized Congress policy toward the *adivasis,* Pratap Gamit, the chairman of the *adivasi* corporation in Gujarat and an MLA (Independent), criticized some well-known Congress *adivasi* leaders for not having defended *adivasi* interests. Because most Congress leaders have been found wanting in most respects, Hinduization has progressed to such an extent that the Congress influence is rejected and only BJP is tolerated. The result of this development is visible in the elections for panchayats, corporations, and parliament.

Adivasi Consciousness

Many *adivasis* now feel that the Hindu religion is their own. "We are Hindus" is a widespread feeling among them. They identify themselves with a larger religious *quam* (community). Their customs and codes of social behavior are guided by the Hindu religion. They want to be recognized as Hindus, and therefore they enter Hindu names in the census paper as well as in school certificates and other documents. Today *adivasis* are accepted, at least nominally, as part and parcel of the Hindu community. This phenomenon came to light at the time of communal riots, when *adivasis* proved their solidarity with the Hindu community by turning against the Muslims. A small group of politically aspiring *adivasis* has been instrumental in securing votes of the *adivasi* masses for the BJP upper-caste politicians. In return, these *adivasi* politicians have been rewarded.

A special kind of *adivasi* self-consciousness is now emerging. It is interesting to observe that on the one hand, the religious leaning toward Hinduism has been increasing, especially over the past ten years, but on the other hand, *adivasi* self-consciousness and self-respect and insistence on rights have also shown a rising trend. A few *adivasi* leaders are now becoming aware of their situation. They increasingly feel that the Aryans (Hindus) have made their lives intolerable. They have begun to realize that the present government will not solve their problems. They see how biased the state is, not only toward *adivasis* but also toward other lower social groups. Their demand for autonomy should be seen in this context. This demand, however, is not new. It was made in the 1960s also (I. P. Desai, 1971), but now it has erupted so violently that it has embarrassed the government.[24]

Adivasi leaders claim that they are the original inhabitants of the land but were driven to the hills by the conquering Aryans. In contrast to those who embrace Hinduism, others feel growing hatred toward the Hindus, particularly toward the upper castes.[25] They allege that the Hindus have imposed their beliefs, their faith, and their culture on the *adivasis* in the name of the so-called mainstream tradition (see the handbill by Adijati Vikas Paksha, n.d.). Some *adivasi* leaders demand autonomy and are suspicious of democracy. According to them, the democratic system made up of MPs, ministers, and bureaucracy is a Western invention and quite incompatible with their own *sanskriti* tradition. *Adivasi* leaders are trying hard to unite the *adivasis* against upper-caste exploitation. On the basis of their own experience, the oppressed groups of Indian society, including the *adivasis,* have begun to critically observe the day-to-day behavior and attitudes of the upper castes. They have become aware of their numerical strength and the fact that they have been politically manipulated by non-*adivasi* Hindus. To remedy this situation, they have begun to assert themselves. Of course, this new self-consciousness has been frowned upon by BJP *adivasi* leaders, who realize that *adivasis* and other groups from the lower social orders have begun to think for themselves. Upper-caste Hindus have begun to realize the long-term consequences of this development and are taking preventive measures (Adhvaryu, 1981; Augustine, 1984; Lobo, 1993; Parmar, 1993; Shah and Shah, 1993).

Conclusion

Theoretically, *adivasis* do not have caste, but castelike elements are found in *adivasi* society. The influence of Hinduism on the social and religious life of *adivasis* has been considerable, particularly in the last ten to fifteen years. The slow process of Sanskritization, which has been going on for a long time, has prepared the ground for the Hinduization of the *adivasi* people. This is reflected in their social consciousness, in the vision they have for themselves and their society, and in their hopes and expectations. The Hinduization of *adivasis* has indirectly resulted in a consolidation of inequality. Ghanshyam Shah (1994) has rightly observed that the Sanskritization of backward classes has reinforced the caste system and the dominance of upper-caste Hindus.

Although there has been a significant influence from Hindu society on the *adivasis,* it is also a fact that they have not given up their traditional values and belief systems altogether. But the BJP and other Hindu organizations such as the RSS, the AVBP, Bajarang Dal, Shiv Sena, the Hindu Milan Mandir, the Arya Samaj, saints and *sadhus,* and some *adivasi* politicians have succeeded in inculcating the Hindutva ideology in the minds of the *adivasi* people. In fact, many have seized the opportunity to embrace Hinduism, which is the religion of the majority and considered to be one of the oldest religions in the world. The adoption of a wider identity is the crux of the matter for the *adivasis,* but Hindutva supporters are also aware of the importance of keeping the *adivasis* within the Hindu fold in order to secure Hindu hegemony. Thus it may be said that both *adivasis* and Hindutva devotees have a common interest in promoting the process of Hinduization. Having chosen Hinduism, *adivasis* have accepted the social and theological implications of their new religion and indirectly recognized the supremacy of the upper castes. Whether this consolidation of the Hindu social order will last, only time can tell.

Notes

1. *Adivasis* are considered to be the original inhabitants of the country. They are known by various names, such as Vanyajati, Vanvasi, Paharia, Adimjati, and Janjati. In the various census papers the *adivasis* are referred to under the following headings: *adivasi* from the religion, animists, hill or forest *adivasi,* primitive *adivasis, adivasis,* and so on.

2. K. S. Singh (1993) does not agree fully with such a typology. He argues

that "the great and little traditions are conceptual categories set up by scholars. They are based on the intellectual perception from above, not people's perception from below. For an adivasi, worshipping in the sacred groves . . . is neither great nor little. It is his own tradition which gives him his identity and a feeling of cultural continuity."

3. In South Gujarat, the total *adivasi* population is distributed as follows: Dang 93 percent, Valsad 55 percent, Bharuch 45 percent, and Surat 42 percent. Within this district, *adivasis* are found concentrated in a few *talukas*. For instance, in Bharuch they are more common in *talukas* such as Dediyapada, Sagbara, Valia, Rajpipla, and Jhagadia. In Surat they are concentrated in Uchchal, Vyara, Mahuva, and Songdh *taluka*. In Valsad, they are found in *talukas* such as Vansada and Dharampur. The whole Dang district is full of *adivasis*.

4. The building of temples in the *adivasi* belt and its impact on the *adivasi* people need an extensive and systematic study. The role of Hindu kings is also important to study, mainly because they invited numerous Hindus from outside to settle in their kingdom. These settlers increased the Hindu pressure on local *adivasis*.

5. Hindu movements are basically well structured. These Hindu revival movements have spawned numerous groups, which have concentrated in different pockets and also reached many *adivasi* villages. It is widely believed that Hindus promoted this movement in order to prevent the conversion of *adivasis* to Christianity. Christian missionaries have been working in the *adivasi* region for the past 100 years. Some *adivasis* have been converted to Christianity, mainly because they were exploited by Hindu landlords, rajas, traders, and police officers. The missionaries gave the *adivasis* material benefits and protection and helped them fight their exploiters.

6. They try to make the *adivasis* abstain from meat, liquor, tobacco, and so on. They try to make them "human," teach them to respect others, and to set apart time for devotion to the divine spirit. They also teach them the importance of certain symbols and wearing the sacred thread, putting *tilak* on the forehead, and making certain saints their gurus. They give them a new identity that is supposed to be socially and economically higher and more attractive than the one they at present have.

7. The *adivasis* worship malevolent spirits mainly because they want to protect themselves from natural calamities such as droughts, earthquakes, or epidemics. They offer special sacrifices to these spirits at certain occasions to win their favor. Most of the names of *adivasi* gods refer to forests, hills, rivers, and the like. Now some Hindu gods and goddesses have crept in. They also worship their ancestors and invariably invoke the blessings of ancestors at every social occasion. Functionalists like Durkheim, Radcliffe-Brown, and Malinowski have interpreted this phenomenon as a source of stability.

8. There are many reasons for *adivasis* to join the Hindu fold. K. S. Singh (1993), who has done admirable work in the "People of India Project," considered three factors in the Hinduization of *adivasis*. First, Hindu Mahasabha had identified as Hindus those persons whose religion has not originated outside India. Second, some *adivasi* groups have demanded to be recognized as Hindus, and third, a majority of the census officials were Hindus, and they have registered *adivasis* as Hindus.

9. For instance, Morari Bapu is working full-time for the survival of Hindu *sanskriti* (culture). He has performed *Ram katha* at several places in *adivasi* towns such as Shinor, Vyara, Mandvi, Santrampur, and Sisodra. He has also been invited on several occasions to give speeches. The first *Ram katha* in an *adivasi* area was

organized at Vyara in October 1995. On this occasion, Bajarang Dal organized a 4-kilometer Pothi Yatra. Morari Bapu has tried to introduce Ram to the *adivasis,* and every day more than half-a-lakh of *adivasis* participated in the *katha* where meals were also served. Morari Bapu's birthday was celebrated with Ramotsav and distribution of Ganges water. Expenses were covered by a wealthy trader from Surat. On the last day, Bapu performed *arti* (an act of veneration) and representatives from each *adivasi* group, Harijans, and Muslims participated in the ceremony, and Babu finally gave to his devotees the mantra *Ram hi keval prem pyala* (only Ram is full of love; therefore he should be worshipped).

10. Morari Bapu is one of the well-known saints, who recites the *Ramayana* in most *adivasi* areas of Gujarat. He has an influence not only on educated and urban *adivasi* but also on the illiterate *adivasi* masses. Nandu Bhagat is an example of a devotee from the village Khroda. He gave up *dacoiti* and drinking habits after listening to Morari Bapu ten years ago. He began chanting *Ram jap* (invocation of Ram in prayer) and gradually learned the whole *Ramayana* by heart. From evening to early morning, he performs the *Ramayana katha* with a small group of *adivasis* as part of a campaign. He has also begun to expose tricks employed by Christian missionaries to convert *adivasis* to Christianity; instead he advises them to embrace the Hindu religion. He has probably organized more than 150 *kathas* with thousands of participants.

11. Drastic change has taken place in Hindutva policy, especially after the mass conversion of Harijans to Islam in 1981 at Minakshipuram, Tamil Nadu. Dalit demands are no longer directly opposed; instead Hindus have begun to present themselves as the true well-wishers of the *adivasi* cause.

12. He has written extensively in local newspapers and has published more than twenty books. The purpose of his writings is to bring out the orthodox and inhuman practices of Hindu religion. Swami seems to be strongly opposed to the traditional Hindu *varna* system. He has devoted a whole book to it in which he highlights the inhuman and discriminatory attitude of *savarnas* (upper-caste Hindus) toward those at the bottom of society.

13. Temple building activity occurs on a large scale. Local people are mobilized. Temples have been considered at several *adivasi talukas.* Twenty-five years ago the first temple of Akshar Purushottam Swaminarayan was built at Mandvi. This was the first temple in the eastern belt in South Gujarat, but now there are many. Recently, the Mahilas of Vyara *taluka* arranged a *Ram katha* of Nilesh Bapu to last for nine days in the interior village of Chodchit in order to collect money for the construction of a Jalaram Bapu temple at Songdh.

14. The Jagannath temple in Orissa was probably an *adivasi* temple originally, but gradually it was changed into a Hindu temple. A study made by Annacharlotte Eschman (1986) shows how Hinduization has been at work in many places. In Orissa, in Bastar, at Mysore, and in West Bengal we meet the same pattern: deities from the Hindu pantheon replace local folk deities.

15. The teachings of Shri Pandurang Shastri Athvale, a Brahmin from Maharashtra, are focused on the study of self. He has been active as a teacher of spirituality for fifty years. Today he probably has a following of more than three million people, spread over 1.25 lakh villages in India and abroad. Devotees are mainly recruited from the lower levels of society. They are invited to participate in activities such as (1) *Swadhayaya,* (2) *Bhakti-Pheri* (devotion march), *Trikal Sandhiya* (three-time prayer), (3) *Yogeshwar Krishi* (community farming), (4) *Matsyagandha,* and (5) *Bal Samskara Kendra, Shri Darshanam* (visit and homage to the Lord). The upper and lower castes often work together. Shastri Athvale is try-

ing to bring about a social, economic, emotional, and political "revolution" through spiritual revolution. *Swadhayaya* is a study of self through group encounters. This self-understanding is holistic in nature and includes the social, economic, political, psychological, and philosophical dimensions of the human personality. *Bhakti-Pheri* is a devotional tour of *Swadhyayees* for spiritual development. They do not seek any material things. With the Lord in their hearts, they visit villages to spread the message of Gita. *Swadhyayees* spend a minimum of fifteen days in a year in villages. *Yogeshwar Krishi* is farming in the name of God in which *Swadhyayees* cultivate plots of land in the name of the almighty and use their farming skill in service. *Matsyagandha* is the construction of floating temples. A crew of six to ten *Swahyayee* fishermen working as devotees are carried on these floats. The sons of these devotees offer a part of their earnings from the sea to the Lord Yogeshwar. When enough money is accumulated, it is used to buy motorized fishing boats. These boats are called *Matsyagandhas*. *Bal Samskara Kendras* are the centers for child development that *Swadhayaya* runs in each locality, a neighborhood or a village, where it is at work. In such centers, women participants of *Swadhayaya* spend time with children. Usually this service is done once a week.

16. There is a belief that God comes weekly to each of the *adivasi* families, and that their house becomes a *Gharmandir*. The *Swadhyay adivasi* families meet in such houses every evening to pray to God. The campaign has had some impact as far as cleanliness, rejection of liquor and meat, and the like are concerned.

17. *Amrutalaya* is a simple structure for worship. By using locally available materials, the *adivasis* build a hut for their *Shram Bhakti* (devotion). There is no idol in the temple except the photos of Krishna, Shiva, and Pandurang Shastri. It is also used as a community center where people deliberate on their problems. *Amrutalaya* is open to all, including Harijans. Even Muslims come to perform *namaz* (worship) there.

18. At one such campaign a BJP minister said that his party had found solutions to questions concerning housing, allotment of residential plots, distribution of 10 kilograms (kg) of grain free of cost, interest-free loans of Rs 2,000 for petty businesses, legalization of forest land, clothes for schoolchildren, wheat at the rate of Rs 2 per kg, Rs 5,000 at the time of marriages, Rs 200 for widows, working women hostels in cities, debt relief of up to Rs 10,000, and so on. The BJP minister and his assistants contacted 200–300 Halpatis in the adjoining areas.

19. A second multiple-wedding ceremony for *adivasis* was held under the auspices of the Adivasi Vikas Mandal of Kamrej-Palsana Vibhag. This ceremony was held at Swami-narayan Sanskriti Dham at Ladvi. Many *adivasi* leaders and saints were present. The Social Welfare Minister also honored the function with his presence. Blessings were bestowed on the forty-five couples. The minister pointed out that the present government was much concerned about the welfare of people from the lower classes, including *adivasis*. He announced some government schemes to be implemented soon, including *Kurvarbai nu Mameru, Saraswati Sadhana Vojana, Manav Garima Yojana,* and so on. Premswaroop Shastriji, who is in charge of Swaminarayan Sanskrit Dham of Ladvi, advised them to seek education and to assimilate with mainstream Hindu tradition. He was also in favor of helping people enslaved by addiction.

20. Some *adivasi* leaders have become strong supporters of Hindutva organizations. At one *adivasi* gathering to which I was invited as a guest speaker, I saw that a few *adivasi* party leaders shared the dais with upper-caste leaders from the BJP. In their speeches, upper-caste leaders did not miss the opportunity to drum into the heads of their listeners that BJP was a real friend working for the uplift of the

adivasi people. They also called attention to the fact that they had given high positions in politics to *adivasi* leaders. Finally they turned against the Congress Party, whom they strongly criticized for the injustices committed against the *adivasi* people.

21. In October 1995 (from 2 to 20 October) an *Ekatma Yatra* was organized by the VHP. This *Yatra* covered the distance from Kanyakumari in the south to the Himalayas in the north, the purpose being to promote Hindutva awareness in the nation. A national and religious awakening was to take place at the same time. The *Yatra* was attended by twenty crore people from 3.5 lakh villages. It comprised about 45,000 public meetings. The *Yatra* was attended by fifty-four lakh people in five zones of the Surat district. Sub-*Yatras* were visited by twenty-two lakh people. Twenty-two sub-*Yatras* and an equal number of *Dharma Sabhas* were held. This *Yatra* covered 790 kilometers and in 976 villages, a pot of water from the holy river Ganges was set up. About 21,100 villages have been included in the campaign. Kamedrasinh, in charge of the Gujarat *Ekatma Yatra,* said in his address that such a *Yatra* was necessary to save the country and its religion (Nandy et al., 1995).

22. Some of the faculty members of the Centre for Social Studies in Surat have launched a study of their own in order to investigate communal riots among *adivasis* in Gujarat in 1993. I was associated with this project and collected some information through personal interviews and observation of the communal situation in Sagbara and Dediyapada *talukas* of the Bharuch district. I also read reports from other parts of South Gujarat.

23. In the last week of February 1995, a published meeting of *adivasis* was held at the *adivasis* village Uchchal. State President Kashiram Rana said that the Congress was losing its importance in the South Gujarat region. The *taluka* presidents invited were *adivasis* from Uchchal *taluka,* Nizar *taluka,* and Navapur *taluka.* They emphasized in their speeches that *adivasis* have now realized that the Congress has not been a spokesperson for the poor or for the *adivasi* people.

24. Recently, Chhotubhai Vasava, Ramanbhai Chaudhari, and some others held a meeting in the *adivasi* area, first in Nizer and later in Mandvi on the eve of the last parliamentary election. They have succeeded in mobilizing lakhs of *adivasis* from all over the *adivasi* belt of Gujarat. For the first time, all seats on the dais were occupied by *adivasi* leaders only.

25. *Adivasi* leaders appeal to *adivasi* masses to free themselves from the clutches of the Hindus. In a handbill published by *adivasi* Vikas Parishad in Panchmahal district, an emphatic appeal was made for *adivasis* to demand their own state—Bhilistan. *Adivasis* were encouraged to liberate themselves from Hindu slavery. The handbill described how in former times the invading Aryans developed the *varnavyavastha* (hierarchical division of social group based on race and color) to keep *adivasis* down, and to make their ideology of suppression perfect they made it part of a religious cosmic order.

References

Adhvaryu, Bhanu. 1981. *Agnigarbh Valia.* Surat: Socialist Study Centre.
Adijati Vikas Paksha (Handbill). (n.d.). Dahod: Adijati Vikas Paksha Trust.
Allen, Douglas (ed.). 1993. *Religion and Political Conflict in South Asia, India, Pakistan, and Sri Lanka.* Delhi: Oxford University Press.
Augustine, P. A. 1984. *Suppression of Valia Tribals: A Case Study of Human Rights Violation.* Delhi: Indian Social Institute.

Bajaj, Jitendra (ed.). 1993. *Ayodhya and the Future of India*. Madras: Centre for Policy Studies.
Banerjee, S. 1968. *Ethnographic Study of the Kuvi-Kandha*. Memoir No. 21, Calcutta: Anthropological Survey of India.
Bidwai, Praful, Harbans Mukhia, and Achin Vanaik (eds.). 1996. *Religion, Religiosity and Communalism*. Delhi: Manor.
Bose, N. K. 1941. "The Hindu Method of Tribal Absorption," *Science and Culture* (Calcutta) 7 (4), October: 188–194.
Campbell, James M. 1988. *Hindu Castes and Tribes of Gujarat*. Delhi: Vintage Books.
Das, A. 1968–1969. "Impact of Christianity of Tribals," *Adibasi* (Orissa) 10 (1), April: 87–96.
David, Hardiman. 1984. "Adivasi Assertion in South Gujarat: The Devi Movement of 1922–23," in Ranajit Guha (ed.), *Subaltern Studies*. Vol. 3. Delhi: Oxford University Press.
Dehon, P. 1906. "Religion and Customs of the Uraons," *Memoirs of the Asiatic Society of Bengal:* 121–181.
Desai, I. P. 1971. "The Slogan of a Separate State by Tribals of South Gujarat," *ICSSR Research Abstract Quarterly* 1 (4), February: 118–127.
———. 1976. *Profile of Education Among the Scheduled Tribes of Gujarat*. Surat: Centre for Social Studies.
———. 1982. *Vedchhi Andolan* (in Gujarati). Surat: Centre for Social Studies.
Desai, Kiran. (n.d.). "Adivasis of South Gujarat" (unpublished typescript). Surat: Centre for Social Studies.
Eschman, A. 1986. *The Saorias of the Rajmahal Hills*. Berkeley: University of California Press.
Ferreira, John V. 1965. *Totemism in India*. Bombay: Oxford University Press.
Fuchs, Stephen. 1973. *Aboriginal Tribes of India*. Delhi: Macmillan India.
Gazetteer of India. 1979. *Gujarat State: South Gujarat Districts*. Ahmedabad: Gujarat State Publications.
Ghurye, G. S. 1963. *The Scheduled Tribes*. Bombay: Popular Prakashan.
Graham, B. D. 1990. *Hindu Nationalism and Indian Politics: The Origins and Development of Bhartiya Jana Sangh*. Cambridge: Cambridge University Press.
Gujarat State Gazetteers. 1979. *Vadodara District*. Ahmedabad: Government Printing Stationery and Publications, Gujarat State.
Guru, Gopal. 1991. "Hinduisation of Ambedkar in Maharashtra," *Economic and Political Weekly* 26 (7), 16 February: 2819–2823.
Hajra, D. 1970. *The Dorlas of Bastar*. Memoir No. 16, Calcutta: Anthropological Survey of India.
Hasan, Mushirul. 1991. "Adjustment and Accommodation: Muslims After Partition," in K. K. Panikkar (ed.), *Communalism in India: History, Politics and Culture*. New Delhi: Manohar, pp. 62–79.
Herbert, Spencer. 1976–1896. *The Principles of Sociology*. 3 Vols. London: William and Norgate.
Iyer, V. K. Krishna. 1991. *Politics and Religion*. Delhi: Konark Publishers.
Jayaprasad, K. 1991. *RSS and Hindu Nationalism*. New Delhi: Deep and Deep Publications.
Joshi, Satyakam. 1992. "Forest Co-operatives of South Gujarat" (Ph.D. diss.). Surat: South Gujarat University.
———. 1995. "Congress Debacle in Panchayat Poll," *Mainstream* 33 (44), 23 September: 11–14.

———. 1996. "Gamits of South Gujarat," in N. N. Vyas (ed.), *Tribal Encyclopedia*. Delhi: Discovering Publishing House.
Joshi, Vidyut. 1980. *Ashramshalao Ek Adhyayan: Adivasi-Shikshano Ek Samajshastriya Abhyas*. Ahmedabad: Gujarat Samajik Seva Mandal.
Kalia, B. 1961. *Tribal Elements in Hinduism*. Delhi: Munshiram.
Lal, R. B. 1977. "Socio-Religious Movements Among South Gujarat Tribes" (mimeograph). Ahmedabad: Gujarat Tribal Research and Training Centre.
———. 1982. "Socio-Religious Movements Among South Gujarat Tribes," in K. S. Singh (ed.), *Tribal Movements in India*, Vol. 2. Delhi: Manohar Publication, pp. 285–308.
Lobo, Lancy. 1990. "Communal Riots in Tribal Dediyapada and Sagbara During October–November 1990: A Report." Unpublished typescript. Surat: Centre for Social Studies.
———. 1992. "Religious Sects Among the Tribals of South Gujarat" (mimeograph). Surat: Centre for Social Studies.
———. 1993. "Suppression of Valia Tribals and Their Assertion," paper presented at a seminar at Nagpur, Bastar: "Pro-Imperialist Development Strategy Versus People's Struggles." Surat: Centre for Social Studies.
———. 1994. "Suppression of Valia Tribals," *Economic and Political Weekly*, 15 January: 1189–1196.
———. 1995. "Religious Movement Among Tribals of Gujarat," paper presented in National Seminar on Social Identities: "Religion, Region and Language in Contemporary India," 14–15 September, Surat.
———. 1996. "Choudhuries of South Gujarat," in N. N. Vyas (ed.), *Tribal Encyclopedia*. Delhi: Discovery Publishing House.
Malik, K. Yogendra, and V. B. Singh. 1994. *Hindu Nationalists in India: The Rise of the Bharatiya Janata Party*. Delhi: Vistaar Publications.
Mohapatra, E. B., and J. Swain. 1969. "Conversion to Christianity," *Man in India* 49 (3), September: 253–258.
Nandy, Ashis, Shikha, Trivedi, Shail, Mayaram and Achyut Yagnic. 1995. *Creating a Nationality: The Ramajanmabumi Movement and Fear of the Self*. Delhi: Vistaar.
Panikkar, K. K. (ed.). 1991. *Communalism in India: History, Politics and Culture*, New Delhi: Manohar.
Parmar, Rameshchandra. 1993. *Agnikund Valia, Bhartiya Dalit Panther*. Ahmedabad: Bharatiya Dalit Panther.
Patel, Arjun. 1996a. "The Dungari Bhils of Baroda District of Gujarat," in N. N. Vyas (ed.), *Tribal Encyclopedia*. Delhi: Discovery Publishing House.
———. 1996b. "The Rathwas of Baroda District of Gujarat," in N. N. Vyas (ed.), *Tribal Encyclopedia*. Delhi: Discovery Publishing House.
———. 1996c. "The Tadavis of Bharuch District of Gujarat," in N. N. Vyas (ed.), *Tribal Encyclopedia*. Delhi: Discovery Publishing House.
Patel, Arjun, and Kiran Desai. 1988. "Review of Literature on Adivasis Studies," *Souvenir, MRS. Dept*. Surat: South Gujarat University.
———. 1992. *Migrant Labour in Rural Gujarat*. Surat: Centre for Social Studies.
Patel, Arjun, and Ghanshayam Shah. 1993. "Tribal Movements In Western India: A Review of Literature." Occasional Paper No. 15. Surat: Centre for Social Studies.
Patnaik, N. 1963. "From Tribe to Caste: The Juangs of Orissa," *Economic and Political Weekly* 15 (18), 4 May: 741–742.
Paul, K. T. 1919. "How Missionaries Denationalise Indians," *International Review of Missions* 8 (4), October: 92–105.

Pinto, Stany. 1995. "Communalisation of Tribals in South Gujarat," *Economic and Political Weekly*, 30 September: 2873–2877.
———. 1996. "Vasavas of South Gujarat," in N. N. Vyas (ed.), *Tribal Encyclopedia*. Delhi: Discovery Publishing House.
Punalekar, D. S. 1996. "Choudhuries of South Gujarat," in N. N. Vyas (ed.) *Tribal Encyclopedia*. Delhi: Discovery Publishing House.
Punalekar, S. P. 1980. "Descriptive Study of Dhodias of Surat" (Ph.D. diss.). Surat: South Gujarat University.
———. 1993. "Structural Constraint in Tribal Education: A Case Study of Tribal Community in South Gujarat," *The Indian Journal of Social Science* 6 (1): 32–47.
———. 1996. "Dhodias of South Gujarat," in N. N. Vyas (ed.), *Tribal Encyclopedia*. Delhi: Discovery Publishing House.
Radcliffe-Brown, A. R. 1964. *Andaman Islanders*. Cambridge: Cambridge University Press. (First published in 1922.)
Rajkishore, C. (ed.). 1995. *Ayodhya Aur Use Age* (Hindi). Delhi: Vani Prakashan.
Roy, Sarat Chandra. 1925. *The Birhor: A Little Jungle Tribe of Chotanagpur*. Ranchi: Man in India Publications.
Sachchidananda, S. 1964. *Culture Change in Tribal Bihar*. Calcutta: Bookland P. Ltd.
———. 1970. "Tribe-Caste Continuum: A Case Study of the Gond in Bihar," *Anthropos* 65: 973–997.
Sahay, K. N. 1962. "Trends of Sanskritization Among the Orans," *Bulletin of the Bihar Tribal Research Institute* 4 (2), September: 89–102.
———. 1967. "A Study in the Process of Transformation from Tribes to Caste: Parahiyas of Lolki: A Case Study," *Journal of Social Research* 10 (1), March: 64–89.
———. 1980. "The Transformation Scene in Chotanagpur: Hindu Impact on the Tribals," in P. Dasha Sharma (ed.), *Sarat Chandra Roy Commemorative Volume: The Passing Scene in Chotanagpur*. Ranchi: Maitryee Publications.
Sen, Jyoti. 1968. *Community Development in Chotanagpur*. Calcutta: Asiatic Society.
Shah, Dilip. (n.d.). "Rural Reforms through Swadhyay Bhakti" (unpublished typescript). Surat: South Gujarat University.
Shah, Ghanshyam. (n.d.) *Gujaratna Adivasio*. Surat: Centre for Social Studies.
———. 1991. *Choudhary Adivasio: Gaikale ane Aje*. Surat: Centre for Social Studies.
———. 1992. *Caste Association and Political Process in Gujarat*. Bombay: Popular Prakashan.
———. 1993. "Tenth Lok Sabha Elections, BJP's Victory in Gujarat," in Asghar Ali Engineer and Pradeep Nayak (eds.), *Communalisation of Politics and 10th Lok Sabha Elections*. Also in 1991, *Economic and Political Weekly* 16 (51), 21 December: 2105–2108.
———. 1994. "The BJP and Backward Castes in Gujarat," *South Asian Bulletin* 14 (1): 35–42.
———. 1995. *Politics of Scheduled Castes and Tribes*. Bombay: Vora and Company Publications Pvt Ltd.
———. 1996. "Gujarat: BJP's Rise to Power," *Economic and Political Weekly*, 13–20 January: 1023–1028.
Shah, Ghanshyam, and H. R. Chaturvedi. 1983. *Ghandhian Approach to Rural Development: The Valod Experiment*. Delhi: Ajanta Books International.

Shah, Ghanshyam, and Arjun Patel. 1984. *Economic Differentiations and Tribal Identity.* Delhi: Ajanta Books International.
——. 1985. "A Profile of Education Among the Scheduled Tribes in Gujarat," in Ghanshyam Shah (ed.), *Tribal Education in Gujarat.* Delhi: Ajanta Books International.
——. 1991. "Tenth Lok Sabha Elections. BJP's Victory in Gujarat," *Economic and Political Weekly* 26 (52), 21 December: 1827–1831.
——. 1993. "Tribal Movements in Western India: Review of Literature." Occasional paper No. 15. Surat: Centre for Social Studies.
Shah, Ghanshyam, and Kalpana Shah. 1993. "Police Adivasio par Gujarelo Atanb: Maljipura Gamni Dastur," *Padkar* Year 10, No. 4: 62–75.
Sharkir, Moin (ed.). 1989. *Religion, State and Politics in India.* Delhi: Ajanta Publications.
Shourie, Arun. 1987. *Religion in Politics.* New Delhi: Roli Books International.
Singh, K. S. 1993. "Hinduism and Tribal Religion: An Anthropological Perspective," *Man in India* 11 (2), March: 74–87.
Sinha, Surajit. 1965. "Tribe-Caste and Tribe-Peasant Continuum in Central India," *Man in India* 45 (1), January–March: 57–83.
Skaria, Ajay. 1992. *A Forest Policy in Western India: The Dangs: 1800s–1920s.* Cambridge: University of Cambridge.
Srivastava, S. K. 1958. *The Tharus: A Study in Culture Dynamics.* Agra: Agra University.
Swain, J. 1969. "Conversion to Christianity," *Man in India* 49 (3), September: 128–135.
Troisi, J. 1979. *Tribal Religious Beliefs and Practices Among the Santhals.* Delhi: Manohar.
Tylor, E. B. 1920. *Primitive Culture* (6th edition), Vol. 1. New York: G. B. Putnam's Sons.
Vidyarthi, L. P. (ed.). 1967. *Applied Anthropology.* Allahabad: Kitab Mahal.
Yagnic, A. 1995. "Hindutva as a Savrana Purana," *Communalism Combat* 5 (45): 31–35.
Yagnic, S. 1995. *Saffronite Swagger.* Madras: Earthworm Books.

Part 3

DALITS AND DEVELOPMENT

8

State, Market, and the Dalits

B. L. Mungekar

In July 1991, India adopted the New Economic Policy (NEP), which constituted a major break with the economic policy pursued since independence. The main thrust of the NEP is on liberalization, privatization, and globalization. Further, the NEP is composed of two parts: (1) short-term "stabilization" measures such as devaluation of the Indian rupee by about 20 percent; and (2) a long-term structural adjustment program (SAP), which, as the name suggests, is intended to restructure the Indian economy. Obviously, the scope of the SAP is so wide and comprehensive that it seeks to alter, in a major way, policies with respect to monetary and fiscal management; trade and prices; location, ownership, structure, management, and control of industries; foreign capital, multinational corporations (MNCs), and technology; agriculture and other activities; and investment in social sectors such as health, education, and other infrastructural services. India was also a party to the General Agreement on Tariffs and Trade (GATT) and subsequently became a member of the World Trade Organization (WTO).

The NEP is based on the following three basic premises:

1. The process of competition, both internal and external, would help achieve optimum allocation of resources and secure their efficient utilization;
2. Opening the economy would enable the country to have greater access to modern foreign technology, which, on the one hand, would strengthen the forces of competition and efficiency, and, on the other, help promote exports; and,
3. The above two together would help the country achieve a higher rate of economic growth.

Thus, in essence, the NEP aims to progressively reduce the role of the state in the economic management of the country and to secure a transition from the "centrally planned" Indian economy to a free market economy. What is a matter of concern is that, first, the transition is going to erode, perhaps considerably, the welfare role of the state. Second, the NEP has blind faith in the "trickle-down" theory of distributing the benefits of economic growth among different socioeconomic groups in the country.

In this chapter I seek to examine in a broader macro perspective the impact of the NEP on the Dalits. Here, the term "Dalits" is used in a comprehensive manner and includes all the depressed and disadvantaged sections of Indian society. My central argument is that in all probability the NEP, by dismantling the welfare state, will adversely affect the social and economic interests of all the weaker sections, but most of all of the Dalits. Again, relevant empirical information, wherever available, is provided about the Scheduled Caste/Scheduled Tribe (SC/ST) communities with a view to representing the conditions of the Dalits as a whole.

The chapter is divided into three sections. First, the socioeconomic profile of the SC communities is presented. Among other things, it will make clear the highly unequal opportunity structure that worsens the already low capacity of these communities to benefit from the prospective growth to be achieved through economic reforms. Second, I examine the impact of dismantling the welfare state on the advancement of these communities, with specific reference to the prospective erosion of the reservation policy (RP) and process of commodification of social services. The last section presents the conclusions.

Socioeconomic Profile of Scheduled Castes

Indian society is highly stratified, with many glaring inequalities among different socioeconomic groups. The worst positioned among them are the Dalits and tribals. The caste system segregated the Dalits from the rest of the society to such an extent that they were denied even the basic human rights that one must enjoy in order to ensure one's bare existence. Denial of the right to drink water from any public well and to walk on the road in broad daylight were some of the notable examples of social persecution of the Dalits at the hands of the upper-caste Hindus. They were forced to cook their food in broken earthen pots. They wore dirty clothes, if they did so at all, because their wearing clean and neat clothes would irritate the upper castes. Further, the torn and dirty clothes would enable the upper castes to easily identify Dalits. They were destined to live in *kachcha* houses on the outskirts of villages because their living in *pukka* houses would insult the upper castes, and their living in the vicinity of a village would result in intermingling with the members of the upper castes and "pollute" them. This description could be infinitely prolonged.

However, the caste system could not have persisted for centuries only through the subjective prejudices and the idea of pollution. One of the most formidable factors that provided enduring sustenance to the caste system was its solid economic foundation. Again, what needs to be emphasized is that the economic aspects of the caste system were sanctified by the Hindu religious scriptures, and like discrimination, they were deeply internalized.

To begin with, caste played an "ascriptive" role inasmuch as it allocated economic functions in the society. Such distribution of economic activities among different individuals has been a characteristic feature of every human society, either in crude or in very complex form. But the unique feature of the caste system was that it assigned an occupation not to an individual but to a group of individuals. A particular individual was ordained to undertake a particular occupation just because he or she belonged to a particular group, that is, caste. This led B. R. Ambedkar to argue that the caste system not only resulted in "division of labour" but culminated in the "division of labourers" (Ambedkar, 1979). The former is the result of the preference, choice, and aptitude of an individual; the latter is independent of the individual will. As in the social sphere, in the economic sphere the caste system amounted to a violation of individual freedom.

But the effects of the birth-based occupational distribution on different castes were entirely opposite in nature. It proved to be a divine privilege to the upper castes, who enjoyed a virtual monopoly on education, industry, trade, commerce, and so on; for the lower castes, it spelled disaster because the latter were assigned the tasks involving only manual labor. They were thus prevented from earning and accumulating wealth, which restricted them to subsistence. In addition, menial labor was stigmatized. Thus, the absence of freedom of occupation, low earnings (mainly in kind), an implicit restriction on needs, and the stigma of menial labor destroyed the economy of the lower castes. They came to be wholly dependent on the upper castes for their bare economic existence. As a result, the Dalits remained socially outcaste, economically dependent, politically powerless, and culturally backward.

Caste thus creates and sustains an unequal opportunity structure, which is anathema to the egalitarian principles that are the basis of a modern democratic society. What is worse, it intensifies and perpetuates the sufferings and servitude of the disadvantaged caste–class groups by reducing their access to development benefits vis-à-vis the higher caste–class groups. In the context of the NEP, the unequal opportunity structure warrants special attention for two reasons. First, as mentioned at the beginning, the NEP is based on the trickle-down system inherent in the postwar theories of economic growth. Second, not only have the advocates of the NEP grossly neglected the role of the caste system in the distributional aspect of the prospective gains of the NEP, but even the opponents of the NEP (mainly the "leftists") do not seen to have paid due attention to the caste system as one of the major factors in assessing adverse impacts of the NEP on Indian society. To make this point clear, in Table 8.1 I show the socioeconomic profile of the SCs for the year 1986–1987.

Table 8.1 Socioeconomic Profile of Scheduled Castes

S. No.	Indicator	Status
1.	Population (1981)	10.48 crore
2.	Urbanization	16.00%
3.	Literacy	21.38%
4.	Agricultural laborers	48.22%
5.	Cultivators	28.17%
6.	Average status of cultivators	marginal
7.	Industrial employment	4.00%
8.	Percentage of people below poverty line	50.00%
9.	Percentage of bonded laborers who are SCs	66.00%

Source: Government of India (1990a).

After three and a half decades of planned economic development and all the rhetoric about the "socialist pattern of society," the rate of literacy of these communities was barely 22 percent and that of urbanization 16 percent; nearly 50 percent of them were agricultural laborers; out of every 100 bonded laborers in the country, 66 come from the SCs; their share in industrial employment was an abysmally low 4 percent. As a consequence of all this, the extent of poverty among the SCs was as high as 50 percent, compared with 30 percent for the population as a whole.[1]

Size Distribution of Landholdings Among SCs

The importance of landholding as a main source of livelihood in rural areas can hardly be overemphasized. Further, access to land largely determines the overall asset-base of rural households inasmuch as size of asset-base in rural areas generally tends to vary directly with the size of landholding. Thus, size of landholding/asset-base determines the extent of access to agricultural prosperity and the overall social prestige of an individual in the rural society.

In 1985–1986, the percentage of marginal farmers among the SCs was as high as 71, versus 58 for the population as a whole. The extent of semi-medium and large farmers among the SCs is obviously low compared with the general population. However, one also notices inequality among SC farmers with respect to landholding, inasmuch as less than 1 percent of the large SC farmers cultivated about 11 percent of the total land cultivated by them all, compared with 71 percent of them cultivating less than 24 percent (Government of India, 1990b).

The condition of agricultural laborers, most of whom belong to the SC/ST communities, is pathetic. They have to toil in heat, rain, and cold alike. They stand a better chance of employment during busy agricultural seasons such as sowing and harvesting, but during lean periods they remain largely either jobless or underemployed. Constant increases in prices of essential commodities such as foodgrains depresses their already meager purchasing power. Further, they suffer from chronic inadequacy of housing, clothing, and primary medical facilities. They can seldom afford to send their children to school because of their abject poverty, and wherever they do, the dropout rate among their children is very high. Except in a state like Kerala, they are not organized or unionized, and consequently their bargaining power vis-à-vis their masters is low. If they dare to make an attempt in an organized way to demand higher (in fact, "due") wages, the landed interests retaliate with all sorts of actions, such as intimidation and even physical coercion. Occasionally, their houses are burned and the women molested to "teach them a lesson." It is distressing to note that in some parts of the country, landlords have raised "private armies" to deal with agricultural laborers who muster some strength and question their exploitation. To make matters worse, the various state governments are very reluctant to revise agricultural wages upward periodically, as required under the minimum wages legislation enacted in 1948, and are not even enthusiastic about the implementation of the prevailing wage rates.

The writers of free India's constitution duly recognized this tragic situation and incorporated into the constitution the principle of "preferential treatment" in the form of the RP. Through this policy, along with the reservation of seats in the central and state legislatures, places for the SC/ST communities in proportion to their numbers came to be reserved in the central and state government/civil service offices as well as in the educational institutions run by them (12.5, 7.5, and 4.0 percent of places, respectively, for the SCs, the STs, and the Denotified and Nomadic Tribes in proportion to their population). The purpose of the RP was to mitigate, at least partially, centuries-old pervasive injustices inflicted upon the SC/ST communities and to enable them to participate in the process of development and social change. In other words, creating the RP was tantamount to accepting the fact that the benefits of economic growth would not automatically trickle down to the weaker sections of society, still less to the socioeducationally disadvantaged groups like the SCs and the STs. This made positive discrimination in their favor by the state a historical necessity.

Against this background it is pertinent to review the nature and quality of the implementation of the RP in India. Table 8.2 reveals the status of the

136 DALITS AND DEVELOPMENT

Table 8.2 Percentage of Scheduled Castes in Central Government, PSUs, and Nationalized Banks, 1 January 1987

	Central Government		
Class/Grade	Total	SC	Percentage
A (I)	57,654	4,746	8.23
B (II)	75,419	7,847	10.40
C (III)	2,130,453	307,980	14.46
D (IV)	1,167,759	234,614	20.09
Total (excluding sweepers)	3,431,285	555,187	16.18

	PSUs (total: 211)		
Class/Grade	Total	SC	Percentage
A	161,815	7,862	4.86
B	162,339	10,010	6.17
C	1,394,015	258,500	18.54
D	399,000	123,010	30.82
Total (excluding sweepers)	2,117,169	399,382	18.86
Sweepers	38,900	30,150	77.51

	Nationalized Banks		
Class/Grade	Total	SC	Percentage
Officers	215,805	15,775	7.29
Clerks	449,144	61,891	13.77
Class IV	167,136	37,272	22.30
Total (excluding sweepers)	832,085	114,938	13.81
Sweepers	17,794	8,740	49.11

Source: Government of India (1987–1988).

implementation of job reservation in the central government services, the public sector undertakings (PSUs), and the nationalized banks.

According to Table 8.2, in none of the organizations—central government, PSUs, or the nationalized banks—are the Class I posts reserved for the SC people fully filled. The implementation of reservation with regard to these posts is the worst in the PSUs, with 4.86 percent, compared with 8.23 percent and 7.29 percent in the central government and the nationalized banks, respectively. Of the Class II posts in PSUs, no more than 6.17 percent (that is, half of those reserved) were filled. The extent of implementation of the Class II reserved posts is relatively better in central government services. Class III posts meant for the SC communities are filled in proportionate to their percentage of the population. Most important, in the case of the Class IV jobs, the SCs were overrepresented; they held 20.09, 30.82, and 22.30 percent of the posts in the central government, PSUs, and the nationalized banks, respectively. In the PSUs, 77 percent of the sweepers come from the SCs alone. Even in the nationalized banks, about 50 percent of the sweepers belong to SCs.

The scenario in the educational institutions with respect to the RP is explained in Table 8.3. It is distressing to observe that in the year 1987, in as many as forty-one universities in the country the share of the SC communities in the grades of professors, assistant professors, and lecturers was 0.61, 1.04, and 3.16 percent, respectively. The number of reserved posts filled in the categories of Class I, Class II, and Class III is also worse in these universities than in the central government and in PSUs. Here, one ought to remember the dictum of the infamous *Manusmriti* that the Shudras are ordained to perform only menial jobs. The nature and quality of the implementation of the RP discussed above clearly demonstrates how faithfully Indian society, even today, is obeying this dictum.

Table 8.3 Percentage of Scheduled Castes in Employment in Forty-one Educational Institutions, 1987

Class (Category)	Total	SC	Percentage
Teachers			
Professors	2,133	13	0.61
Associate professors	3,261	34	1.04
Lecturers	5,341	169	3.16
Research assistants	674	71	10.53
Administrative Staff			
A Class	3,525	118	3.35
B Class	4,833	221	4.57
C Class	19,811	1,686	8.51
D Class	17,607	2,628	14.97

Source: Government of India (1987–1988).

I have dealt somewhat extensively with the implementation of the RP, because notwithstanding all the limitations and shortcomings of that implementation, the RP has undoubtedly helped the SC/ST communities to overcome their centuries-old socioeconomic, political, educational, and cultural subjugation. It is the RP that has enabled them to partially break the shackles of bonded labor and that has been instrumental in creating in these communities a small middle class consisting of officials, lawyers, professors, engineers, and doctors, whose enhanced economic status has not only increased the pace of social mobility but given some sort of mental stability and confidence to the communities as a whole. As a result, they have started to contribute to art and literature and thus seek cultural advancement. It is indeed gratifying that they are producing their own literature. Dalit literature in Maharashtra is a case in point. Although in the context of the present theme what is stated above may appear to be disproportionately lengthy, I hope it may enable us to comprehend correctly the prospective impact of the NEP on the Dalits.

Impact of the NEP on Dalits

I mentioned at the beginning that the main thrust of the NEP is on the primacy of the market, implying thereby a progressive erosion of the role of the state in the economic affairs of the country. This transition, I believe, is very likely to have adverse consequences for the Dalits. But before I deal with that issue, it would be proper for me to mention, in brief, the nature and quality of state intervention that I have in mind.

To begin with, I believe that in a society characterized by the "private ownership of means of production," the state primarily protects the interests of the ruling classes. These interests are not economic alone but also social, educational, and cultural. Thus, the intervention of the state in the overall management of "social relations" in an "unequal" society generally (if not every time) implies championing the interests of the ruling classes. In the Indian context "ruling classes" implies the so-called upper castes, who have greater command over the material and nonmaterial resources. Consequently, the intervention of the state in favor of the ruling classes in India, who also happen to belong to the upper castes, is bound to affect adversely the interests of the poor in general and the Dalits in particular.

However, even in an unequal society, the ruling classes cannot remain totally neutral toward the minimal requirements of the vast majority of the poor. They have to take care of the socioeconomically disadvantaged sections of the society by devising economic and other policies intended to give lower classes purchasing power, for three reasons. First, maintenance of social stability requires that all socioeconomic groups in the society feel that they stand to benefit from development. Second, in a competitive democratic system, the ruling classes are always constrained to obtain as much support as possible with a view to widening their social base. Third, in a capitalist economy, creation of additional purchasing power is one of the objective conditions for sustaining, if not enlarging, the size of the market, so vital for maintaining the rate of economic growth. The RP for the SC/ST communities (now effectively extended to the Other Backward Castes, or OBCs) is a case in point.

One of the major consequences of the NEP is the contraction of the public sector. Whatever rewards such a policy may bring for the economy, it is likely to have an adverse effect on the SC/ST communities because the contraction of the public sector will certainly restrict the scope of the RP, which, in turn, will result in the erosion of job opportunities for the SCs and STs.[2] In this context, three pertinent questions may be raised. First, will the overall process of privatization of the economy and all the attendant policies create enough jobs to compensate for the loss of jobs caused by the contraction of the public sector? Second, assuming for a while that the private sector does so, what is likely to be the nature of these prospective jobs? Third, and most important, what chance do the SC/ST communities stand of getting a fair share of these jobs so as to compensate them for the adverse consequences of the RP?

To answer the first question, it is a matter of grave concern that during the last one and a half decades or so the overall growth of the economy has not been accompanied by a proportionate increase in the level of employment. This may be attributed mainly to the decline in the elasticity of employment with respect to growth of the economy (Mundle, 1992; Kundu, 1993; Mungekar, 1993; and Gupta, 1994). Earlier, agriculture was the last resort of employment, but over the years there has been a growing tendency among the better-off farmers to replace labor by machinery. As a consequence, the labor-absorption capacity of Indian agriculture is declining (Tyagi, 1981; Vaidyanathan, 1986; Bhalla, 1987). The organized sector as a whole is a great failure in contributing to employment generation. For instance, the total estimated employment in the organized public and private sectors rose from 26.73 million in 1991 to 27.37 million in 1994, that is, by merely 640,000. Again, within the organized sectors, the performance of the manufacturing sector (both public and private) is deplorable. Between 1991 and 1992 this sector generated barely 80,000 jobs (Government of India, 1997a). The small-scale industrial units that contribute enormously to employment generation are less likely to sustain the forces of overall competition and, as a result, may either slowly vanish or opt for such technological upgrades as to erode their employment generation capacity. The MNCs that are rushing to India are most likely to adopt capital-intensive techniques of production because they are/will be increasingly catering to the consumption requirements of the elites; therefore their coming does not brighten the employment prospects in the country. In fact, some even fear that too much emphasis on trade as an engine of economic growth may lead to deindustrialization of the country, resulting in a fall in both growth and employment (Nambiar and Tadas, 1994). Further, the banking and insurance industries—the two major areas of the service sector—are being increasingly computerized, again leading to a trade-off between efficiency and employment. How the employment prospects in India are becoming gloomier is demonstrated in Table 8.4.

Table 8.4   Employment Scenario at a Glance, 1992–1997 (in millions)

1.	The backlog of unemployment at the outset of the Eighth Plan	23.0
2.	Addition to the labor force during the plan period	36.0
3.	Total employment to be provided (1 + 2)	59.0
4.	Likely employment generation during the plan period	31.5
5.	Backlog of unemployment at the end of the Eighth Plan (3 – 4)	27.5

Source: Government of India (1996).

I do not mean to suggest, however, that the economic reforms will not create any jobs. Far from this. What is germane is that the jobs created will not be proportionate either to the prospective rate of economic growth or to the number of people who will be demanding them. Recently, this view has been shared even by the minister of labor, when he expressed a serious concern over the continuously widening gap between job-seekers and the availability of jobs (Government of India, 1997b).

With regard to the second question concerning the nature and quality of the jobs, it seems logical to argue that the jobs the economy may create will demand relatively more technical skill and professional competence. I must hasten to add that I am not at all averse to our labor force acquiring higher technical skills and professional capabilities. My only concern is that the SC/ST communities lag far behind in possessing these capabilities. This also answers the third question: How are these jobs going to be distributed among the SC/ST communities? The chances of their sharing these jobs are indeed bleak. I am aware that this is a pessimistic view, but I am constrained to hold it because when the job interests of these dispossessed and disadvantaged groups are less than adequately protected even in the presence of a constitutionally prescribed (and hence obligatory) reservation policy, how will their interests be protected with the erosion of the very same reservation policy? In other words, prospective erosion of the reservation policy on the one hand and the prejudiced, caste-ridden social arrangement on the other are more likely to create an unfavorable situation in the labor market even for the meritorious among the SC.

What, then, is the prospective scenario with respect to their job opportunities in the era of economic reforms? The answer seems to be inescapable. The Dalits will crowd themselves still more into the unorganized and informal sectors of the economy than they are today. This, in turn, will result in their economic marginalization. How the NEP is likely to set in motion and also strengthen the process of marginalization of the Dalits will be further evident once we understand what I would describe as the commodification of social services.

Commodification of Social Services

One of the characteristics (one may even call them obligations) of the modern welfare state is that it takes the responsibility of making available to the relatively poor sections of society certain services either free of cost or at lower-than-market prices. The rationale for such a policy stems from the failure on the part of a large section of society to enter the market for want of adequate purchasing power. Since the market is guided solely by the consideration of private profit, it does not care for those who are unable to enter it. Thus, the market is useless for the poor, and the poor are useless for the market. This makes it obligatory for the welfare state to take special care of the relatively vulnerable sections of society by implementing specially designed policies and programs such as comprehensive social assistance/security measures (old-age pensions and unemployment allowances) and spending on social services (health and education). To illustrate and emphasize my point, I present in Table 8.5 the share of welfare expenditure in the total public expenditure incurred by some of the Organization for Economic Cooperation and Development (OECD) countries.

Table 8.5   Welfare Expenditure as Percentage of Total Public Expenditure in Selected OECD Countries, 1977

OECD Countries	Percentage
United States	52.3
Japan	41.6
France	65.3
Germany	54.8
Italy	56.5
United Kingdom	45.0
Netherlands	55.9
Sweden	59.2

Sources: ILO (1981: Table 2); OECD (1982: annex); Goram Therborn (1984: 29, national table 9).
Note: Welfare expenditure includes expenditure on income maintenance, health care and social service, and education as a percentage of total public expenditure, excluding public employees and war victims schemes.

Table 8.5 shows that in the advanced industrial countries the welfare expenditure on income maintenance, health care and social services, and education constituted between 45.0 percent (United Kingdom) and 65.3 percent (France) of the total public expenditures in 1977. In India, rather a

142 DALITS AND DEVELOPMENT

contrary scenario has existed. As mentioned earlier, as a result of the overall process of privatization, the state is set to withdraw even more from its welfare obligations by reducing its expenditure on social sectors. This is and will continue to be justified on the ground of containment of fiscal deficit, a strict condition imposed by the International Monetary Fund (IMF) and the World Bank. In Table 8.6 I present the combined expenditure of the center, states, and the Union Territories on social services (education, medical and public health, family welfare, housing, urban development, and other social services) as a percentage of the gross domestic product (GDP) during the period from 1985–1986 to 1996–1997.

Table 8.6 Expenditure by Center, States, and Union Territories on Social Services as Percentage of GDP, 1985–1986 to 1996–1997

Year	Expenditure per of GDP
1985–1986	14.7
1986–1987	15.1
1987–1988	16.3
1988–1989	16.8
1989–1990	16.5
1990–1991	16.5
1991–1992	15.9
1992–1993	15.5
1993–1994	15.9
1994–1995	17.2[a]
1995–1996	19.4[a]
1996–1997	14.6[b]

Sources: Government of India (1996–1997, tables 2.7–2.10).
Notes: a. Revised estimates.
b. Budget estimates.
Other figures show actual expenditure.

Table 8.6 shows that the expenditure on social services in the country increased from 14.7 percent of GDP in 1985–1986 to 16.5 percent in 1991–1992.[3] However, during 1992–1993 to 1993–1994 (the first three years of economic reforms), it ranged from 15.5 to 15.9 percent of GDP. The estimates of expenditure for 1994–1995 and 1995–1996 are 17.2 and 19.4 percent, respectively, and the budget estimates for 1996–1997 themselves have fallen to 14.6 percent of GDP. Thus, on the whole in the postreform period, the expenditure on social services as proportion of GDP has either remained stagnant or, at its worst, declined. In other words, taking into account the scope and severity of the prevailing vulnerability in our society, the expenditure on social services is far from adequate. Further, when adjusted for inflation it may prove to be even more inadequate.

I would like to cite just one illustration to support my contention. In 1995, the Planning Commission had voted down a proposal that only those SC/ST students who secured more than 60 percent marks in the SSC or equivalent examination should qualify for the postmatriculation Government of India Scholarships. The proposal was dropped only because of political intervention. Viewed in the light of the conditions in which the SC/ST students are struggling to acquire education, the proposal not only amounted to a travesty of wisdom on the part of the Planning Commission but also indicates the direction in which the wind has begun to blow. In other words, social services like health and education will be more commodified than they were in the past or are even today, and the results will be borne by all the poor, particularly the disadvantaged among the Dalits.

Conclusion

The central argument of this chapter is that India's NEP, based on liberalization, privatization, and globalization, may enable the country to secure economic growth, perhaps at a relatively high rate. But the highly unequal social system creating and sustaining an unequal opportunity structure will deprive socioeconomically and culturally disadvantaged and dispossessed groups such as the Dalits of any opportunity of sharing meaningfully in the benefits of this prospective economic growth. It is therefore imperative for the Dalits, and along with them all the disadvantaged and dispossessed sections in the country, to wage a united battle to see that the welfare state is not dismantled by the ruling classes.

Notes

1. Comparable information about the non-SC population is not available.
2. This is because, at present, jobs are reserved only in the public sector undertakings or organizations owned or run by the central and the state governments.
3. It needs to be noted that during the Seventh Five-Year Plan (1985–1990), the outlay provided for the social services was 17.5 percent of GDP, whereas the actual expenditure incurred turned out to be only 16.0 percent of GDP (Government of India, 1997a).

References

Ambedkar, B. R. 1979. *Babasaheb Ambedkar: Writings and Speeches.* Vol. II. Bombay: Government of Maharashtra, Education Dept.
Bhalla, Sheila. 1987. "Trends in Employment in Indian Agriculture, Land and Asset Distribution," *Indian Journal of Agricultural Economics* 42 (4), October–December: 537–560.

Government of India. 1987–1988. *Report of Commissioner for the SCs/STs.* New Delhi: Ministry of Social Welfare.

———. 1990a. *Report of the Study Group Appointed During the VII Five-Year Plan to Look into the Progress of the SCs and STs.* New Delhi: Ministry of Social Welfare.

———. 1990b. *Agricultural Situation in India.* New Delhi: Ministry of Agriculture, June.

———. 1996. "Planning Commission, Draft Mid-Term Appraisal of the Eighth Five-Year Plan: 1992–1997." New Delhi: Government of India.

———. 1996–1997. *Economic Survey: 1996–1997.* New Delhi: Ministry of Finance, Economic Division.

———. 1997a. *Economic Survey.* New Delhi: Ministry of Finance.

———. 1997b. *Labour Bureau, Indian Labour Journal.* Simla: Ministry of Labour.

Gupta, S. P. 1994. "Recent Economic Reforms and Their Impact on the Poor and Vulnerable Sections of Society," NCAER, mimeograph, New Delhi.

International Labour Organisation. 1981. *The Cost of Social Security 1975–77.* Geneva: ILO.

Kundu, Amitabh. 1993. "Growth and Changing Structure of Employment in Urban India: An Analysis in the Context of the New Economic Policy," *Indian Journal of Labour Economics* 36 (4), October–December: 537–552.

Mundle, Sadipto. 1992. "The Employment Effects of Stabilization and Related Policy Changes in India," *Gandhian Journal of Labour Economics* 35 (3), July: 227–237.

Mungekar, B. L. 1993. "Investment, Growth and Employment in India, 1972–72 to 1987–88," *Indian Journal of Labour Economics* 36 (4), October–December: 589–598.

Nambiar, R. G., and Gopal Tadas. 1994. "Is Trade Deindustrialising India?" *Economic and Political Weekly* 29 (42), 15 October: 2741–2746.

Organization for Economic Cooperation and Development. 1982. *National Accounts 1963–80. Vol. II.* Paris: OECD.

Therborn, Goram. 1984. "The Prospects of Labour and the Transformation of Advance Capitalism," *New Left Review* 145, May–June.

Tyagi, D. S. 1981. "Growth of Agricultural Output and Labour Absorption in India," *Journal of Development Studies* 18 (1), October: 104–114.

Vaidyanathan, A. 1986. "Labour Use in Rural India: A Study of Spatial and Temporal Variations," *Economic and Political Weekly* 21 (52), 27 December: A-130–A-146.

9

Dalits and Economic Policy: The Contributions of B. R. Ambedkar

Gail Omvedt

"Ambedkar would have supported devaluation!" This claim by Narendra Jadhav of the Reserve Bank of India shocked me at a time when all progressives seemed to be automatically opposing devaluation as a part of liberalization.[1] But whereas this most highly placed economist of Dalit background was a supporter of liberalization, others have been equally vociferous in arguing that the New Economic Policy (NEP) will affect Dalits most harshly, with much-needed reservations lost to privatization and cutbacks in social spending hitting the rural poor the hardest (see Teltumbde, 1997; Thorat, 1997).[2] Still others have argued that participation in a world economy has been part of the Dalit heritage since Mohenjodaro, whereas the Aryan Brahmins and their heirs prefer a closed economy.[3]

There was a time, before the collapse of communism in the Soviet Union, when debates on economic policy had a clear left-right, progressive-conservative lineup. Socialists and progressives pushed for a greater role for the state, if not in building socialism then at least in ensuring welfare where markets failed, whereas rightists hailed the market. These days are gone. Today the most notorious reactionaries on social issues, from Pat Buchanan to Zhirinovsky, join with old leftists and trade unionists in calling for protectionism. The former socialist countries are forging a path toward capitalism, the Asian ones are under the leadership of their communist parties, and fervent free-marketers such as the "Freshmen Republicans" in the United States have discovered the virtues of at least some subsidies. In India, the Bharatiya Janata Party (BJP) and CPI(M) alike have opposed "Dunkel" tooth and nail while in opposition but have promised that "reforms will not stop" while in power: the effective debate now is only over the speed and type of reforms. Socialism is seemingly dead, but the market has hardly triumphed, welfare survives, and people everywhere behold the doings of their political classes and intellectual leaders with scorn and puzzlement. Rethinking is clearly necessary.

145

Bhimrao Ramji Ambedkar, "Babasaheb" to his Dalit followers, received his degree in economics from Columbia University. In spite of an event-filled political life, he found time to write numerous books, many dealing directly or indirectly with economic theory. In these days of intellectual confusion, can we find any guidance in the Dalit tradition, as compared with the Marxist one? In this chapter I take a brief look at Ambedkar's theorizing.

Ambedkar's Economic Theory: The Stage of Economic Traditionalism

Ambedkar—even more than Marx—was primarily a political activist, though with a Ph.D. in economics. He had little time for deep academic research but was immersed in the turmoil of his times. This is reflected in his economic thinking, which broadly went through three stages. The first was in his early, more academic economic writings of the 1920s (especially *The Problem of the Rupee* and *The Evolution of Provincial Finance in British India* [Moon, 1990c]), which gave strong anti-imperialist but fairly orthodox liberal economic assessments of British rule.[4] The second was in the 1930s and 1940s, when as a central figure in the social and national movements of the period, he was heavily influenced by traditional Marxism in the field of economics, a period that climaxed with the slogans of "state socialism." During this period, Ambedkar used a kind of "dual systems" approach in which Brahminism and capitalism were seen as parallel systems of exploitation. The third period came toward the end of his life, marked by his historical researches on caste, Hinduism, and Buddhism, when he sought a total alternative in Buddhist philosophy.

In the 1920s, employed as a professor at Sydenham College, Ambedkar spent his time reading and working and preparing the base for a surging Dalit movement. This included the organization of the Bahishkrut Hitakarni Sabha and the first great campaign (later to be memorialized as "Untouchable Liberation Day") for water in the Mahad tank satyagraha. (This organizing of Mahad tank satyagraha in the Konkan region, it might be noted, was in an area that was later to become a center for a united Mahar-Kunbin movement against the Khoti landlord system.) But with a pace somewhat slower than that of later years, Ambedkar found time to write two major economic treatises. Both followed fairly conventional economic thinking, and both also had important similarities with works by the Indian economic nationalists—with *The Evolution of Provincial Finance in British India* taking a harsh stand against much of British policy.

The *Problem of the Rupee* was the book that justified Narendra Jadhav's contention that Ambedkar would have supported devaluation. In the final section of the book, Ambedkar dealt with the devaluation controversy of his day. Strikingly, at that time it was the Indian bourgeoisie who wanted a low rupee against the pound, whereas the British bureaucracy wanted a high rupee—the first, undoubtedly because they were primarily in an industry that had been a world leader from the very beginning (the textile industry), the second at least partly because they preferred to be able to buy more pounds from their rupee salaries when they retired.

Ambedkar's own position was to argue for a moderately low rupee. In the course of his discussion, however, he did something that few in the devaluation debate of the 1990s had done: he gave a class analysis of the (at least temporary) effects of devaluation—arguing that entrepreneurs and the self-employed (from businesspeople to farmers) would benefit from a low rupee, whereas wage and salary earners (from bureaucrats to daily laborers) would benefit from a high one that would keep consumer goods cheaper.[5] Ambedkar's recommendation was therefore one that he consciously saw as a compromise between workers and capitalists—devalue the rupee, but not quite as much as the Indian bourgeoisie would have liked.

Against Brahminism and Capitalism

Ambedkar did not remain a "conventional economist" for long. In the 1930s and 1940s, under the impact of a mass upsurge, the pressures of the Great Depression, and the evidently successful economic progress of the USSR and the working-class radicalism this gave birth to, he turned to the left. This was the period when his Dalit-based Independent Labour Party joined with communists to organize peasants and workers, and he formulated the struggle as being against both capitalism and Brahminism. In the largest peasant march of the 1930s, organized to demand abolition of the Khoti landlord system in the Konkan, he had told the rally that "in regard to the toiler's class struggle, I feel the Communist philosophy to be closer to us" (*Janata*, 15 January 1938). Later that year at a conference of Dalit railroad workers, he said:

> There are in my view two enemies which the workers of this country have to deal with. The two enemies are Brahmanism and Capitalism. . . . By Brahmanism I do not mean the power, privileges and interests of the Brahmins as a community. By Brahmanism I mean the negation of the spirit of Liberty, Equality and Fraternity. In that sense it is rampant in all classes and is not confined to the Brahmins alone though they have been the originators of it. (reported in *The Times of India*, 14 February 1938)

These were years in which the pages of *Janata*, Ambedkar's weekly, were filled with reports of the struggles of workers and peasants against "capitalists and landlords" as well as the fights of Dalits against atrocities.

Ambedkar did not have much time for theoretical writing in this period of tumultuous organizing, but his programs and speeches indicate that he accepted the Marxist analysis of class struggle so far as economic issues were concerned. What this led to, though, was a kind of "dual systems" theory that saw capitalism and Brahminism (casteism) as separate systems of exploitation, the one to be fought by class struggle, the other by caste struggle.

The climax of this approach in many ways came with the writing of *States and Minorities* (Moon, 1990a), proposed to be a draft of sections of the constitution. Here Ambedkar gave a severe critique of capitalism and called for the nationalization of land and basic industries, explicitly calling this "state socialism." In a sense the term "state socialism" indicated his difference with the communists, in that in contrast to a revolution under "working class leadership," state ownership was to be written into a democratic constitution. At another level, the phrase simply made the assumption of a mechanical Marxism that socialism, or collective ownership of the means of production, was equivalent to *state* ownership.

There were, however, many problems with the dual system of Brahminism and capitalism. These became clear in *State and Minorities* itself, which seemed to contain two rather disparate sections, one advocating land nationalization and state socialism, the other calling for separate village settlements of Dalits. The connection between the two was not clear. The problems of any dual systems theory remained: seeing separate systems of class and caste exploitation left unchallenged by a class analysis, and accepting the idea that "class" dealt with the economic issues, whereas the "caste" system of exploitation was at a cultural and ideological (superstructural) level. The dual system of capitalism and Brahminism provided useful rhetoric and a yardstick for analysis, but it left the question of the connection between the two systems completely unresolved. And if other systems of oppression (for instance, "patriarchy" and "national oppression") were also included, then such an approach simply would yield to an unwieldy amalgam of many disparate systems of exploitation. In other words, the dual system theory could not give an integrated, holistic explanation. It reflected Ambedkar's initial grappling with Marxism, when he insisted that caste be added to a class approach (and even that it should have priority) but did not develop an overall alternative theory.

Buddhism Versus Marxism

If capitalism and Brahminism were the themes of the 1930s and 1940s, the last years of Ambedkar's life were preoccupied with Buddhism and from time to time with the question of Buddhism and Marxism. But his framework of thinking was different. Whereas in the 1930s and 1940s Ambedkar had tended to see dual systems of exploitation, increasingly he came to give weight to caste and Brahminism and to try to theorize these in a way that would provide a unifying theme for the entire society. In the process, he also came to question his earlier acceptance of a mechanical class approach and of state socialism as the solution to economic exploitation. In his search for a "single systems" theory, Ambedkar began to look toward Buddhism as the solution not only to problems of caste but also to economic exploitation.

We do not have to go far for the reasons for this change. One was internal: that is, the logic of a dual systems theory was inadequate in the sense that it gave no idea of the connection between Brahminism and capitalism. Making class the economic base and caste a political-ideological superstructure tended to give legitimacy to the Marxist position that the base was primary and that caste was a secondary issue. This was unacceptable to Ambedkar and other Dalit-Bahujan activists. But the other reason for disillusionment with the existing theory of Marxism was *external,* the result of historical experience. On the one hand, Ambedkar had an ongoing struggle with the Indian communists, who saw him only as a party bourgeois misleader. On the other hand, the world context was changing. In the 1930s and 1940s, the revolutionary claims of Marxism appeared justified by world events; depression, war, and revolution abounded, and the Soviet Union seemed to be able to achieve both equality and impressive economic growth. By the 1950s these conditions had reversed themselves. Capitalist growth in the West was showing a new dynamism, and its proletariat was becoming integrated into the system. And the Soviet model was beginning to tarnish; the state was not withering away, it was showing its dictatorial face in a way clear to all. In this context, Ambedkar began to define himself not so much as a socialist but as an egalitarian who was equally devoted to freedom and a moral community life. His earlier definition of Brahminism had seen it as the negation of the ideals of liberty, equality, and fraternity; now he returned to this theme. As his conclusion to a draft essay on Buddha and Marx says:

> Society has been aiming to lay a new foundation as was summarised by the French revolution in three words, fraternity, liberty and equality. The French revolution was welcomed because of this slogan. It failed to produce equality. We welcome the Russian revolution because it aims to produce equality. But it cannot be too much emphasised that in producing equality society cannot afford to sacrifice fraternity or liberty. Equality will be of no value without fraternity or liberty. It seems that the three can coexist only if one follows the way of the Buddha. Communism can give one but not all. (Moon, 1990b: 462)

What did Ambedkar mean by "the way of Buddha"? He could not finish the book he proposed on this, but the essay "Buddha or Karl Marx" gives some indications of his thinking. The essay begins with an outline of Marxist propositions and states that most of these have been historically invalidated: the proletariat has not become increasingly miserable and revolutionary; the state has not withered away after revolutions. Marx's assertion of private property as the origin of exploitation and of class conflict remain, in Ambedkar's words, "a residue of fire, small but still very important" (Moon, 1990b: 444), but now he sees the way to overcome the exploitation of private property in a radically different way. In other words, with this Ambedkar rejects state socialism, nationalization, and the dictatorship of the proletariat as solutions to the problem of exploitation and turns to Buddhism for an alternative. And here he comes up with what may be called a "moral economy" solution to the problems of exploitation, which was not simply a matter of stressing nonviolence.

Ambedkar had never rejected Marxism simply because of the role of force in its philosophy; unlike Mohandas Gandhi he did not see nonviolence as an absolute or religiously based principle. In this essay he expands on what he feels is a more practical Buddhist attitude toward violence. His argument is that we cannot (and Buddha did not) renounce force when it is necessary to obtain justice. Buddha "certainly would not have exempted property owners from force if force was the only means for that end," Ambedkar writes (Moon, 1990b: 451). But this kind of force was not necessary, he argues, first because equality and the abolition of private property was achieved in the Bhikku Sangha through voluntary means and second because morality and a welfare state could ensure that private accumulation of wealth did not lead to impoverishment. Thus, a long Buddhist parable in the essay describes how the rule of "righteousness" rather than the "rule of law (force)" is necessary to maintain the prosperity of the kingdom. The role of the state (as symbolized by the righteous king) seems to be twofold: one is the guarantee of property and protection to all in the kingdom, and the second is direct action to remove poverty by "providing wealth to the destitute." The second is crucial; in fact it is the failure to remove poverty that leads (in the parable) to the downfall of the society.

But Ambedkar assumes here that property and wealth accumulation will continue, though under state regulation. In regard to this, he makes an important contrast between Buddhism and Christianity. Christianity gives a high value to poverty and otherworldliness; Buddhism does not—and Ambedkar believes Buddha was superior precisely for this reason: "There is no Sermon on the Mount to be found in the Buddha's teachings. His teaching is to acquire wealth" (Moon, 1990b: 460). For householders, lawful and moral accumulation of wealth is praised:

Thus to acquire wealth legitimately and justly, earned by great industry, amassed by strength of the arm and gained by the sweat of the brow is a great blessing. The householder makes himself happy and cheerful and preserves himself full happiness; also makes his parents, wife and children, servants and labourers, friends and companions happy and cheerful, and preserves them full of happiness. (Moon, 1990b: 461)

In this essay, Ambedkar talks of equality but not of socialism. Similarly, in his speech introducing the Indian constitution, he refers to "social democracy" rather than socialism (Ambedkar, 1979, vol. 13: p. 1216). Was he having doubts about the value of socialism as defined in terms of collective ownership of the means of production? Or were these responses due only to the situation: after all, a summing up of the debate on the constitution was not a place to talk of socialist ideals since no one had, at that time, seriously proposed that independent India define itself as socialist.

But, if Ambedkar maintained a socialist ideal, it must have been in a very different form than the traditional understanding of socialism at the time. Socialism was defined in terms of "collective ownership," and Ambedkar's identification of this as "state ownership" was similar to the confusion shown by all the Marxists of his day. Soviet developments (and the continual communist defense of the dictatorship of the proletariat) identified this, in turn, with dictatorship or the use of force. That is perhaps why, in this essay, Ambedkar continues to emphasize equality but does not use the word "socialism" and explicitly rejects the abolition of poverty by force. "Equality" is to be maintained by voluntary communism in the Bhikku Sangha, and poverty is to be remedied by the redistributive activities of the state. Thus, by the end of his life Ambedkar can be called a socialist only if socialism is defined in terms of the value of equality and not as equivalent to the collective ownership of the means of production.

Ambedkar and the Moral Economy

Today, provoked by the failures of state socialism and by the resurgence of issues of identity, culture, and spirituality, many socialist activists and theorists are centering their attacks on the immorality of commercial capitalism and writing about the need for a moral economy. Ambedkar would have agreed—the need for "morality" in the economic and political ordering of society was one of the crucial points of his criticism of the Marxism of his day.

At the same time, Ambedkar's moral economy differed crucially from the version being put forward by many in India (and other countries) today. Today, most of the progressives arguing for a moral economy in the abstract base their criticism on the immorality of the market economy and the meaninglessness and destructiveness of economic growth for its own sake. But the guiding theme for their moral economy is a neo-Gandhian Hinduism, in which "Indian (Hindu) spirituality" and the "limitation of needs" are praised. On these points Ambedkar would have thoroughly disagreed. Morality in economic life required, according to him, a firm rejection of the pseudo-morality of traditional Hinduism; it had to be grounded in the three revolutionary values of liberty, equality, and fraternity, and it presumed the overcoming of poverty through the development of human productive forces. Ambedkar sees these as (not Western but) universal ideals and as necessary for the welfare of the Bahujan Samaj.

Ambedkar makes his views clear in an early essay, a review of a book by Bertrand Russell. In contrast to the Gandhian notion of "limitation of needs," Ambedkar never accepted the equation of morality with suffering, poverty, asceticism, or renunciation of money and consumption.

> This time-honoured complaint of the moralists against "love of money" is only a part of their general complaint against the goods of the world and finds its justification in the economic circumstances which gave rise to this particular belief. . . . At a time when the whole world was living in a "pain economy" as did the ancient world and when the productivity of human labour was extremely low and when no efforts could augment its return, in short when the whole world was living in poverty, it is but natural that moralists should have preached the gospel of poverty and renunciation of worldly pleasures only because they were not to be had. (Ambedkar, 1979, vol. 1: 489)

Ambedkar's moral economy, then, was to be one of abundance and wealth accumulation. His rejection, in "Buddha or Karl Marx," of the Christian glorification of poverty is consistent with this. It seems at the end of his life he returned to his first insight: "The trouble . . . is not with property but with the unequal distribution of it" (Ambedkar, 1979, vol. 1: 491).

At a time when many environmentalists, once again, are preaching an antidevelopment ethic and urging a return to traditionalist practices, this basic philosophical outlook is important. Ambedkar would certainly have been aware of the problems of ecological destruction caused by unregulated overproduction, but he would even more certainly have seen the solution to this in a form of *sustainable development,* not a rejection of development as such. Ambedkar here shares with Marx a positive appraisal of economic development—the development of the forces of production and the potentials of wealth, choice, and freedom made possible by this. He has no inclination toward the ascetic limitation of needs and rejects what he calls a "pain economy." Thus Ambedkar's "moral economy," which is outlined in a very sketchy way in "Buddha or Karl Marx," is not contrasted either to a market economy or a planned economy as such but rather presents some alternatives that will make both market and state work for the good of the people. His moral economy has three basic elements: (1) the role of the state was to provide "protection" and to remove poverty; (2) the role of the market was to help in the production and accumulation of wealth by individual householders (modified by moral concerns); and (3) the role of community was to develop a voluntaristic egalitarian communism in the Bhikku Sangha.

Ambedkar's Economic Theory and Economic Reforms

One should not make too much of "Buddha or Karl Marx"; it provides at most a direction of economic thinking but by no means provides a fully developed economic theory. Would Ambedkar have opposed privatization or supported liberalization? Statements at this level remain to a large degree speculative. But it seems clear that a large part of his approach, finally, would have been pragmatic, looking for the most effective combination of state, market, and community roles; that he would have been clearly for the kind of globalization that would aid the Dalits and other sections of the poor in establishing their full place in a world heritage; and that he would have been concerned both with all-around economic growth and its impact on the poorest and most deprived sections of the community. He would clearly have been more wary of giving an overriding power to the state than many of those speaking in his name and referring only to his period of advocacy of "state socialism"—and though he would not deny the occasional need for state power to override property rights, he would see acquisition not as an evil but as part of a process of wealth creation and would look to voluntary sharing in a community of concern as the primary means of achieving equality.

Notes

An earlier version of this paper was published in *Fourth World* 4 (1), 1997.

1. At a seminar on the "Dalit Middle Class," Pune University, Department of Politics, 1994. See also his speech at the Vichar Vedh Sammelan in Nashik, December 1996, where he elaborated the distinction between "open economy," or *khule arthavyavastha,* and "free economy," or *mukt arthavyavastha:* the latter is the pure "free market" of ideologues; the former emphasizes a crucial role for the state, especially in regulation, social services, and infrastructure.

2. See Anand Teltumbde (1997) and Sukhdeo Thorat (1997). These were papers for a seminar on the "Impact of New Economic Policy on Dalits," organized by the Department of Sociology on 9–11 December 1996; the collection is to be published in a book edited by P. Jogdand.

3. See the articles in *Bahujan Sangharsh* by Nagesh Chaudhuri (1994), Divakar Bhoyar (1994), and Siddharth Kamble (1994).

4. Where not otherwise cited, references to Ambedkar's writings are to the volumes edited by Vasant Moon and published as *Dr. B. R. Ambedkar: Writings and Speeches*, Bombay: Government of Maharashtra.

5. In evaluating this issue today, it might be noted that salaries of organized-sector workers (both public and private) are three to five times as high as the "self-employed" in the unorganized sector. It might also be asked why the Indian policymakers (the nationalists of the 1920s) changed their position after independence to maintain a currency kept artificially high by world market standards: here the interests of the bureaucracy plus a new push for import-substitution industrialization built a group of industrialists who benefited from a high rupee and hence cheaper imports (reported in *The Times of India*, 14 February 1938).

References

Ambedkar, B. R. 1979. Babasaheb Ambedkar: Writings and Speeches. Vols. 1, 2, 13. Bombay: Government of Maharashtra, Education Dept.

Bhoyar, Divakar. 1994. "Dunkel, GATT and Bahujans," *Bahujan Sangharsh*, April 30.

Chaudhuri, Nagesh. 1994. "What Policy Should We Take Towards Dunkel?" *Bahujan Sangharsh*, April 30, Editorial.

Kamble, Siddharth. 1994. "What Is the Dunkel Draft?" *Bahujan Sangharsh*, April 30.

Moon, Vasant (compiler). 1990a. *Dr. B. R. Ambedkar: Writings and Speeches, Vol. 1: States and Minorities*. Bombay: Education Department, Government of Maharashtra.

———. 1990b. *Dr. B. R. Ambedkar: Writings and Speeches, Vol. 3: Buddha or Karl Marx*. Bombay: Education Department, Government of Maharashtra.

———. 1990c. *Dr. B. R. Ambedkar: Writings and Speeches, Vol. 6: The Problem of the Rupee and the Evolution of Provincial Finance in British India*. Bombay: Education Department, Government of Maharashtra.

Omvedt, Gail. 1997. "Dalits and Economic Policy: Contributions of Dr. B. R. Ambedkar," *Fourth World* 4 (1): 22–26.

Teltumbde, Anand. 1997. "Impact of New Economic Policy on Dalits in India." Occasional Paper Series 1. Pune: Department of Sociology, University of Pune.

Thorat, Sukhdeo. 1997. "New Economic Policy and Its Impact on Employment and Poverty of the Scheduled Castes." Occasional Paper Series 2. Pune: Department of Sociology, University of Pune.

10

Dalits and Rural Development

S. P. Punalekar

In this chapter I am concerned with the rural poor, including the Dalits, who symbolize both sociocultural and economic backwardness in the rural areas of western India, mainly Gujarat and Maharashtra. Here the notion of Dalits represents a larger social category and includes Scheduled Castes (SCs); Scheduled Tribes (STs), including nomadic tribes (*vicharati jati*); Other Backward Castes (OBCs); and minorities. They also include Dalit women, who suffer dual disadvantages, that is, being Dalits and being women. The burden of the argument is that rural development has generated processes and patterns that have tended to subordinate and marginalize the masses, including the Dalits (Brara, 1983; Breman, 1994). I address two questions: (1) What are these subordinating processes and patterns? and (2) What are the perceptions and experiences of the masses, and how do they cope with emerging crises and challenges?

In answering the first question, I try to note and discuss the conditions of the rural poor at the ground level. These processes, I believe, have their roots in the macro developments in the spheres of policy and delivery packages (Adelman, 1975; Frankel, 1978; Haque and Mehta, 1977). These decisions are taken at a distance farthest from the village, *taluka,* or district. Thus, when the Dalits and other poverty-stricken groups come face to face with this "development," the question before them is whether to take it or leave it. There is hardly any third option. But how do they perceive and interpret these changes occurring around them? Do they mutely accept the message of the developers, without searching for rejoinders? This constitutes my second question, and I try to explore this on the basis of my field experience in the region.

Development and Dalit Masses

In this section, I discuss briefly the developments in two states in western India, namely Maharashtra and Gujarat, and argue the nature of contradictions and paradoxes underlying development. For this I utilize my own fieldwork experiences in both states in 1985–1986 and other documentary evidence, including literary sources such as autobiographical narratives of the Dalits and other downtrodden men and women (Punalekar, 1985b, 1986, 1988). In an empirical survey, I covered eight villages; four from Maharashtra and four from Gujarat. The Maharashtra villages (MVs) are Kasbe Digraj and Tung from Miraj *taluka* of Sangli district and Bargaon Nandur and Digras from Rahuri *taluka* of Ahmednagar district. The Gujarat villages (GVs) are Vankaner and Mota from Bardoli *taluka* of Surat district and Narsanda and Pij from Anand *taluka* of Kheda district.

All four districts were involved in varying degrees in contributing to and shaping the social fabric of this region. Ideas of independence from foreign rule, social reform, and moral uprightness of the individuals were quite popular and pronounced in this region. Protest against dominance and misrule was not an alien experience to the people of these districts (Omvedt, 1976; Hardiman, 1981). Political contacts and experiences of the nationalist workers and the freedom fighters helped many of them later, on the eve of independence, to consolidate their position in the Congress Party, the only party that had a broad mass base. The rich and vocal sections of the peasantry dominated such rural institutions as Gram Panchayat, cooperative societies, and development banks, albeit with the support of the lower ranks of peasantry (Jugale, 1987).

The more influential and powerful the leader in the ruling party hierarchy, the more that person's village and the surrounding area benefited in terms of development schemes. Villages such as Kasbe Digraj of Sangli district and Bargaon Nandur of Ahmednagar district provide a vivid testimony to this process. Facilities such as roads, electricity, banks, post offices, telephones, and state transport are more developed in these politically advanced and influential areas. All eight villages covered in this study share certain common developmental attributes. All these villages have extensive irrigation facilities. They receive water through canals, tubewells, rivers, or rivulets. Out of a total land base of more than 20,233 acres in eight villages, 9,641 acres (48 percent) are under canal irrigation. This has helped to increase agricultural production. Cash crops such as sugarcane and tobacco are now grown on an extensive scale. In recent years, lemon and grape orchards have also been planted. A network of local and regional markets has enabled the farmers to sell their produce at favorable prices.

In addition to these regulated marketing outlets, there are cooperatives of sugar and milk producers in these villages, which are vertically linked to *taluka* and district-level organizations. These institutions have provided opportunities for village elites to gain political positions and influence. There are well-developed multipurpose cooperative societies in all four

Maharashtra villages we surveyed. They are locally known as VIKAS agencies, an abbreviation for Vividh Karyakari Sahakari Mandal (Multipurpose Cooperative Society). Annual transactions of these VIKAS agencies run into several lakhs of rupees. They distribute annual gifts to their members in the form of cash certificates, utensils, or other household utility items from a surplus generated in the cooperative venture.

Land distribution is quite skewed. The advantage of cooperatives and the allied network has largely been secured by the upper and middle strata (UMS) of the peasantry. The UMS are known as the progressive farmers. In local parlance, they are referred to as "Dhanik" (rich), "Pragatishil" (progressive), and "Mota Khedut" (big farmer). Most of the developments relating to crop pattern, water management, agricultural technology, credit distribution, and marketing have taken place in the last fifteen to twenty years. Since the mid-1970s, this development has intensified, providing sharp contrasts between the rich and the poor in MVs and GVs. Rising productivity in agriculture and its commercialization has increased the net cash inflow in these villages. There is a perceptible rise in the demand for consumer goods and services, especially from among the upper and middle strata. The latter group seem to be keenly imitating the lifestyle of their urban counterparts residing in the nearby towns like Bardoli, Surat, Anand, and Vallabh Vidyanagar (in Gujarat) and Sangli, Miraj, Kolhapur, Ahmednagar, and Rahuri (in Maharashtra) (Breman, 1974; Punalekar, 1980; Shah, 1991).

In Kasbe Digraj and Tung together, between 2,000 and 3,000 migrant laborers live in the tents on village fields. These laborers have migrated from drought-prone regions, namely from the districts of Beed, Osmanabad, and Latur in Marathwada. There are some from the neighboring districts of Karnataka state also. This number swells when the sugarcane-cutting season reaches a peak. Private doctors, numbering about ten in this village, make a good deal of money. Canal irrigation was introduced in these villages some fifteen or twenty years ago and has brought rapid prosperity to many farming households in this region. However, the ratio of cultivable land to grassland is quite low. Bargaon Nandur and Digras villages have no worthwhile grassland at all. This does cause a great deal of hardship to the poorer households in obtaining fodder for their cattle.

In the study region, the rural poor can be classified into two groups, the locals and the outsiders or migrants. The locals are the longtime residents or natives of Kasbe Digraj and Tung from Miraj *taluka* of Sangli district. The outsiders/migrants are those who have migrated to these villages in recent times, mostly during the last ten to fifteen years. There are two further subgroups among the migrants. These are the early migrants, now settled, that is, those who have some permanent dwelling in a new village and have regular occupational relations with the local farming households; and the seasonal migrants, that is, those who move in and out of the villages at regular intervals in correspondence with the agricultural season (mostly staying for six to eight months between October and June).

The Hindus are in overwhelming majority among the local poor households (91 percent). The Muslim households constitute about 8 percent. The rural poor are predominantly from the lower castes, comprising the artisan or service castes, the Scheduled Castes, and the Scheduled Tribes, including the nomadic tribes. Over 92 percent of local poor households are landless. Some 8 percent have agricultural holdings of less than 1 acre. The principal occupation of the head of the household is agricultural labor. Their other occupational activities are nonagricultural, manual labor; service in the sugar factory or at a public works project; artisan work; or petty trade. Most of them are daily-wage laborers. They lack security of employment (Breman, 1985; Joshi, 1996; Katre, 1987). Only a handful of them have jobs in relatively better-paid occupation like loaders and unloaders in a sugar factory or tractor drivers or as peons in a cooperative society. They get monthly wages with paid leave and holidays. They enjoy some status and respectability because they are a little more educated and earn monthly wages or salary. This is particularly evident in Kasbe Digraj and Tung, both in Miraj *taluka* (Maharashtra), and Vankaner, in Bardoli *taluka* (Gujarat).

Often the boys and girls of ten to twelve years of age assist their parents in petty trade and even in agricultural labor. An early engagement of younger children in the above-mentioned activities serves a definite purpose for the poor households. For the families living below the poverty line, education is "expensive," though formally free. Educational data amply reveal this situation. Nearly half of the respondents (heads of households) are totally illiterate, some 9 percent have reached the 11th standard, and even fewer have reached an even higher level of education.

Out of 411 households, thirty-two (8 percent) have less than 1 acre of land. The rest are landless. Out of these, twenty-four households cultivate their land. Of these twenty-four cultivating households, twenty-one have irrigation facilities. The major source of irrigation is river water. Only five out of thirty-two landowning farmers have access to canal irrigation facilities, despite the fact that all eight villages are well endowed with irrigation resources. A majority of the local poor households are without electricity (64 percent), though all the eight villages are electrified. Also, a majority get drinking water from the water taps owned by others (32 percent) or from the public well (37 percent). Only 16 percent of the households have their own water taps. It was alarming to note that nearly half of the local poor households experience starvation on some days during the year. Some forty-two households (thirteen from Gujarat and twenty-nine from Maharashtra), that is, 10 percent, have to face starvation for more than thirty days during the year, despite the fact the some get "cooked food" from their farmer-employers on various occasions. Pardhis who are nomadic tribals collect leftover food on marriage occasions in the well-off families. Yet, starvation stalks them.

All the study villages have primary health centers (PHCs). These are wholly government-run institutions. Even then, more than two-thirds of the local poor households go to private doctors for their medical treatment (276 out of 411 households). Experience suggests that the PHCs and other such public health systems are not yet widely utilized by the local poor households despite the fact that over one-fourth of them faced acute difficulties in health matters and need help and assistance. A majority of them (59 percent) still do not utilize the PHCs or hospitals for the deliveries of babies. Childbirth takes place at home at the hands of the local *dai* or midwife, who is experienced but "untrained." Modern facilities, including health systems, are still miles away both socially and culturally for these households.

Why do the public health institutions remain unutilized by the marginal sections of rural society? This question underlying the interface between the poor and health institutions is indeed a complex one and needs deeper investigations to get at the circumstances behind inaccessibility. Dominant reasons seem to be poor facility structures at these PHCs as well as the apathy and indifference of the medical and paramedical staff toward the members of poor households.

Divisions Between Local and Migrant Labor

Since the introduction of cash crops and, especially, sugarcane production, there has been a considerable influx of migrant labor in this region from drought-prone regions like Dharampur, Dangs, Songadh, Uchchal, and Nizar in Gujarat state and Beed, Latur, Osmanabad, Parabhani, Sholapur, Bijapur, and Parner in Maharashtra state. As mentioned earlier, some neighboring drought-prone *talukas* of Karnataka state also contribute to the supply of migrant labor to neighboring irrigated villages in Maharashtra. Acute recurrent drought conditions compel many households to move out of their villages with cart, cattle, and children. They seek employment through the contractors for sugarcane cutting or as daily-wage earners on public works. In the latter, they join individually in a gang that works on road, nallah, or dam-building activities. Some join the labor cooperative societies, which are cooperative in name only. As regards distance between the native place of the migrants and the villages where they work, it varies from 35–40 kilometers (km) to more than 250 km. Sugarcane cutters (SCCs) constitute a sizable section of this migrant poor. The SCCs are mostly drawn from the arid region adjoining the lush, green region typical of the study villages but also come from far-off places.

The situation among the sugarcane cutters is worth examining (Katre, 1987; Breman, 1978). As mentioned earlier, the SCCs comprise more than 90 percent of the migrant labor in this region. In Sangli district alone, some 20,000–30,000 SCCs are employed during the crop-cutting season from October to May. Rahuri, Kopargaon, and Srirampur *talukas,* comprising a sugar belt in Ahmednagar district, employ more than 40,000 sugarcane laborers. According to Jan Breman, some 50,000 men, women, and children from Maharashtra work in the sugarcane fields of southern Gujarat, especially in the Chalthan, Palsana, and Bardoli areas. He further writes:

> But what points them out even more definitely as outsiders is the way they live and work, bonded together. The cane cutters are put up in temporary camps close to the field in which they are working. The camps can be seen from the road-rows of little makeshift huts, consisting of a couple of mats which are held aloft with a few sticks. These camps are regularly shifted and the seasonal labour force thus works its way throughout the area to be harvested always, though, separated and apart from the village population. (Breman, 1978: 1317)

Employing migrant labor for sugarcane harvesting operations has been a permanent feature of this region, one that seems to be beneficial to sugar factory management (SFM). The SFM relies on the contractors, or labor brokers called *mukadams* in local parlance. Breman has clearly established that labor recruitment through the *mukadams* is a clever move by the sugar factory management.

> The Mukadam system results in the seasonal migration taking place in a way which is controlled and which assures the sugar factories of a supply of the required number of the labourers at the right time for the least cost and without they themselves having to carry the risks attaching to the process. In short, it is a cheap, reliable, efficient and workable system for making use of temporary labour on a grand scale. (Breman, 1978: 1326)

These migrant laborers are "strangers," "outsiders" to the village people. No one gives them cash loans. Even local private doctors do not give them medicine, if they do not have cash money. "They are here in this village for 10–15 days. Soon they will go to other 'Fads' [canefields]. How can we trust them?" said one doctor in Sangli district. So when the question of medical treatment arises, the SCCs go to local doctors along with their contractors. The contractors pay or promise to pay the doctor. Even shopkeepers in the village give grains on credit to the SCCs only after the contractor puts in a word. In some cases, the contractors settle their accounts with the doctors, shopkeepers, and even liquor shop vendors and later deduct the money from the wages of the SCCs. "We are mostly cheated in these transactions," one laborer said with a deep sense of anguish.

The SCC settlements are known as *bastis*. These *bastis* have no electricity, water supply, or even approach roads. The SCC families have to face scarcities in a variety of things, including foodgrains and firewood. The local laborers also do not always view the SCCs in a favorable light. They consider them outsiders intruding into their work and livelihood chances. The *bastis* of the migrant laborers are usually on the roadside or on the cleared sugarcane fields. Their contacts with local village institutions are fleeting, to say the least. Some SCC families bring their children along with them because no one is left at home to look after them. These children spend their time in tending cattle, playing, or assisting their parents. They do not attend village schools. Neither the village elders nor the schoolteachers are bothered about nonparticipation of migrants' children in school education.

Canal irrigation was introduced in the study villages some fifteen or twenty years ago, and it has brought rapid prosperity to many farming households. However, the ratio of cultivable land to grassland is quite low and declining year after year. Bargaon Nandur and Digras have no worthwhile grassland at all. This caused a great deal of hardship to poorer households in obtaining fodder for their cattle. It is clear from the evidence that agricultural modernization has not brought any noticeable relief to them. In all spheres such as health, housing, and education, there appears to be little advancement in the conditions of the agricultural laborers, the lowest strata of rural society in Maharashtra and Gujarat (Desai, 1987; Jain, 1985; Lobo, 1993).

There have been numerous attempts to organize laborers, but so far all mobilization efforts have achieved little success. The state, through its various programmatic interventions, is attempting to provide some relief to this class. There are a variety of developmental schemes aimed at improving the lot of the landless and poor peasantry. And yet, these schemes have very little impact on their living conditions. The most urgent and immediate question before them is survival on a day-to-day basis. They are in constant search of strategies of survival at the individual or household level. For instance, in some households the labor input is apportioned so that at least there will be a minimum living for each. Use of child labor at home or in the field; use of female labor for a wide range of duties (from caring for one's own household to domestic service in the landowner's household); the keeping of goats, sheep, and fowl at home; rearing of the sick calf of the Dhaniama at home; and seasonal migration to nearby villages exemplify some typical ways that the rural poor cope with problems of survival.

Why do the landless laborers remain the most neglected section of rural society? Why do they not come together and launch a collective struggle? These questions are significant, and to answer them, we need to closely examine the social, economic, and cultural contexts of their life, including their work environment (Kurien, 1978; Punalekar, 1994). It is becoming increasingly clear that they essentially constitute a disaggregated mass that is fragmented into several caste groups with further divisions into religious sects and other primordial loyalties. There are no durable signs of their unity across class lines (Breman, 1978; P. M. Patel, 1981). They do not rise as a single, unified force in solidarity, and hence their demands do not get articulated with sufficient vigor and effectiveness. Also, there are occasions of mutual mistrust and misconceptions among the local and migrant workers about one another. Especially in seasonal, short-term employment sectors like sugarcane cutting, mining, brick kilns, construction, or salt-pan work, such ill will surfaces. There are free-floating myths about the migrant labor in the minds of local villagers, including the local landless laborers. The latter do not generally view the migrant labor in a positive way.

The local poor believe that the migrant laborers are better off economically: "They come from better off economic backgrounds; their staying power in the labour market is superior. They are cunning, shrewd and selfish. They are always for their own monetary gains and least concerned with the woes and discomforts of others working with them." Such myths prevail, yet conditions at their native villages are not any better (Breman, 1985; Patel and Desai, 1992). Most of them barely manage to pull through on the earnings they have gained while on migration. But even then, the local laborers are not able to understand the real situation of the migrant laborers. Such notions or myths prevail among the local laborers and drive a wedge between the migrant labor and local labor. How these myths are sustained is a question for a separate inquiry. But I learned from field experiences that some unscrupulous elements like local contractors, Sarpanchs, and sugar factory management officials concoct such stories and float these among the local population. On cannot also rule out the role of some disgruntled local laborers in spreading such myths.

The poor get divided, first in mutual perceptions and then in practice. The social and cultural distance between the two groups increases, which further reduces the chance of their coming together and mobilizing themselves as a united class. Seasonality of employment, separate lives in the camps (on fields or *gaothan/gauchar* lands), their concentration in a particular activity where there is hardly any chance to meet the local poor, and above all, the deliberate efforts of the contractors, *mukadams,* and others from the employers' class are the known factors that are responsible for isolating and distancing the migrant laborers from the local laborers.

Insecurities built into the work process also discourage the migrant laborers from interactions with the local or native laborers.

I observed that a small section of the cane cutters did speak well about their contractors. They felt a sense of gratitude toward them for providing them a chance to work and earn their livelihood. This was a small section, mostly comprising older people and those without any formal educational background. But the majority spoke negatively about their *mukadams* or contractors in a hush-hush voice. Similar mixed reactions were visible when the SCCs talked about their co-workers, local farmers and laborers, and the village community at large. A few older people wisely chose to remain silent on these issues, but there were quite a few young, educated SCCs who did not wish to conceal their anger and fury. They were agitated about their own forced migration, inhuman working conditions, low wages, and insecurities of all kinds. "We are living like our cattle; dumb and dependent," said a laborer from Tasgaon *taluka*. "These sugar factories are built on our sweat and blood. These sugar barons prosper and we languish year after year. This is a miserable life indeed," added another young migrant laborer from Valve *taluka*.

Thus, there were clear signs of protest and militancy (Katre, 1987; Breman, 1978, 1994), especially among the younger generation from the SCC households, who were unwilling to submit to the highhandedness of the farmers and the contractors. Tensions in work, life, and relationships were getting projected into the domestic front also. There were instances of conflict between husband and wife, father and son on petty matters as well as physical fights. All this was due to insecurity and instability built into the very mode of their migratory existence.

It is also evident that the situation of the former Untouchable castes has shown only marginal change in terms of social and cultural relations and behavior of the village community. Even the members of the different Scheduled Castes (Mahars, Mangs, Chamars, Dhors, Vankars, Rohits, Meghwals, Bhangis, and so on) were not united among themselves socially and culturally. They believed in and upheld their separate identity based on social and occupational rankings. This fact of separation and disunity among the Scheduled Castes themselves and between them and other lower Untouchable castes (Nhavi, Luhar, Suthar, and Vanjari) demands deeper sociological attention. Though poverty was a common factor enveloping all or most of them and subjecting them to equally brutalizing experiences, they were slow to learn the ways of closing their ranks and uniting. As the present situation stands, both in Maharashtra and Gujarat, they seem to lack a sense of social solidarity and unity of purpose and exhibit differential social consciousnesses.

Another set of questions needs to be directed toward the ground-level manifestations among the rural poor: Why do the rural poor, including women, hesitate to join development activities or express doubts about the outcome of such projects? Why do they desist from displaying a forward-looking, future-oriented outlook? Why are they so much tied to the questions of mundane, day-to-day living?

To answer such questions, we must recognize the experience and the perceptions of the rural poor. Their views matter a great deal in formulating strategies to initiate development that meets their needs. Their doubts and fears, their anxieties and agitation are rooted in their own past encounters and interaction with local structures of power, authority, and control. This can easily be discovered through the reactions of the sugarcane cutters to prevailing conditions.

Scheduled Tribes

I now focus my attention on the Scheduled Tribes, which constitute more than 14 percent of Gujarat's and 7 percent of Maharashtra's population and include Bhils, Varlis, Thakurs, Dublas, Dhodias, Katkaris, and Chodhras. Other significant tribal groups are Gamits, Nayakas, Tadvis, and Dhankas. An overwhelming majority of them live in rural areas, mostly in hills and forests. During the last 150 years, there have been substantial changes in the ecology and landscape of their habitat. Thanks to state planning and development efforts, tribals living in the command area or in villages having developed infrastructure are relatively better off. A few among them are getting closer to the mainstream peasant communities such as Marathas of Maharashtra and Patidars of Gujarat. Education has increased among some tribal groups like Dhodias, Chodhras, Gamits, and Nayakas in southern Gujarat. Also, in Maharashtra, there has been a rise in the educational level of Thakurs and Mahadev Kolis (Shah and Chaturvedi, 1983; Shah and Patel, 1984; Punalekar, 1985a, 1985b).

The benefits of development, including education, have reached a small segment of this community. Only a few tribal households have advanced economically and socially. They have acquired a somewhat privileged position in their own social milieu and outside. A few of them have acquired a place in the mainstream political parties as well, giving them an opportunity to enjoy some political power. They are the new elites whose major attention is on improving their own socioeconomic and political profile. Evidence suggests that they have achieved some measure of success in the present social system. However, the common tribals who constitute a majority and belong to the lower economic strata are outside the vortex of this development (Desai and Choudhary, 1977; Punalekar, 1996).

We must note that tribal societies were relatively homogeneous some decades ago. Now they are getting internally differentiated and stratified. There is a distinct upper strata of the literate and educated tribals (Bose, 1981; Punalekar, 1985b; Shah and Patel, 1984). They come from the landowning groups with better access to input markets including seeds, fertilizers, credit, and labor. Their closer acquaintance with (as well as membership in) other resource structures, including cooperatives, has also helped them to strengthen their position. Among them, the households that have a larger share of development and prosperity in tribal regions belong largely to Dhodia, Kokna, Chodhra, Gamit, and Mahadeo Kolis. Other groups such as Varlis, Dubias, Rathwas, or Katkaris are socially and economically far behind. These backward groups live in relatively underdeveloped and sometimes inaccessible areas. Their struggle for existence is still very difficult and sometimes grim. Their experience with outsiders (be they contractors, traders, moneylenders, or petty officials) is not altogether happy.

They are exploited in exchange and credit markets. They feel frustrated and agitated. This is evident in the transactions that take place in the *hats* or *hatwadas* (i.e., weekly markets). And as mentioned earlier, whenever a "development" project is launched in their territory, they become the first victim. Their ecological milieu is severely disturbed and their forest resources depleted. Their social and cultural relations are dislocated (Joshi, 1987; Mankodi and Gangopodhyay, 1983; Arjun Patel, 1994). In some cases, the tribals become "oustees," meaning those who have been displaced, and are forced to shift to other places and community milieus where it takes them years to readjust and resettle.

The effects of dislocation on tribal communities are not known (for example, Koyana, Likai, Jaikwadi, and other smaller dams in Maharashtra and Gujarat). The emergence of Naxalites and similar militant outfits among the tribals is largely rooted in these exploitative relations, which tend to destabilize their society, economy, and culture (Lobo, 1992; Punalekar, 1996; Joshi, 1996). The answer is not to persecute Naxalites or other militants who are spearheading the movement, but to urgently address and resolve the basic socioeconomic issues confronting the tribal masses.

In recent years, there has emerged a distinct group from among the tribals of Maharashtra and Gujarat—seasonal migrants. They live away from their villages and families for over six months every year. In Maharashtra, this trend is visible since the severe droughts in the state in the early 1970s. In Gujarat also, such migration has become a regular feature since the mid-1970s. Not only do these tribals migrate to irrigated villages for agricultural labor, but they have begun to migrate to towns and cities in search of their livelihood. In major towns and cities of Gujarat, the large congregation of such tribal migrant labor is seen in the city squares, vegetable market yards, railway stations, and goods transport depots. In

Gujarat these markets are known as *chakla* market, and the persons who assemble there to sell their labor are known as *chakla* workers. In fact, their labor share in urban services like loading, unloading, grass-cutting, and construction of roads and buildings is considerable. This is a distinctly postindependence phenomenon.

Bhils of Dhulia district work as casual laborers in Surat City, and Bhils of Panchmahals are seen in the urban labor markets at Ahmedabad, Anand, Nadiad, Baroda, and Bharuch. Many of them migrate with their families. Obviously, their children's education suffers. But the question of survival precedes the question of education and other pursuits. What are their conditions of living in the urban areas? Do they get fair wages for their output? Does the settled urban population help them in coping with the problem of housing, health, water, and other social and cultural amenities? These and related questions need to be explored.

Denotified Tribes

Another important social group is the nomadic, or denotified, tribes, some of whom were labeled as criminals during the British regime. Their number is considerable, both in Maharashtra and Gujarat, and includes the Berad, Kaikadi, Kanjar Bhat, Banjara, Vadar, Vaghari, Gosavi, Joshi, Kolhati, Bhoi, and Raval. In a changing socioeconomic order, their problems of survival are becoming increasingly acute. Their traditional skills of trade, earth digging, entertainment, and repair services, do not enable them to compete with modern technology and the service sector. The basis of their social relations with traditional clients is also getting eroded due to "new" forces of production. Until recently, there was no awakening among them. Even now, all nomadic groups have not come together. Also, perceptions of the common people and legal authorities have not sufficiently altered. To cite just one example, Paradhis of Maharashtra are still suspect in the eyes of the police *patil* and village headman. Vaghris and Chharas of Gujarat are still perceived as "unreliable and untrustworthy," as are Kaikadis of Maharashtra, who suffer severe humiliation and indignities.

Laxman Mane, himself a Kaikadi, did a great service to the cause of his community by writing an autobiography, *Upra* (1992). The literate world outside could then know the woes and travails of the nomadic group. This also tells us how effectively a sociological account can be written by a literate and sensitive member of an oppressed community. *Upra* is a reflection on the living conditions of nomadic tribals. So are the autobiographical novels *Balut* by Daya Pawar, *Athavaniche Pakshi* by Sonkamble, *Taral Antaral* by Shankarrao Kharat, *Katyavarchi Pot* by Uttam Bandu Tupe, and *Majhya Jalmachi Chittarkathe* by Shantabai Kamle. They depict the lives of ordinary men and women from lower social groups. Literature of this kind provides vital sociological insights into the agonies and aspirations of marginal groups and their wounded consciousness (Punalekar, 1994).

The SCs, STs, nomads, and others are now beginning to find their "voice" and insist on rigorous implementation of constitutional safeguards, protective schemes, educational assistance, legal support, and more vigorous monitoring of the existing schemes. Outside intervention, including leadership, can achieve but little in terms of political mobilization. Internal awakening of the community itself can achieve a great deal, once they begin to reflect on their own conditions in the light of their relations and experiences with other relatively better-off, settled sections of the society.

Conclusion

This chapter has outlined the rural situation in Maharashtra and Gujarat, the premier industrializing, fast-developing states in the Indian Union. Signs of growth and economic development are too clear to miss. But this growth is lopsided, creating in its wake a series of contradictions and paradoxes, which give rise to another significant set of questions, namely those relating to social justice.

Rural development as evidenced in the countryside has bifurcated and broken the region in two parts; one is better endowed with externalities of irrigation facilities and developed infrastructure in input markets. It is richer in terms of production levels and productivity, buttressed further by a vigorous network of cooperatives and other institutions. A larger share of state resources seem to be concentrated in this part of the region. Political leadership at the state level is more attentive to demands from this area, so bureaucrats seem to concentrate on these pockets.

On the other end of the spectrum are the villages in the underdeveloped region. They are dry, unirrigated, and facing recurring drought and famine. People there are faced with the perennial question of survival and search for dependable means of livelihood. They have lands but no means to irrigate them with any certainty. Consequently, they have to migrate and join a swelling army of casual laborers in the irrigated fields in their own district or outside. This migration stream from the arid villages to green villages is becoming a permanent feature in the rural economy of both Maharashtra and Gujarat.

This migration is seasonal for some and, as years pass by, becomes a step in a permanent severing of their social and cultural linkages with their native village. They then live in the far-off host villages or in the town or city. I have shown that their conditions of living are indeed critical, whether they live in the open fields or in the city slums. Also, their conditions of work are poor, leaving them no space for creative, productive enterprise. Both their work and domestic life are full of tensions and unease, often leading to violence or self-abuse.

The question of survival obliterates all chances of meaningful participation in creative, constructive activities. As migrants, they are denied help and support in the host environment. Even the local poor families do not confide in or trust them. Rather, they are hostile and indifferent to the migrant families. Many myths supporting such chasms are prevalent in these rural areas, which further dim the prospects of their unity or solidarity. Alienated from the bonds of sympathy from the local populations, the migrant poor are further pushed into the network of their contractors or *mukadams*, who often take maximum advantage of such critical situations. Thus, the migrant laborers are subject to endless miseries and hardship. Women too suffer a great deal. They have to work along with the men and share the family support burden amid greater exploitation and abuse. The health and education of children suffer. They cannot aspire for a settled, secure, and steady life for themselves. Denial of education restricts their scope for social mobility.

The situation of the local, native poor is also similar to that of the migrants, but they have local roots and linkages. Their caste and other primordial loyalties enable them to survive a little better, and their bargaining capacity is a bit higher. But these assets do not always work. If they are too curt or militant, they are shown their place by their employers, including the rich village peasants. The latter then invite and encourage migrant laborers and exclude the local labor. Long spells of unemployment force the local poor to fall in line and obey the dictates of their employers without any protest or appeal.

When survival is at stake, the basic strength or capacity of the individual and his or her family is undermined. A larger proportion of their time and energy is then devoted to somehow meeting the basic needs of shelter, food, and health. Questions of education and other cultural pursuits then become a last priority, forcing them to opt out of participation in more creative, meaningful avenues of life. This condition is a starting point in the denial of justice to them in their desire for the basic rights of shelter, food, a healthy life, and education.

How can they be brought into the main arena, where they can play their role as citizens endowed with basic human rights? How can they be empowered to successfully win this battle of becoming equal citizens with guarantees of a stable residence, family life, and full participation in the region's social and cultural institutions? These are basic and critical questions, on the resolution of which rests the success of the efforts at social emancipation of marginalized sections of society (Kurien, 1978).

Looking at the micro level, all these segments, such as SCs, STs, nomadic groups, minorities, and women, have a special social location in the system, with all its niceties and complexities. No one can deny this. But micro realities do not exist in a vacuum or in isolation. They are also the products of larger externalities like the market, which is now globalizing and also deregulating itself. They seemingly struggle harder and harder to stay at the present subsistence level in a free, competitive economy. How can they compete and come out ahead, when they are lacking settled conditions of living and working, without a reasonable level of education, shorn of social and political contacts and networks?

In this changing situation, they need more—and not less—support and protection from the state. They need more stringent application of protective legislation; more and more help and guidance from the labor unions and their leadership. Above all, there is need for more and better "politicization" of this class of the underprivileged to fight against the onslaught of liberalization if it cuts into their needs for survival and growth. That means the coming together of similarly placed individuals and groups (be they SCs, STs, women) to take a more comprehensive view of their immediate future. Issues of development and social justice are not merely matters of state-sponsored schemes or programs; they essentially constitute a site of struggle of relations of equal power. These political issues hence need political answers.

References

Adelman, Irma. 1975. "Growth, Income Distribution and Equity-Oriented Development Strategies," *World Development* 3 (2–3): 283–298.
Bose, Pradip Kumar. 1981. "Stratification Among Tribals in Gujarat," *Economic and Political Weekly* 16 (6), 7 February: 214–216.
Brara, J. S. 1983. *The Political Economy of Rural Development: Strategies for Poverty Alleviation.* New Delhi: Allied Publishers, p. 20.
Breman, Jan. 1974. *Patronage and Exploitation: Changing Agrarian Relations in South Gujarat, India.* London: University of California Press.
———. 1978. "Seasonal Migration and Cooperative Capitalism: Crushing of Cane and Labour by Sugar Factories of Bardoli," *Economic and Political Weekly* 13 (31, 32, and 33), special number: 1317.
———. 1985. *Of Peasants, Migrants and Paupers: Rural Labour Circulation and Capitalist Production in West India.* Bombay: Oxford University Press.
———. 1994. *Labour Nomads in South Gujarat.* I. P. Desai Memorial Lecture. Surat: Centre for Social Studies.
Desai, A. R. 1987. *Rural Development and Human Rights of Agrarian Poor in Independent India.* I. P. Desai Memorial Lecture Series. Surat: Centre for Social Studies.
Desai, I. P., and Banwarilal Choudhary. 1977. *History of Rural Development in Modern India.* Vol. 2. New Delhi: Impex India.
Frankel, F. R. 1978. *India's Political Economy, 1947–77.* Princeton: Princeton University Press.

Haque, V., and Niranjan Mehta et al. 1977. "Towards a Theory of Rural Development," *Development Dialogue* 2: 11–137.
Hardiman, David. 1981. *Peasant Nationalists of Gujarat: Kheda District 1917–1934*. Delhi: Oxford University Press.
Jain, L. C. 1985. *Grass Without Roots: Rural Development Under Government Auspices*. New Delhi: Sage Publications, p. 14.
Joshi, Vidyut. 1987. *Submerging Villages: Problems and Prospects*. Delhi: Ajanta International.
———. 1996. "Adivasi Samashyanu Swarup." Mimeograph.
Jugale, V. B. 1987. "Role and Perspective and Sugar Cooperatives in Rural Development and Poverty Alleviation," in seminar proceedings on "Rural Development and Rural Poor." Surat: Centre for Social Studies.
Katre, M. M. 1987. "Maharashtra Sherdi Kamdarono Sangharsh," *Setu Patrika* (Gujarati) 1 (5), September: 27–32.
Kurien, C. T. 1978. *Poverty, Planning and Social Transformation*. Bombay: Allied Publishers.
Lobo, Lancy. 1992. "Ethnocide and Pauperisation of Oustees of Large Dams," *New Quest* 92, March–April: 85–96.
———. 1993. *An Assessment of Integrated Tribal Development Programme in Songadh, 1980–90*. Surat: Centre for Social Studies.
Mane, Laxman. 1992. *Upra*. Sangli: Kaikadi Welfare Trust.
Mankodi, Kashyap, and Tanushri Gangopodhyay. 1983. *Rehabilitation: The Ecological and Economic Costs*. Surat: Centre for Social Studies.
Omvedt, Gail. 1976. *Cultural Revolt in a Colonial Society: The Non-Brahmin Movement in Western India, 1873–1930*. Pune: Scientific Socialist Education Trust.
Patel, Arjun. 1994. "Social and Cultural Implications of Displacement: A Case of SSP," paper presented in a seminar on "Development, Displacement and Rehabilitation." Centre for Social Studies, Surat, May 11–13.
Patel, Arjun, and Kiran Desai. 1992. *Gramin Gujartma Shram Sthalantar*. Surat: Centre for Social Studies.
Patel, P. M. 1981. "Impact of Irrigation on Power Relationship in a Village: A Case of Tundi," in seminar proceedings on "Political Economy of Rehabilitation." Surat, Centre for Social Studies, 23–24 December.
Punalekar, S. P. 1980. "Descriptive Study of Dhodias of Surat City" (Ph.D. diss.). Surat: South Gujarat University.
———. 1985a. "Growth, Inequality and Tensions: A Case Study of Sangli District in Maharashtra," in seminar proceedings on "Rural Development and Rural Poor." Surat: Centre for Social Studies, February.
———. 1985b. "Social Stratification and Educational Inequalities: A Case Study of Tribals from Maharashtra, Gujarat and Rajasthan," in Ghanshyam Shah (ed.), *Tribal Education in Gujarat*. Delhi: Ajanta Books International.
———. 1986. *Rural Poor in Western India: A Case Study*. Surat: Centre for Social Studies, December.
———. 1988. "Rural Poor in Western India: A Case Study," in I. P. Getubig and A. J. Ledesma (eds.), *Voices from the Culture of Silence: The Most Disadvantaged Groups in Asian Agriculture*. Kuala Lumpur: Asian and Pacific Development Centre.
———. 1994. "On Demystification of Methodology in Social Sciences," *Indian Journal of Social Sciences* 7 (2): 28–36.
———. 1996. *Tribal Society and Social-Legal Interventions*. Surat: Centre for Social Studies.

Shah, Ghanshyam. 1991. *Choudhary Adivasio: Gaikale ane Aje.* Surat: Centre for Social Studies.
Shah, Ghanshyam, and H. R. Chaturvedi. 1983. *Gandhian Approach to Rural Development: The Valod Experiment.* Delhi: Ajanta Publications.
Shah, Ghanshyam, and Arjun Patel. 1984. *Economic Differentiations and Tribal Identity.* Delhi: Ajanta Publications.

The Contributors

Timothy Fitzgerald graduated from King's College, London, and the London School of Economics. He has been to India three times to research Ambedkar Buddhism. He has lived in Japan for ten years, where he teaches at Aichi Gakuin University near Nagoya.

Mahesh Gavaskar is an assistant editor at *Economic and Political Weekly* (Mumbai). He is doing research on the works of Jotirao Phule and B. R. Ambedkar. He has published articles on culture and contemporary politics in *EPW, Mainstream, Manushi,* and *Humanscape* and also writes for Marathi newspapers and magazines.

Gopal Guru is professor of politics and public administration at the University of Pune. His area of specialization is contemporary social movements in India with special reference to Dalits in Maharashtra.

S. M. Michael is a lecturer in sociology at the University of Mumbai. He is also the honorary director of the Institute of Indian Culture, Mumbai. He has studied the Ganapathi cult in India and has also done studies on culture and urbanization.

B. L. Mungekar is professor of industrial economics at the University of Mumbai. He has worked for two years as a member of the Task Force on Terms of Trade, government of India. His main publication is *The Political Economy of Terms of Trade* (Bombay: Himalaya Publishing House, 1992).

Gail Omvedt is professor of sociology at the University of Pune. She is a scholar-activist working with new social movements, especially women's groups and farmers' organizations. Her academic writings include several books and articles on class, caste, and gender issues, most recently

Reinventing Revolution: New Social Movements in India and *Dalits and the Democratic Revolution.*

Arjun Patel is a scholar-activist working with the exploited masses of Gujarat. He is a fellow at the Centre for Social Studies at Surat, Gujarat. His publications are in the field of empowering tribals and Dalits.

S. P. Punalekar is a senior fellow at the Centre for Social Studies at Surat, Gujarat. He has concentrated his research on the weaker sections of Indian society.

S. Selvam is a reader at the Department of Social Work, University of Delhi. His publications are in the areas of secularization, community development, and communication.

John C. B. Webster taught history at Baring Union Christian College in Batala, Punjab (1963–1976) and served as director of the Christian Institute of Sikh Studies there (1971–1976). He is at present editor of the *Dalit International Newsletter.* Among his most recent publications are *The Dalit Christians: A History* and *From Role to Identity: Dalit Christian Women in Transition.*

Index

Absolute deprivation, 96, 99–100
Acchutanand, 25
Adi Shankara, 6
Adivasis: BJP influence on, 112–117; Brahmin values among, 108; caste, 109, 119; cultural change, 108–109; on democracy, 118; diet, 106, 108, 109, 120*n*6; dislocation among, 165; economic status, 105–106; education, 164; Hinduization of, 9, 106–107, 109; opposition to Hinduism, 118–119, 123*n*25; opposition to Islam, 115–116, 117, 118; in politics, 112; pollution as concept among, 109; religious identity, 117–118; religious practices, 108–112, 120*n*7; religious studies on, 103–105; rural development among, 164–166; of southern Gujarat, 105, 120*n*3
Advani, Lal Krishna, 116
Agamas, 85, 86
Ahimsa, 30
Alcohol consumption, 106, 108–109, 120*n*6
All-India Conference of Indian Christians, 16
Ambedkar, Bhimrao Ramji: as Bodhisattva, 65–66; British rule, 55*n*19; on capitalism, 147–148; on caste, 133, 147–149; conflict with Gandhi, 6, 7, 33, 59–60; conversion to Buddhism, 34–35; economic traditionalism in, 146–147; education of, 58; on Hinduism, 63; Hindu use of writings of, 38, 104; on liberation, 58; on Marxism, 145, 146, 148–151; moral economy of, 150, 151–153; on nonviolence, 150; origin of untouchability, 4, 11; politics, 67–68; on poverty, 150–152; sanskritization, 95; upper-caste denunciations of, 38; vision of just society, 25
Amrutlaya, 111, 122*n*17
Andhra Pradesh: Buddhist conversion, 100; Christianity, 20*n*15; Dalit militancy, 96; Dalit relative deprivation, 97
Annihilation of Caste (Ambedkar), 58, 59
Antiuntouchability campaign, 13
Appadurai, A., 87
Arthasastra (Kautilya), 3
Aryabhats, 51
Aryan culture: Dravidian opposition to, 31–33; Indian nationhood based on, 26–27; theory of race, 27
Aryans, 3
Arya Samaj, 110, 119
Asharam Bapu, Shri, 110, 114
Athavaniche Pakshi (Sonkamble), 166
Athvale, Shri Pandurang Shastri, 111–112, 114, 121*n*15
Ayodhya, 100, 104

Babari Musjid, 104, 115
Backward, Adivasi, and Muslim Caste Federation, 100
Bahishkrut Hitakarni Sabha, 146

Bahujan Samaj, 37–38, 152
Bajarang Dal, 119, 121*n9*
Bajirao II, 46
Bali, King, 28, 29, 49, 52
Balut (Pawar), 166
Balutedari, 44
Bastis, 161
Bedevos, 108
Beef eating, 4, 12
Beidelman, T. O., 84
Berreman, G. D., 82
Bhagavad Gita, 111, 112
Bhakti Hinduism, 78, 79, 81, 85–86, 107
Bhangis, 17
Bharatiya Janata Party (BJP): *adivasi* support for, 113, 119; Dalit support for, 100; political strategies, 116–117; programs sponsored by, 113–114, 122*n18;* rise of, 104, 112–113; sponsorship of marriages, 114, 122*n19*
Bhartiya sanskriti, 110
Bhatiji movement, 111
Bhed, 51
Bhikku Sangha, 150, 151, 153
Biardeau, M., 84
Bihar, 96
Bodhisattvas, 65–66
Bose, N. K., 109
Brah-man-anche Kasab (Phule), 50
Brahminism. *See* Caste
Brahmins: bhakti Hinduism and, 78, 79, 81, 85–86; as colonial power, 43–45; control of temples, 86, 87; education as source of power, 50–51; Indian nationalism as tool of, 51, 55*n18;* as intermediaries, 51, 54*n1;* as lower castes' enemy, 27–28, 48–50; miscegenation by, 3; in Peshwai, 46; priviliged world of, 47–48; threat to social order of, 110–111; under the British, 45, 53; values of, 108; vision of society, 30–31, 77
Brahmo Samaj, 26
British colonialism: Brahmins under, 45, 53; caste, 14, 43; education, 50–51, 54*n6;* electoral reservations for Dalits, 7; role in Dalit struggle of, 47, 50, 52–54, 55*n19;* temple reform, 88

Buchanan, Pat, 145
The Buddha and His Dhamma (Ambedkar), 58, 59, 64
The Buddha and the Future of His Religion (Ambedkar), 58, 59, 62
"Buddha or Karl Marx" (Ambedkar), 150, 152–153
Buddhism: caste in, 15, 67, 70*n11;* compared to other religions, 62–63; conversion movement, 100; as doctrine of salvation, 63–64; in Maharashtra, 65, 68, 100; Mahayana, 63–64; Marxism vs., 148–151; politics, 67–68; poverty, 150–151; in South India, 86; Theravada, 63, 67

Capitalism, 147–148, 149
Caste: among *adivasis,* 109, 119; as basic social institution, 82; British approach to, 14, 43; in Buddhism, 15, 67, 70*n11;* capitalism and, 147–148; in Christianity, 14, 15–18, 19*n10;* class analysis, 11–14; communal analysis, 11, 14–18; elimination of, 59–60; endogamy, 67, 69, 109; Gandhian approach, 15, 31; in Islam, 14; in labor unions, 13; low vs. high, 27–28; New Economic Policy and, 133–134; origins, 2–6; persistence of, 75; ranking as function of power, 83–84; segregation by, 132–133; in Sikhism, 14, 15, 19*n7;* sociology and, 1, 11
Caste in India (Hutton), 4
Catholics, 17
Census of India, 12, 14
Centre for Social Studies, 108, 123*n22*
Chakla workers, 166
Chandalas, 2, 3. *See also* Dalits
Chand Bapu, Saint Shri Laxmi, 110
Chaudhare, Amarsingh, 117
Chhote Morari Bapu, 110
Chikhaliya, Dipika, 116
Childbirth, 159
Chitnis, Suma, 15
Christianity: caste in, 14, 15–18, 19*n10;* Catholicism, 17; conversion to, 16, 19*n10;* among Dalits, 14, 15–18; Hindu interaction with, 110, 116, 120*n5;* history in, 28; influence on Dalit struggle of, 48, 49; pollution

in, 18; Protestantism, 17; rural populations, 18, 20*n16;* Syrian Orthodoxy, 17, 20*n15;* view of poverty, 150, 152
Chuhras, 17
Civil society, 43–44
Class struggle, 63, 148
Colebrooke, H. T., 27
Commodification, 141–143
Communal riots, 115, 116, 117, 123*n22*
Community, 76
Competition, 131
Congress Party, 113, 115, 116, 117, 156
Conversion: of Ambedkar, 34–35; Buddhist movement for, 100; to Christianity, 16, 19*n10;* to Islam, 121*n11*
Cooperatives, 156–157
Corruption, 117
Crime, 35, 36, 96

Dalit Bandu, 11
Dalitization, 78
Dalit Maha Sabha, 37
Dalit movement: British role in, 47, 50, 52–54, 55*n19;* Christian influence, 48; fragmentation of, 98–99; liberal view of, 93; relative deprivation as threat to, 98; state's response, 99
Dalit Panther movement, 2, 11, 98–99
Dalits: alienation among, 95–96; art and literature, 137–138, 166–167; in the BJP, 100, 113; Christian, 14, 15–18; crimes against, 35, 36, 96; government expenditures on, 100; labeling of, 2, 8, 11–20; Muslim, 121*n11;* New Economic Policy's effect on, 37, 132, 138–143; pollution, 13, 89; poverty among, 36–37; relative deprivation among, 96–98; in rightist Hindu movements, 104; in rural areas, 18, 95–96; rural development, 155–159; sanskritization, 94–95, 99; socioeconomic profile, 132–138; temple use, 101*n1;* in urban areas, 96; vision of society, 1–2. *See also* Employment of Dalits
Dalit Sangharsh Samiti, 37
Dalits Sena, 38
Democracy, 118

Denotified and Nomadic Tribes, 135, 166–167
Depressed Classes. *See* Dalits
Deshmukh, Chandu-bhai, 117
Devaluation, 145, 146–147
Devasthan, 108
Dharma, 62, 64, 77
Dharmasutras, 3
Dravidians, 4, 31–33
Dumont, Louis, 75, 82–84

Education: of *adivasis,* 164; as agent of Hinduization, 110, 112; under the British, 50–51, 54*n6;* under economic reform, 143; higher, 35; literacy, 36; of lower castes, 28; of migrant laborers, 161
Egalitarianism, 153
Electoral reservations, 7, 135
Employment of Dalits: BJP programs, 113; under the British, 44–45; under economic reform, 139–140; in the public sector, 36, 37, 135–137, 139
Endogamy, 67, 69, 109
Evans-Pritchard, Edward E., 103
The Evolution of Provincial Finance in British India (Ambedkar), 146

Fanon, Franz, 7–8
Festivals, 109
Fitzgerald, Timothy, 9, 57
Forest land, 114, 122*n18*
Fuchs, Stephen, 4–5, 109

Gaashala, 110
Gaikwad, Dadasaheb, 98–99
Gamit, Pratap, 117
Gandhi, Mohandas: antiuntouchability campaign, 13; on caste, 15, 31; conflict with Ambedkar, 6, 7, 33, 59; Harijan uplift campaign, 13; nonviolence, 150; religion of, 29–30
Gavaskar, Mahesh, 8, 43
Gayatri mantra, 49
Gayatri Parivar, 112
Gayatri Shaktipath, 110, 112
Gellner, Ernest, 53
General Agreement on Tariffs and Trade (GATT), 131
Gharmandir, 111, 122*n16*
Globalization, 131, 153

Gokhale, Gopal Krishna, 29
Gokul Gram, 114
Gokul Gram Yojana, 113
Golwalkar, M. R., 30
Government on the Doorstep program, 113
Gram Panchayat, 156
Gramsci, Antonio, 85, 94
Guha, Ranajit, 94–95
Gujarat: *adivasi* populations, 105, 120*n3;* education, 164; Hindu communalism, 104, 116; migrant labor, 160–161, 166–167; nomadic tribes, 166–167; rural development, 155–159
Gulamgiri (Phule), 48–50
Guru, Gopal, 9, 93, 104
Guru, Narayan, 6, 25

Habib, I., 83–84
Harijans, 13, 37. *See also* Dalits
Harijan Sevak Sangh, 31
Harijan uplift campaign, 13
Health care, 159, 160
Hedgewar, Keshab Baliram, 30
Hegemony, 80, 84–89
Hindi, 32
Hinduism: *adivasi* opposition to, 118–119, 123*n25;* bhakti, 78, 79, 81, 85–86, 107; Brahmin view of, 30–31, 57; Christian conflict with, 110, 116, 120*n5;* class struggle in, 63; communalism in Gujarat, 104, 116; history, 28–29; labeling of Dalits and, 12; militancy in, 115–116; mythology, 48–50; nationalism in, 104; rationalist approach to, 26; revival movement, 107; sects within, 107; sociology and, 78; unity and diversity in, 78–79
Hinduization: of *adivasis,* 9, 106–107, 109; of Dalits, 94–95, 99, 104; education as agent of, 110, 112
Hindu Mahasabha, 30
Hindu Milan Mandir, 115, 119
Hindu Nationalists in India: The Rise of the Bharatiya Janata Party (Malik and Singh), 104
Hindu Religious and Charitable Endowments Department (HRCE), 88

Hindu Religious Endowment Board, 88
Hindutva, 30, 99, 104, 110, 115, 119
History, 28–29
Hume, Allan Octavian, 29
Hutton, J. H., 4, 12–13, 14

Impurity. *See* Pollution
Independent Labor Party, 147
Indian Dalit Federation, 37
Indian National Congress, 29–30, 32, 51
Indian renaissance, 26
Informal economy, 140
Integrated Rural Development Programme (IRDP), 99
International Monetary Fund (IMF), 142
Ireland, 4
Irrigation, 156, 157, 158, 161, 167
Islam: *adivasi* opposition to, 115–116, 117, 118; caste in, 14; Dalit conversion to, 121*n11;* Dalit view of, 49, 52; Gandhian approach to, 29–30; history in, 28

Jadhav, Narendra, 145, 146, 153*n1*
Jainism, 86
Janata, 147
Jones, William, 27
Just society, 25, 27–29

Kale, Govind Ganapat, 45
Kalia, B., 109
Kamle, Shantabai, 166
Karma, 58, 64, 70*n1,* 77
Karnataka, 81, 157, 159
Kathas, 110, 111, 112
Katyavarchi Pot (Tupe), 166
Kaviraj, Sudipta, 48
Kerala, 17, 20*n15,* 135
Kharat, Shankarrao, 166
King Bali, 28, 29, 49, 52
Kisan Sabhas, 13
Kothari, Rajni, 25–26
Kshatriyas, 80, 81
Kuvar Bainu Memeru, 113

Labor: agricultural, 135; bonded, 58; caste and, 133; child, 158; local, 162–163, 168–169; migrant, 157, 159–163, 166–169; productive, 52, 54*n7;* seasonal, 105, 158, 165–166

Labor unions, 13, 135, 161
Lal, R. B., 107
Land: disputes over, 36; drought-prone, 167; nationalization, 148; ownership patterns, 44, 157; size distribution of holdings, 134–135
Language, 30, 32
Lassen, C., 27
Liberation, 58, 65, 66, 70*n7*. *See also* Soteriology
Literacy, 36
Literature, 137–138, 166–167
Lobo, Lancy, 107
Lok Sabha, 112

Mahabharata, 85
Mahad tank satyagraha, 146
Mahars, 94, 96–98
Maharashtra: Buddhism in, 65, 68, 100; crimes against Dalits, 96; Dalit relative deprivation, 97–98; education, 164; Mahar emulation of upper castes, 94; migrant labor, 157, 159–161, 166–167; nomadic tribes, 166–167; rural development, 155–159
Mahayana Buddhism, 63–64
Majhya Jalmachi chittarkathe (Kamle), 166
Malik, K. Yogendra, 104
Malinowsky, Bronislaw, 103
Mandal Commission, 43, 113
Mane, Laxman, 166
Mangoo Ram, 25
Mangs, 96–98
Manu, 3
Manusmriti, 3, 58, 59, 61, 137
Marathwada, 97, 157
Marathwada Mitra Mandal, 97
Marriage: BJP-sponsored, 114, 122*n19;* caste endogamy, 67, 69, 109; of widows, 28; without Brahmin priests, 28
Marriott, M., 81–82
Marxism: of Ambedkar, 63, 145, 146, 148; Buddhism vs., 148–151; hegemony, 84–85; on religion, 76
Medical care, 159, 160
Michael, S. M., 1, 8, 25
Minimum wage laws, 135
Miscegination, 3
Mitchell, Murray, 46, 54*n3*

Moral economy, 150, 151–153
Morality, 62
Morari Bapu, 110, 114–115, 120*n9,* 121*n10*
Mosse, C. D. F., 18
Mueller, Max, 27
Mukadams, 160, 163, 168
Multinational corporations, 139
Mungekar, B. L., 9, 131
Munshi, Gaffar Beg, 46, 54*n3*
Myths, 48–50

Naoraji, Dadabhai, 29
Narmada dam project, 108
Narratives, 48
Nath Panthi Bhakta Parivar, 109–110
Nationalism, Indian, 51, 55*n18,* 115
National Rural Employment Programme (NREP), 99
Nationhood, 25–27
Naxalites, 165
Neo-Hinduism, 107
New Economic Policy, 9; adoption of, 131–132; caste and, 133–134; effect on Dalits of, 37, 132, 138–143
Nilesh Bapu, 110, 121*n13*
Nirmik, 51–53
Nirvana, 64
Nishadas, 3
Nomadic tribes, 135, 166–167
Nonviolence, 150

Omvedt, Gail, 9, 145
Oommen, T. K., 94, 95, 99
Organization for Economic Cooperation and Development (OECD), 141
Oustees, 165

Panchayats, 112–113
Panth, 109
Patel, Arjun, 9, 103
Pawar, Daya, 166
Periyar, E. V. Ramaswamy, 25, 31–33
Peshwai, 46
Phule, Govindrao, 46
Phule, Jotirao: Brahmanic colonialism, 43–45; British rule, 47, 50–51, 52–54; Christian influence on, 48, 49; education of, 46; founder of Dalit movement, 6, 8–9; on gender relations, 54*n10;* on Islam, 52; just

society of, 25, 27–29; on the *Nirmik,* 51–53; productive labor, 52, 54*n7;* upper-caste denunciations of, 38; work life of, 45–46
Pinto, Stany, 111
Political parties. *See* Bharatiya Janata Party (BJP); Congress Party; Republican Party of India
Politics: *adivasi* role, 112; Buddhist, 67–68; class struggle, 63; divisions among Dalits, 38–39; of Hinduization, 105; influence in rural development of, 156, 169; of numbers, 35; participation by Christian Dalits, 16
Pollution: as *adivasi* concept, 109; in Christianity, 18; Dalit beliefs, 89; as separator of Dalits, 13; as sustainer of caste, 82–83, 133
Poverty: among *adivasis,* 105; among Dalits, 36–37; Buddhist view, 150–152; Christian view, 150, 152; divisiveness and, 162–163; in rural areas, 158, 168–169
Praful Shukla, 110, 111, 112, 114–115
Priests: *adivasi,* 108; Brahmin, 28, 106, 108
Prinsep, James, 27
Privatization, 100, 131, 153
The Problem of the Rupee (Ambedkar), 146–147
Protestants, 17
Protest movements, 80, 93
Punalekar, S. P., 9, 155–156
Pune pact of 1932, 7
Puranas, 28, 85
Purity, 5. *See also* Pollution

Race, 27
Radcliffe-Brown, A. R., 78, 103
Radha Krishna, 115
Rajagopalachari, C., 32
Rajas, 106, 120*n4*
Ramayana, 85
The Ramayana: A True Reading, 32
Ram, Jagjivan, 13
Ram, Mangoo, 25
Ram Krishna, 115
Ram Sevak Samitis, 110
Ramshila Pujan, 115
Ranade, Madhava Govinda, 29

Rao, M. S. A., 80, 93
Rashtriya Swayamsevak Sangh (RSS): *adivasi* membership in, 115, 119; founding of, 30, 54*n4*
Rathyata campaign, 115–116
Rationalism, 26
Reference groups, 93–94
Relative deprivation, 93–94, 95–100
Religion: *adivasi* practices, 108–112, 120*n7;* as community, 76; as concept, 57; economic role of, 76–77; Gandhian view of, 29–30; in Indian society, 76–77; Marxist view, 76; origin of, 103; rules vs. principles, 58–61; Western principles in, 60, 61
Renunciation, 59, 60–61
Republican Party of India, 7, 35, 69, 99
Reservation policy, 35, 132, 135–138, 140
Ritual, 66–67
Ritual purity, 5. *See also* Pollution
Rojgar Mela, 113
Roy, Rammohun, 26
Runciman, W., 99
Rural development: Dalit masses and, 155–159; denotified tribes, 166–167; migrant and local labor, 159–164; Scheduled tribes, 164–166
Rural populations, 18, 20*n16,* 95–96
Russell, Bertrand, 152
Ryotwari system, 44, 54*n1*

Sachchidanand, Swami, 114, 121*n12*
Sacred thread, 49, 54*n6,* 120*n6*
Saints, 110, 111, 114–115
Saiva Siddantha, 85
Samsara, 77
Sangharakshita, Venerable, 68
Sangh Parivar, 115
Sannyas, 59, 60–61
Sanskrit, 30
Sanskriti Parivar, 110
Sanskritization, 78–82, 94–95, 99
Saraswati, Dayananda, 27, 33
Sarvajanik Sabha, 51
Satsang, 110
Satvalekar, Pandit, 110
Satyagraha, 30
Satya Shodhak Samaj, 28, 51, 54*n2*
Savarkar, V. D., 30
Scheduled Castes. *See* Dalits

Scheduled tribes, 164–166. *See also* Adivasis
Seasonal workers, 105, 107
Segregation, 132–133
Self-Respect Movement, 32, 81
Selvam, S., 9, 75
Shah, Ghanshyam, 104, 113, 119
Shastras, 60, 110
Shiv Sena, 115, 119
Shoshits, 25
Shourie, Arun, 38
Shudras, 3, 27, 137
Sikhism, 14, 15, 19*n7*
Simon Commission, 13, 16
Singh, V. B., 104
Sitaram Seva trust, 110
Social democracy, 151
Socialism. *See* Marxism
Social mobility, 93–94, 95
Social services, 141–143
Society, Indian: Brahmin vision of, 30–31, 77; Dalit vision of, 1–2; functionalist interpretation of religion in, 77–82; Gandhian view, 29–30; local traditions, 80; rational approach to, 26, 29; religious role in, 76–77; ritual in, 66–67; social stratification as characteristic, 75; structuralist interpretation of religion in, 82–84; upper-caste hegemony, 84–89; vedic approach to, 26, 29
Sociology: caste and, 1, 11; Hinduism and, 78; questioning assumptions in, 100
Soteriology, 63–64, 66, 67–68. *See also* Liberation
Soviet Union, 145, 147, 149
Srinivas, M. N., 75, 78–81
Staal, T. F., 80
Starvation, 158–159
State intervention, 138, 169
States and Minorities (Ambedkar), 148
Stein, Burton, 86
Storytelling, 110
Structural adjustment program (SAP), 131
Structural holism, 82–84
Sugar cane cutters, 159–161, 163
Sureshanandji, Shri, 110
Sustainable development, 152
Swadhyay Parivar, 111, 112, 115

Swaminarayana, 115
Swaraj, 35
Syrian Orthodoxy, 17, 20*n15*

Tamil Nadu: bhakti Hinduism in, 78, 79, 85–86; Christianity in, 20*n15*; Self-Respect Movement in, 81; temple reform in, 88
Taral Antaral (Kharat), 166
Technical training, 112
Telangana, 97
Temples: Brahmin control of, 86, 87; British reform of, 88; Dalit use of, 101*n1*; government support for, 87, 106–107; Hindu *adivasi*, 111, 120*n4*, 121*n13*; Hinduization of, 121*n14*; traditional *adivasi*, 108
Theravada Buddhism, 63, 67
Tilak, B. G., 29
Trickle-down economics, 132
Trilokya Bauddha Mahasangha (TBMSG), 68, 87*n5*
Tritya Ratna (Phule), 47, 54*n3*
True Religion, 60, 61
Tupe, Uttam Bandu, 166

Untouchability: occupation and, 3; origin of, 2–6, 11; political opposition to, 13, 35
Untouchables. *See* Caste; Dalits
The Untouchables (Ambedkar), 4, 11
Upanishads, 59
Upra (Mane), 166
Urban populations: Christians in, 18; Dalits, 96, 113; migrants, 165–166

Vaishyas, 80, 81
Vajpayee, Atal Bihari, 112, 113
Values, 61
Vanvasi Kalyan Parishad-Sidumbar, 112
Varna, 3, 4, 31, 77, 121*n12*
Vedic culture, 26–28, 29
Vegetarianism, 106, 108, 120*n6*
VHP. *See* World Hindu Council (VHP)
Vicharati jati, 155
Vidarbha, 97
Viditatmanand Saraswatiji, Swami Shri, 110
Village life, 81–82
Visions, 1–2

Vividh Karyakari Sahakari Mandal (VIKAS), 157
Wages and salaries, 135, 154*n5*
Wales, 4
Weber, Max, 76
Webster, John C. B., 8, 11
Welfare expenditures, 141–142, 143*n3*
Western thought in India, 26
Widow remarriage, 28
Wilkins, Charles, 27
Williams, Monier, 27
Wilson, H. H., 27
Women, 28, 36–37
World Bank, 142
World Hindu Council (VHP), 100, 115
World Trade Organization (WTO), 131

Yagnas, 112
Yagnic, Achyut, 104
Yeola Conference of 1935, 34
Yog Vedant Samiti, 110

Zamindari system, 44
Zhirinovsky, Vladimir, 145

About the Book

Exploring the enduring legacy of untouchability in India, this book challenges the ways in which the Indian experience has been represented in Western scholarship.

The authors introduce the long tradition of Dalit emancipatory struggle and present a sustained critique of academic discourse on the dynamics of caste in Indian society. Case studies complement these arguments, underscoring the perils and problems that Dalits face in a contemporary context of communalized politics and market reforms.

S. M. Michael is a senior lecturer in sociology, University of Mumbai (India), and honorary director of the Institute of Indian Culture. He is the author of *Culture and Urbanisation*.